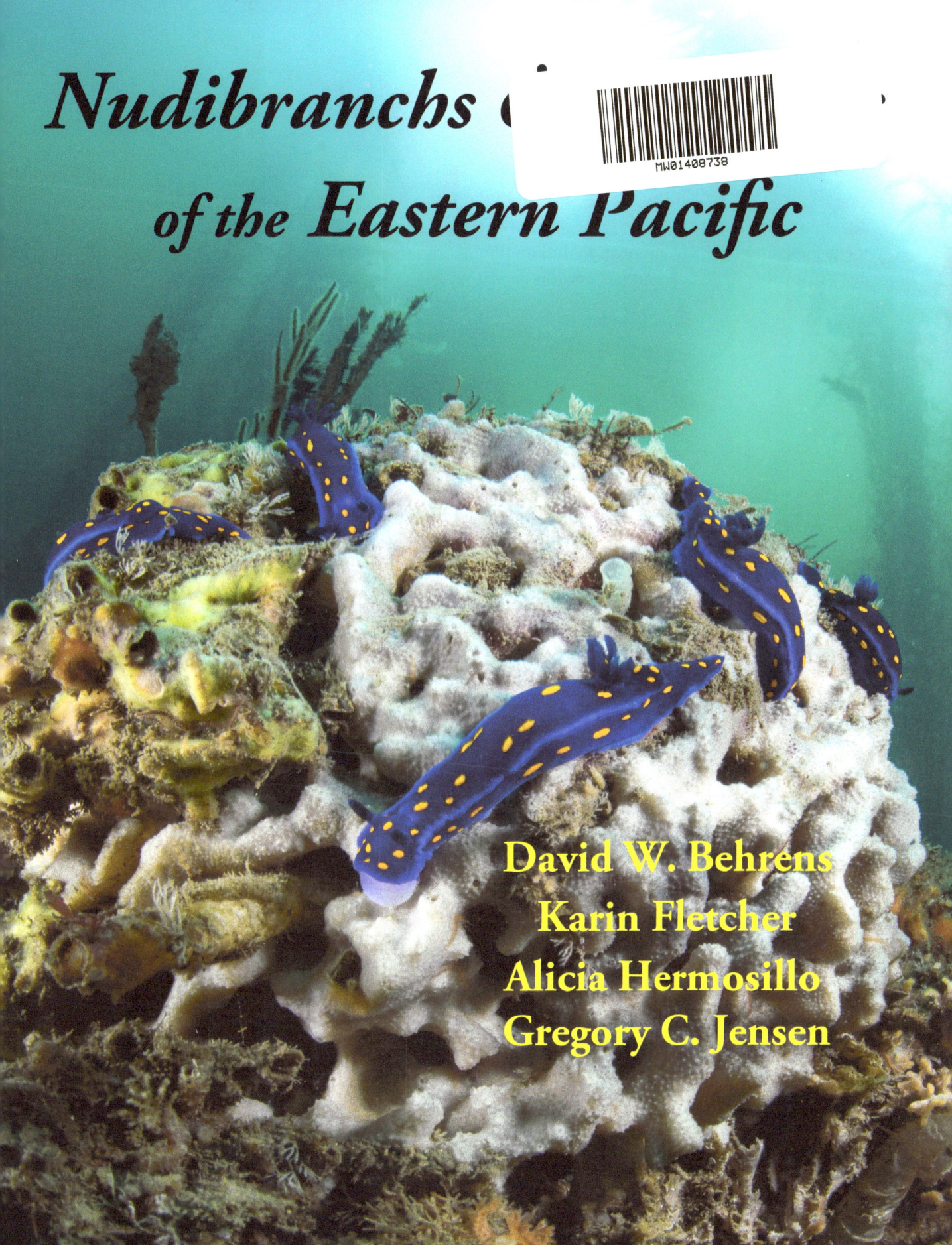

Nudibranchs of the Eastern Pacific

David W. Behrens
Karin Fletcher
Alicia Hermosillo
Gregory C. Jensen

A MolaMarine Publication

Copyright © 2022 David W. Behrens Karin Fletcher Alicia Hermosillo Gregory C. Jensen
All rights reserved. No part of this book may be reproduced or transmitted in any form or by any means, electronic or mechanical, including photocopying, recording, or by any information storage retrieval system, without permission in writing from the publisher.

First printing: 2022

ISBN 978-0-9898391-2-9

Design and layout by MolaMarine

MolaMarine

3808 Sundown Dr., Bremerton, WA 98312

CONTENTS

Photo credits..iv

Preface..v

Acknowledgments..vi

Introduction..1

Pictorial glossary..14

Superfamily Acteonoidea...17

Order Runcinida...17

Order Cephalaspidea..18

Order Aplysiida..28

Order Pleurobranchida...32

Superorder Sacoglossa...37

Order Systellommatophora..45

Order Nudibranchia: Suborder Doridina...46

Suborder Cladobranchia..100

Superfamily Tritonioidea...101

Superfamily Dendronotoidea...106

Superfamily Arminoidea..117

Superfamily Proctonotoidea..118

Superfamily Aeolidida...121

Selected references..156

Index..157

PHOTO CREDITS

Robin Agarwal: 25; 32; 35; 52; 56; 58; 72; 77; 84; 88; 111; 112; 119; 123; 129; 139; 140; 144; 147; 151; 152; 154
Orso Angulo Campillo: 136
Amy Baldwin: 117
David Behrens: 22; 27; 30; 34; 35; 69; 78; 79; 85; 89; 115; 132; 145; 146
Hans Bertsch: 74; 80; 83; 86; 96; 97; 140
Ryan Boerema: 36; 63
Marc Chamberlain: 30; 32; 59; 72; 75; 82; 96; 102; 103; 108; 111; 116; 124; 155
Sarah Douglas: 53
Karin Fletcher: 21; 25; 44; 52; 55; 56; 57; 59; 60; 61; 62; 63; 71; 72; 74; 76; 78; 87; 89; 107; 109; 110; 112; 113; 122; 125; 127; 131; 132; 133; 137; 146; 153; 154
Phil Garner: 26; 59; 75; 79; 80; 82; 84; 87; 97; 108; 118; 119; 143
Charles Gibbs: 49
Jeff Goddard: 62; 79; 100; 104; 112; 120; 123; 127; 131
Terry Gosliner: 20; 27; 51; 71; 153
Brenna Green: 33; 131
Rhoda Green: 71
Ed Gullekson: 120
Jeff Hamann: 42; 43: 48; 54; 58; 67; 71; 93; 100; 130; 133; 149; 150
Rick Harbo: 20
Alicia Hermosillo: 22; 23; 25; 27; 29: 31; 32; 34; 35; 36; 38; 39; 40; 41; 48; 50; 51; 52; 53; 54; 55; 62; 63; 64; 65; 66; 68; 73; 74; 75; 76; 77; 78; 81; 85; 86; 88; 89; 90; 91; 92; 93; 94; 95; 97; 98; 99; 102; 105; 107; 112; 114; 115; 116; 120; 123; 126; 127; 128; 130; 132; 133; 135; 136; 137; 138; 139; 141; 142; 144; 145; 148; 149; 150; 151; 152; 155
Craig Hoover: title page; 10; 34; 38; 62; 67; 68; 83; 84; 90; 92; 93; 98; 99; 101; 104; 105; 125
Jackie Hildering: 148
Bill Horist: 42
Paul Humann: 7; 67; 98; 106;
Gregory Jensen: 10; 19; 22; 23; 24; 29; 30; 33; 37; 43; 45; 46; 49; 52; 57; 60; 61; 63; 69; 75; 76; 77; 78; 82; 83; 84; 90; 96; 103; 107; 108; 110; 111; 117; 118; 120; 121; 123; 128; 130; 134; 143; 148; back cover
Scott Johnson: 114
Jan Kocian: 13; 24; 39; 69; 74; 105; 110; 124; 143
Jim Lance†: 44; 138; 146
Kevin Lee: 6; 17; 26; 28; 33; 47; 56; 57; 58; 59; 65; 70; 72; 73; 76; 77; 80; 82; 86; 88; 89; 90; 93; 94; 95; 98; 107; 109; 113; 116; 119; 124; 129; 133; 137; 146; 147; 149; 153; 163
Robert Lee: 51
Ron Long: 20; 21; 59; 125
Neil McDaniel: 104; 128
Gary McDonald: 19; 21; 151
Siena McKim: 155
Robin McMunn: 32
Mike Miller: 54; 99; 117
David Mulliner: 41
Merry Passage: front cover; 18; 44; 47; 49; 50; 57; 61; 63; 67; 69; 72; 75; 82; 83; 85; 98; 103; 111; 113; 135; 136; 140; 143; 153
Gustav Paulay: 20; 87; 112; 143
Brook Peterson: 43
Marina Podddubeskaia: 39
Marta Pola: 65
Richard Roller†: 19; 20; 41
Eric Sanford: 17
Jovan Shepard: 53
Ron Shimek: 48
Mark Silberstein: 42
Alan Smith: 129
Jeff Adams Stauffer: 45
Hiroyuki Tachikawa: 25
Sarah Thiebaud: 124
Kei-iche Ueda: 147
Ángel Valdés: 5; 122
Jim Valle: 84
Sula Vanderplank: 45
Allison Vitsky: 111
Margaret Webb: 114
Bruce Wight: 29

PREFACE

By way of introduction, I have been scuba diving and photographing sea slugs since 1982 and am the webmaster of the Sea Slug website (slugsite.us). I developed the site because of my love for these fascinating and diverse creatures, and my perception has not changed some 40 years later. It started with underwater photography; my dive mates at the time thought the love affair began because sea slugs were colorful but largely inanimate subjects that were an easy target for less gifted photographers such as myself. Since then, sea slug photography has evolved into an art form that has greatly facilitated visual identification in the field.

Back then, the "bible" for west coast slug aficionados was Dave Behrens' 1980 book, *Pacific Coast Nudibranchs*. Once tide poolers and scuba divers had the means to identify Pacific coast sea slugs, interest in these captivating mollucs grew. Dave published a second edition in 1991 that incorporated a plethora of new and undescribed species this surge in interest had uncovered. In 2005 Dave joined with Ali Hermosillo to produce a third edition, expanding coverage to include the Mexican fauna and leading to even more sea slug enthusiasts, both casual and professional. Since then, the numerous name changes and newly described species have left many copies well-worn, dog-eared, and marked up. An update was long overdue!

So, after 17 years an updated and revised guide to eastern Pacific sea slugs has finally arrived. *Nudibranchs & Sea Slugs of the Eastern Pacific* simplifies species identification with updated descriptions, more detailed photos, color variations, egg ribbons, and comparisons to similar species, as well as the usual size, range, and habitat information. Species names have been updated to reflect either the most recently published morphological and molecular conclusions as noted in WoRMS, or conclusions drawn from comparisons of publicly-available CO1 sequences of eastern Pacific specimens from BOLD and GenBank. The index includes both the old species names and the new names, a real boon to the citizen scientist slugger!

Dave and Ali, together with Karin Fletcher and Greg Jensen, have compiled an exhaustive list of range extensions, new information, and documented dozens of likely new and undescribed species gleaned from photo collections and genetic sequencing data. These new finds and the changes they have made represent giant strides in what we now know about our sea slug friends.

Michael Miller
San Diego, Calif
June, 2022

Line drawings by David Behrens

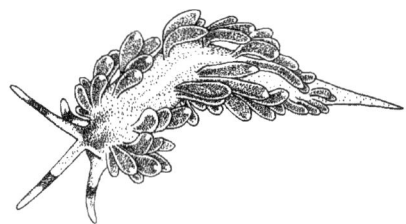

ACKNOWLEDGMENTS

It is difficult to recall or thank all the people assisting us over the years to produce this fourth edition. However, the big guns have always been there for us: Terry Gosliner, Ángel Valdés, Hans Bertsch, Sandra Millen, Yolanda Camacho-Garcia, Jeff Goddard, and Mike Miller. Their dedication to all things heterobranch has truly made such a project possible.

We also extend our sincere thanks to the following who provided expertise and enthusiastic encouragement to us:

Robin Agarwal	Bernard Hanby	Janna Nichols
Clinton Bauder	Craig Hoover	Merry Passage
Don Cadien	Paul Humann	Gustav Paulay
Marc Chamberlain	Jan Kocian	Bernard Picton
David Cowles	Elizabeth Kools	Linda Schroeder
Megan Dethier	Tanya Korshunova	Ron Shimek
Sven Donaldson	Andy Lamb	Craig Staude
Nancy Elder	Kevin Lee	Cynthia Trowbridge
Phil Garner	Kennet Lundin	Christiane Waldrich
Joe Gaydos	Alexander Martynov	Bruce Wight
Donna & Charlie Gibbs	Neil McDaniel	Nathalie Yonow
Brenna Green	Gary McDonald	Richard Zade
Josh Hallas	Doug Miller	
Jeff Hamann	Amy Moran	
Rick Harbo	Jim Murray	

It's impossible to overstate our gratitude to all the photographers whose wonderful images appear on these pages. This book would be a mere shadow of its present form without their generous contributions.

David, Karin, Ali, & Greg

This 1905 illustration by Olive MacFarland is of an aeolid nudibranch that was called *Cratena spadix* in the posthumous work she assembled for her husband, Frank MacFarland. After his sudden death in 1951 (see *Platydoris macfarlandi*, page 84), Olive spent ten years assembling his "Studies of Opisthobranchiate Mollusks of the Pacific Coast of North America" but then died five years before its publication in 1966. *Cratena spadix* is currently synonymous with the southern form of *Catriona columbiana* (page 146).

INTRODUCTION

Nudibranchs and other sea slugs have long captivated the interest of tidepoolers, divers, and researchers, and for good reason: their dazzling colors, bizarre body forms, and strange habits fuel a seemingly unending sense of wonder. The rich diversity of species along the west coast of North America provides a fertile source of material for the nudibranch aficionado, be it a photographer seeking to capture their images or a scientist looking for new discoveries. With new species continually being described and named along our coast, it has become necessary to update and expand "Eastern Pacific Nudibranchs – A guide to the Opisthobranchs from Alaska to Central America" (Behrens & Hermosillo, 2005) to bring it up to date and include the new and rare species that were not previously covered. In this volume we include nearly every shallow-water species, described or undescribed, found from Alaska to Central America.

This book is designed to aid divers, amateur biologists, students, and professional biologists in the identification of these organisms. Since the publication of the three previous editions, we have learned a great deal about ways to make this book a more effective tool for you, the reader. We believe we have incorporated most of your suggestions. You will notice that many names have been changed and that many of the undescribed species found in the previous editions have now been formally described in scientific journals and have full scientific names. Systematic and phylogenetic studies, which have now evolved to include DNA analysis and protein sequencing, continue to refine our knowledge of the relationships between genera and species and therefore continue to change many of the names that have long been familiar.

As always, when observing or studying any group of living organisms, the first step to knowledge is identification. By knowing the animal's name one can communicate findings to others as well as investigate pertinent references to increase one's knowledge of this fascinating group of molluscs. Although considerable research has been done on this group, much remains to be discovered. Each observation, whether by trained biologists or casual enthusiasts, can potentially uncover new information to increase our understanding of heterobranch biology.

WHAT IS A HETEROBRANCH?

Heterobranchs are a group of largely shell-less gastropod molluscs, related to the more familiar shelled marine snails like conchs and whelks but lacking the characteristic twisted body form of those other gastropods. Referred to by numerous names – sea slugs, "branchs" (pronounced branks), naked snails, etc., most are only distantly related to the terrestrial slugs that wreak havoc in your vegetable garden. This group of molluscs is extremely diverse, with more than 8400 described species worldwide and many more yet to be named. Its members, while mostly shell-less, include a few with reduced or internal shells. All but a small group occur in saltwater and range in size from 3 mm (0.1 in) to a meter (3.3 ft) in length.

Within Heterobranchia, this guide will cover nudibranchs (literally, "naked gills"), which are perhaps the most familiar sea slugs; Cephalaspidea and Umbraculoidea, most of which possess external shells; the Pleurobranchida, which at first glance may be mistaken for dorid nudibranchs; Anaspidea, or sea hares, and the Sacoglossa, or sap-sucking slugs, many of which superficially resemble aeolid nudibranchs.

Probably the most fascinating characteristics of these marine animals are the diversity of body forms and coloration (Fig. 1). These range from colors and patterns that cryptically resemble their substrate to ones that brightly advertise their presence to all.

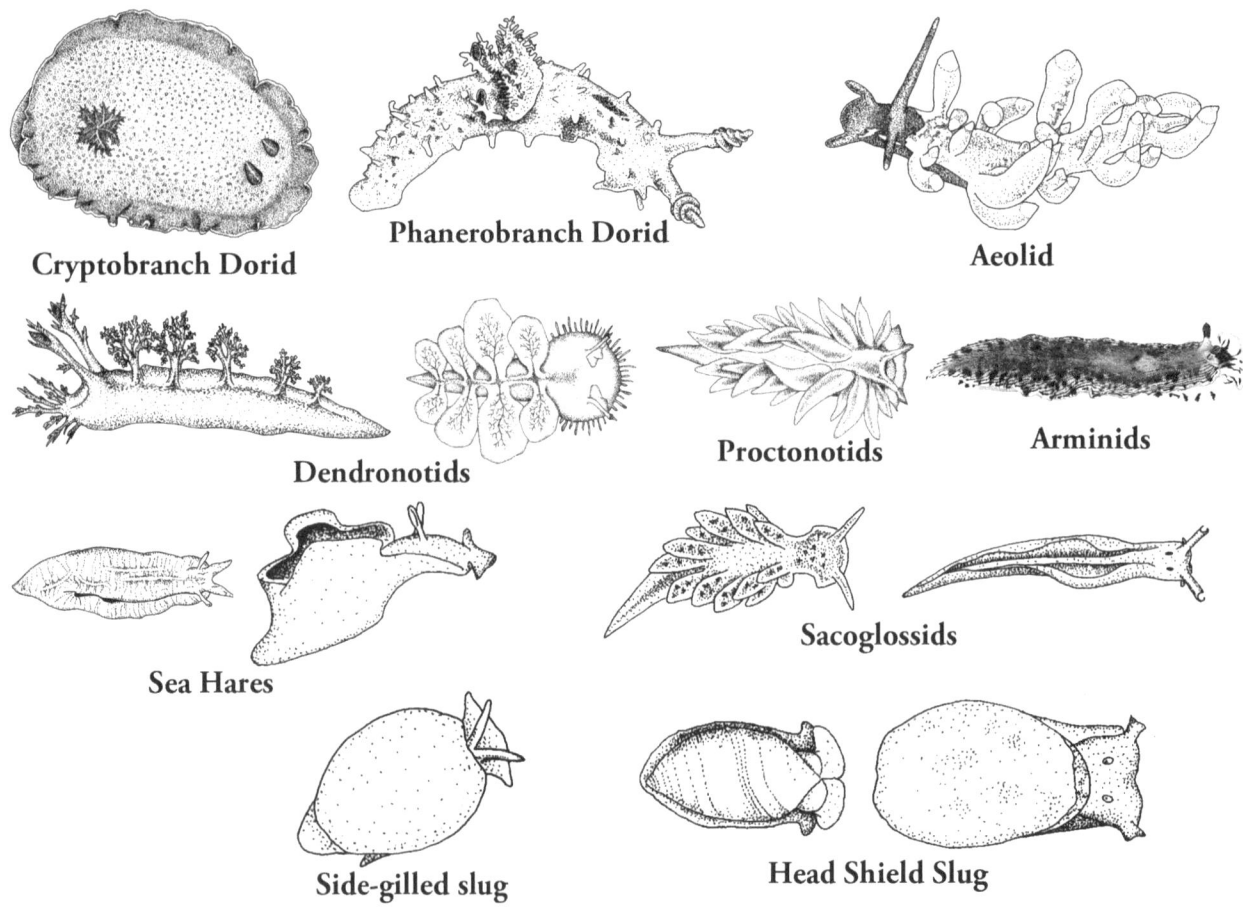

Fig. 1- Typical Heterobranch Body Forms

Coloration in heterobranchs, like that of butterflies, birds, and coral reef fishes, is not for our enjoyment but rather serves an important biological function. The bright coloration of these soft and seemingly vulnerable creatures seems incongruous- why would such an animal want to advertise itself to predators? Animals with brightly colored, distinctive patterns can be exhibiting warning coloration. Many have a foul taste of acids and toxic chemicals (often derived from their own prey) and the bright colors are a warning to predators- a sort of, "Don't eat me, I don't taste good." Fish have been observed to swallow a nudibranch, only to spit it out. Fish learn quickly of this chemical defense and rarely repeat the mistake. These visual signals do not work for some predators: the head-shield slug *Navanax* is blind and dines regularly on both colorful and drab cousins, and the aeolid *Favorinus* feeds upon brightly colored, often toxic, heterobranch eggs. These species have apparently developed a tolerance to the toxins in their prey.

Many heterobranchs are so brilliantly colored and extroverted in their behavior, often crawling on a rock in the open, that there is little question they are employing warning coloration advertising their unpalatable taste. However, other species can be extremely difficult to see as they blend in with their surroundings, a defense mechanism termed cryptic coloration. Cryptic coloration can be viewed under two separate categories: crypsis and special resemblance. Crypsis includes those species which blend in with a generally confused, heterogeneous background (termed "disruptive coloration") and those like *Tylodina fungina*, which are cryptically colored when on yellowish sponges but stick out like a sore thumb when not. Similarly, the eggs of these nudibranchs often blend in with the surrounding substrate.

Special resemblance refers to those species which resemble a specific feature or characteristic of the substrate or prey item. Examples include *Cumanotus*, resembling the hydranths of the hydroid *Tubularia* and *Corambe* resembling the encrusting bryozoan *Membranipora*. The size and spacing of the spots of *Aldisa sanguinea* precisely match the diameter and spacing of the oscula of the red sponge upon which it feeds.

Another category of coloration is mimicry. Mimicry refers to those species or groups of species resembling co-occurring species with demonstrated unpalatability to predators. On this coast only a few examples of mimicry are known. In two of these, the heterobranch acts as a model for another more palatable marine species. These are the resemblances of *Coryphella trilineata* and *Flabellinopsis iodinea* with similarly-colored podocerid amphipods (Goddard, 1984, Gosliner and Behrens, 1990). It has been suggested that the similarity in color between *Triopha catalinae*, *T. modesta*, *Limacia cockerelli. L. mcdonaldi,* and *Crimora coneja* might also form a mimetic complex. The mimetic importance of the convergent coloration between these species may only be a superficial similarity of appearance, however. For a detailed discussion of the forms of mimicry and its distinction as either Batesian mimicry or Mullerian mimicry, see Behrens (2005).

Another defense employed by some nudibranchs is to fire stinging cells (nematocysts) derived from the cnidarians (corals, hydroids, etc.) on which they feed. Although most heterobranchs spend much of their lives resting undisturbed or crawling about in search of food, some have the ability to avoid predation by swimming. For most of these, the swimming response seems to be a transient means of escape from predators that is invoked only when alarmed, and not used as their primary means of locomotion. On this coast, the accomplished swimmers are species of *Gastropteron*, *Tritonia*, *Melibe*, *Notobryon*, *Cumanotus*, the former flabellinids, and *Dendronotus*. The swimming movement is produced by muscle contractions resulting in various lateral flexions, undulations, and subtle flapping of cerata. Such a response usually continues for several seconds, allowing the animal to move out of the area of danger or elevate enough to be carried by currents, but may be sustained for several minutes under some circumstances.

Some heterobranchs even have commercial and tangible importance. Several species, including *Aplysia californica*, *Pleurobranchaea californica*, *Tritonia exsulans*, *Hermissenda crassicornis,* and *H. opalescens* are invaluable in medical research. *Aplysia* are being cultivated at commercial slug farms to meet this need. Because of their large soft bodies and slow movement, they are ideal for physiological research involving various ganglia and nerves. There is also a growing scientific interest in the ability of certain heterobranchs to store functional photosynthetic organelles, such as chloroplasts. Significant efforts are also being made in natural products research in the isolation and production of active chemical compounds, which may serve as antibiotics and chemotherapeutic agents. Strictly from the point of the purists, heterobranchs provide pleasure to all in the recreational dive industry. They are one more reason you enjoy spending your weekends and vacations underwater, and need to spend money on cameras and dive gear (and books!). Their allure has spawned the creation of dozens of sea slug web sites on the Internet.

Unfortunately, their popularity is a double-edged sword, having an impact on populations of some species. The exploitation of tropical nudibranchs by the seawater aquarium trade is directly reducing numbers in the wild. It offends us that so many in the commercial aquarium industry continue to buy and sell these beautiful animals knowing that most are nearly impossible to keep alive for long in home aquariums. Most naturally have very short lifespans even under ideal conditions; removing them from the wild only reduces the reproductive potential of their populations.

This book includes nearly all described and undescribed species of heterobranchs known to occur at depths of 60 m (200 ft) or less, from southeastern Alaska to Central America. Pteropods- graceful, pelagic sea slugs that resemble transparent gelatinous butterflies, are not included. They are rarely seen by scuba divers, fishermen, and students, and species identification is extremely difficult. Some small, rare cephalaspidians have also been omitted, as have non slug-like marine pulmonates.

NOMENCLATURE

Most of the names used here are those currently accepted by biologists as published in refereed scientific journals. Some names are inferred from publicly available genetic sequences in BOLD and GenBank. Over the past decade, taxonomic nomenclature has been changing rapidly and long-accepted names have been changed as new genetic information has become available. Systematic studies are still underway evaluating the characteristics being used to separate groups, particularly at the family level. These studies will continue to uncover past oversights and identify more valid anatomical discriminators, resulting in the reshuffling of species and subsequently, the revision of names. That is the nature of science.

There are two words in a scientific name. The first ("generic") is the name of the genus to which the animal belongs. The second is its specific or trivial name. Together, the genus and trivial names make up the complete name of a "species." Generally speaking, the term "species" is used to differentiate groups of organisms that theoretically do not interbreed. In the main, however, species separation is based on morphological and genetic characteristics. "Genus" is the smallest organizational grouping for closely related species.

Following the scientific name is the name of the author(s) who originally described the species, with the year in which the description was first published. When these are bound by parentheses, it means that there have been subsequent revisions from the original description and it is now in a different genus. In those cases where a name has changed since the previous (2005) edition, the former name has also been included (preceded by the word "Previously"), to draw your attention to the revision or name change. In some cases you will see "cf" between the genus and species name; this is used when there is uncertainty regarding the species. For example, a particular form may closely resemble a recognized species, but subtle differences suggest that it may be a separate species. When there is little doubt that a form represents an undescribed species, only the genus is given, followed by "sp."

We have included common names for many species in this guide. These are often fabricated from the etymology, or the basis for the scientific name, when that selection is known (e.g., the name *Doriopsilla spaldingi*, is to recognize George Spalding, the person who discovered the species, or the name *Dendronotus albus* denoting the white color of this species). Others are names long established in field guides or used by the dive community.

FEEDING

Heterobranchs tend to feed on organisms that are rarely eaten by other marine animals. Most have highly specialized diets, often feeding on only a single genus or species. Except for the Orders Anaspidea, Sacoglossa, and certain cephalaspideans, all heterobranchs are carnivores.

Like most other molluscs, sea slugs usually possess a ribbon of chitinous teeth called a radula (Fig. 2).

Fig. 2 – Scanning Electron Micrographs (SEMs) of the radular teeth of various species (SEMs by Ángel Valdés)

The number of rows of teeth on the radula as well as the shape of each individual tooth are important taxonomically; when quantified, they become the "fingerprint" for an individual species. Unfortunately, the use of radulae as an identification tool involves dissection of the animal and microscopic examination, so is not included in this field guide.

Ecologically, the form of the radula and its teeth are adapted to correspond well to each species' food preferences. In the cryptobranch dorids, most of the radular area is broad and bears many teeth for grazing on encrusting marine sponges, while the radulae of phanerobranch dorids is somewhat narrower due to the more filamentous and articulating nature of their bryozoan food. The Anaspidea have long broad radulae used for feeding on algae. In the Sacoglossa the radula is a single band of teeth that slides into position for use in puncturing egg capsules of other heterobranch species or algal cells. The old, worn teeth fall off and are captured in a sack-like space in the mouth, but the advantage of saving old teeth is not yet understood. To supplement their diet, sacoglossans usually retain chloroplasts, the intracellular organelles that are responsible for photosynthesis in plant cells. These chloroplasts remain captive in the translucent skin of the digestive branches and continue to produce sugars, which are absorbed by the sea slug.

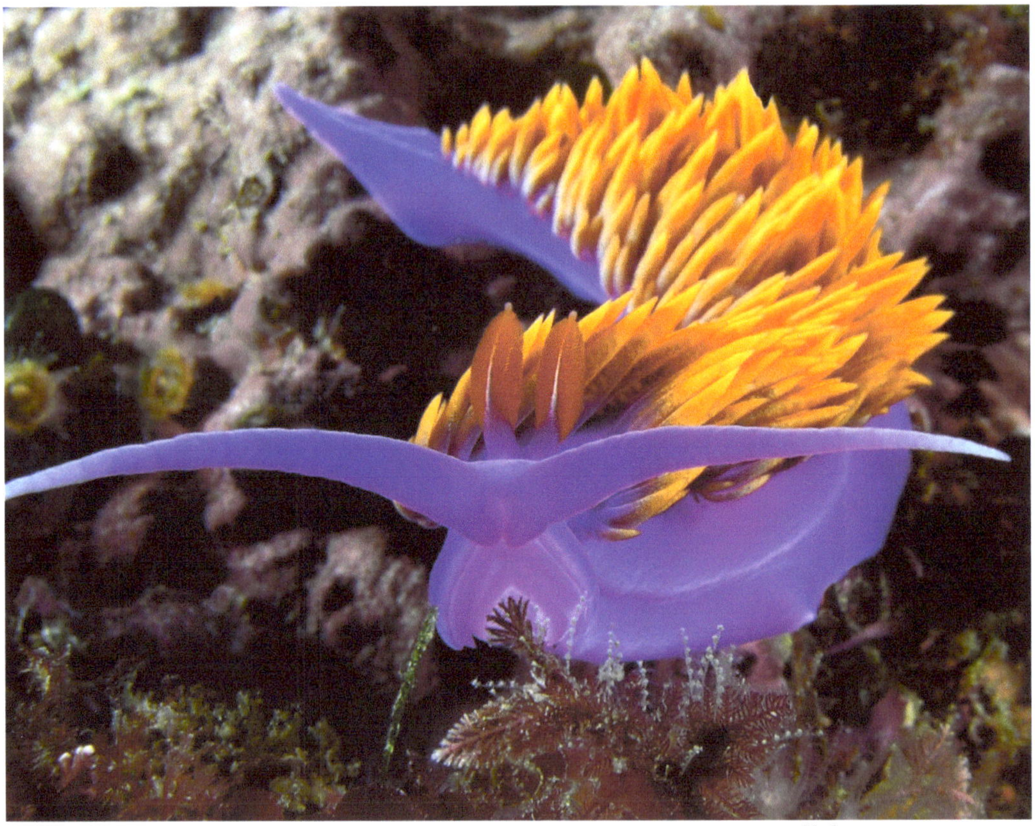

K. Lee

K. Lee

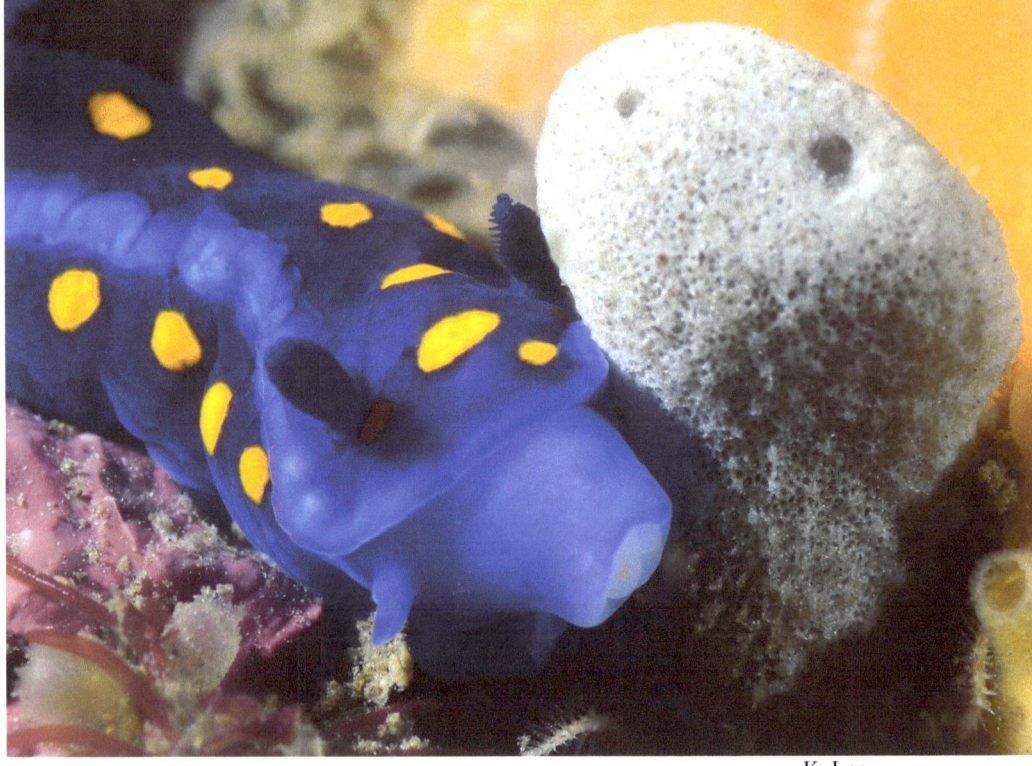

Fig. 3- *Flabellinopsis iodinea* (top) feeding on hydroids, and *Felimare californiensis* (bottom) feeding on sponge.

Besides possessing radulae, many heterobranchs also possess a pair of jaws anterior to the radula which serve to crop their food. Most of the aeolids and a few dendronotid nudibranchs that feed on hydroids and stalked bryozoans have narrow radulae and well-developed jaws; *Dirona albolineata* even uses its strong jaws to crack the shells of small snails. With a few exceptions, dorids lack strong jaws. The radula and jaws of a dorid that eats soft marine sponges differs markedly from that of a dorid feeding on acorn barnacles, or from one that eats encrusting bryozoans. See Behrens (2005) for a detailed discussion of feeding strategies and preferred foods.

Those species without a radula forage in other ways. *Melibe leonina* uses its net-like hood to capture its prey, which it swallows whole. Others, such as members of the genera *Doriopsilla*, *Dendrodoris*, *Phyllidiopsis* and *Tyrannodoris*, suck their prey in with specialized buccal pumps (Fig. 4). Certain cephalaspideans in the Family Aglajidae use their muscular buccal mass to rapidly strike their prey and swallow it whole. This group includes some of the most voracious and dramatic feeders of heterobranchs, on this coastline - *Navanax*.

P. Humann

Fig. 4- The appropriately-named tiger dorid *Tyrannodoris tigris* everting its blue buccal hood to cannibalize a smaller specimen.

SENSORY ORGANS

Heterobranchs rely primarily on their sense of chemoreception (smell and taste), as their vision is extremely limited. The eyespots visible on some species are likely able to only detect the direction and intensity of light; as underwater photographers can attest, many exhibit a "shadow response" and retract their gills when approached.

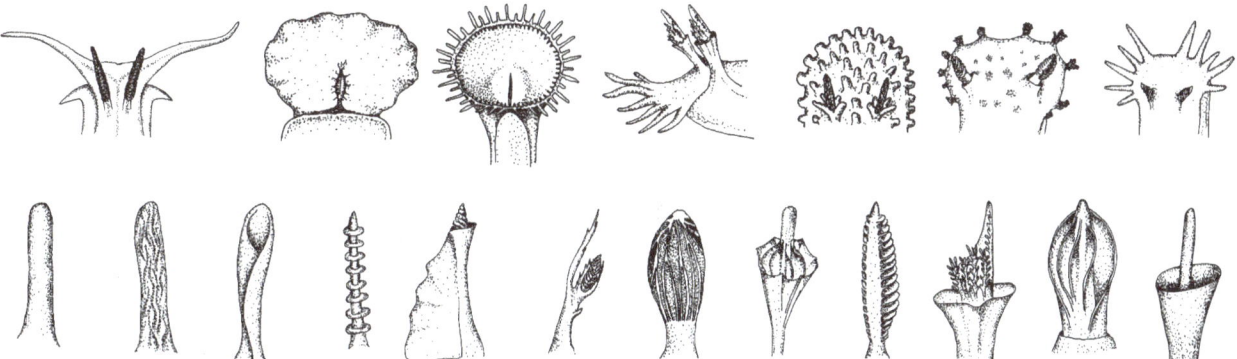

Fig. 5- Shapes of heads and types of rhinophores

The most obvious sensory organs in nudibranchs are the horn-like rhinophores on the top of the head (Fig. 5). Little is known about the function of rhinophores; although they seem to be very important sensory organs, their surface tissue does not differ greatly from that of other areas of the body, except for the absence of secretory glands. The limited studies to date have found that they are used for chemoreception and likely function in both finding food and seeking a mate. The rhinophores of the sea hare *Aplysia* are even light sensitive.

Rhinophores come in myriad forms and are important characters for identifying species. In the Anaspidea, Umbraculida, Pleurobranchomorpha, and most Sacoglossa, the rhinophores are rolled and shaped like a rabbit's ear. They are ciliated on the inner surface to promote water movement, likely enhancing their sensitivity to waterborne cues. The epithelium, or outer surface tissue, contains nerve endings as receptors. Cephalaspideans do not have rhinophores; sensory function in this group is carried out by an external lamellate structure, the Hancock's organ, or by a sensory funnel such as in *Gastropteron*.

Rhinophores are more complicated in the Nudibranchia. The clavus, or distal end, is usually composed of a series of folds resembling gills, although some may be smooth, wrinkled, or elaborately foliate. Nerves of the rhinophores connect directly to the cerebral ganglia. These nerves branch extensively until they reach the surface of the rhinophore. In some species this surface is covered with ciliated cells. In one major group of dorid nudibranchs (the cryptobranchs), the rhinophores can be retracted into the body, presumably for protection.

Many heterobranchs have developed other sensory structures, such as sensory mounds or oral tentacles around the mouth. Some of these undoubtedly play a crucial role in contact chemoreception (taste), both in recognizing prey and in detecting the slime trail of a potential mate (or meal).

RESPIRATION

Unlike the gills of other molluscs that are concealed in a mantle cavity, the respiratory structures of heterobranchs are usually obvious, exposed structures (recall "nudibranch" = "naked gill"). The two main forms of gills in this group are the cerata or the branchial plumes.

Cerata are fingerlike or club-shaped structures arranged in uniform groups of clusters along each side of the dorsum (Fig. 6). They are present in all members of the suborders Aeolidioidea, Dendronotoidea, Proctonotoidea, and most Sacoglossa. In addition to providing extra surface area to aid in respiration, they usually function in digestion and often defense. Histologically cerata, like rhinophores, do not differ from other body surface tissues. In most groups, the cerata usually contain branches of the digestive gland.

In some nudibranchs each ceras contains a terminal cnidosac harboring nematocyst capsules, harpoon-like stinging cells capable of being used in the nudibranch's defense (Figure 7). The nematocysts come from the hydroids, anemones, or corals fed upon by the nudibranchs. Minute juvenile nematocysts pass undischarged through the animal's digestive system and into the cerata where they mature

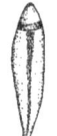

Fig. 6- Types of cerata

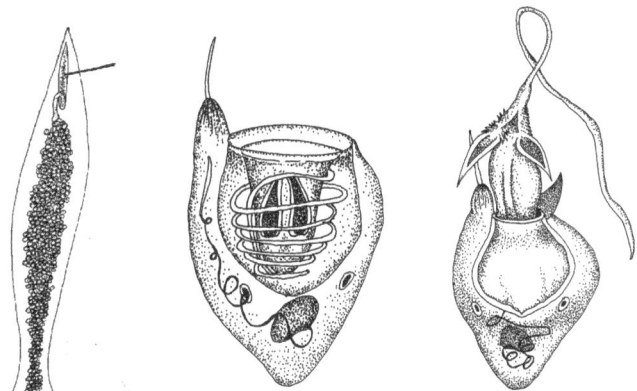

Fig. 7- Cnidosac at tip of cerata, and whole and fired nematocyst

into efficient weapons.

Cerata are easily autotomized, or cast off, and regenerated by many nudibranchs. In some species the cerata are cast off at the slightest provocation. This is thought to be a protective diversionary behavior similar to a lizard losing its tail. When autotomy occurs there is no loss of material from the midgut, as the area at the point of ceratal insertion seems to seal immediately. The cerata are readily regenerated in only a few days.

The other major type of heterobranch gill is found in the dorid nudibranchs, where a circlet of branchial leaves surrounds the anus on the dorsum. In these nudibranchs there are three distinct types of

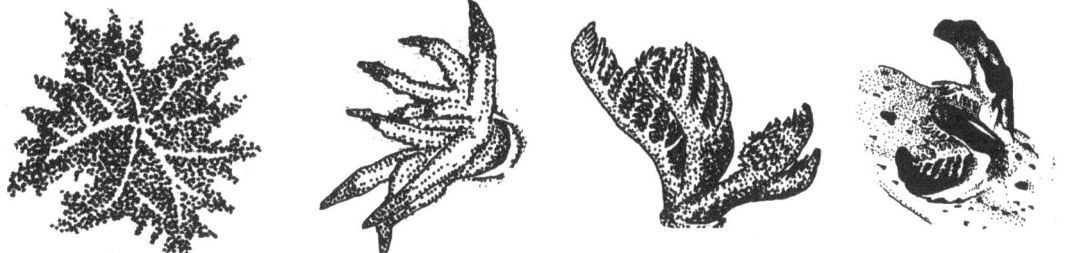

Fig. 8- Types of branchial plumes

gill (Fig. 8). In the cryptobranchs and dendrodorids the gill can be retracted into a distinct sheath; in the phanerobranchs there is no sheath and the gill cannot be retracted.

Members of the Phyllidiidae and Arminoidea lack a gill around the anus, and instead have a series of secondary gill-like folds along the sides of the body, between the notum and foot. The gill in the Cephalaspidea, Anaspidea, Umbraculida, and Pleurobranchomorpha are more developed organs located within the mantle cavity or below the notum.

REPRODUCTION

Virtually all heterobranchs are hermaphroditic, simultaneously possessing active organs of both sexes. One advantage of hermaphroditism is that it increases the probability of finding a suitable mate, since every individual of the same species is a potential partner. Since the sexual organs are located on the right side of the body, mating is in a head-to-tail position (Figure 9). Copulation generally results

Fig. 9- Mating pair of *Polycera tricolor*.

in cross-fertilization of the mating pair, except in cephalaspideans and anaspideans where matings of multiple individuals are common. Self-fertilization is extremely rare. Eggs and sperm develop simultaneously so that exchange of sperm will benefit both individuals; incoming and outgoing sperm and eggs travel through a common aperture, the exceptions being cephalaspideans, anaspideans, and some sacoglossans. Thompson (1976a) and Behrens (2005) give excellent, detailed explanations of heterobranch reproduction. The egg masses spawned by heterobranchs vary in size, shape, and color from species to species. Dorid eggs masses are ribbon shaped, while aeolids and dendronotids lay egg "strings" (Figure 10). Egg masses are highly characteristic and many can be identified to species; when available, images of them have been included with species accounts.

Depending on the species, egg numbers within a spawn range from a few eggs up to a million.

Fig. 10- **Dorid with ribbon-like eggs (left) and egg strings of a dendronotid (right).**

Development of the eggs can take up to 50 days, but is usually much shorter and influenced by temperature. Large individuals of a single species produce larger numbers of eggs than smaller individuals, and early spawns usually produce greater numbers of eggs, with the following ones containing successively fewer eggs.

Three types of egg development occur. Two produce planktonic veliger larvae (incomplete development), the other ends with a fully developed juvenile (complete development). In species with incomplete development, a shelled veliger larva hatches from the egg and is planktonic until it finds favorable substrate upon which to settle. Of these two types, the planktotrophic ones feed on smaller planktonic organisms, while the second variety, referred to as lecithotrophic, can complete development without feeding as they carry a large supply of yolk. This planktonic stage has two phases: the obligatory phase, during which the veliger is growing, and the searching phase, when it is seeking a favorable substrate for metamorphosis. The veliger larva has a thin, oval, spiral shell of about 1 to 1 ½ whorls within which are housed the soft body parts. The larva bears two large extensions resembling wings, which are covered with cilia for locomotion. In most species, the shell is lost at metamorphosis.

Since heterobranchs are slow moving creatures that can only travel limited distances during their adult life, their dispersal to other suitable environments is dependent upon this planktonic larval period. Veligers may extend their life in the plankton if no suitable substrate for their adult life is present; often a specific environmental cue triggers settlement and metamorphosis. Longer larval life increases the chance of greater dispersal.

In contrast, some species of heterobranchs such as *Doriopsilla gemela* and *D. nigromaculata* have complete development. In these, the juveniles develop within the egg capsule into miniatures of the adult, bypassing the free-swimming veliger stage. Since all phases of development take place in the egg mass, there is no planktonic period and the juveniles hatch in close proximity to their food supply. The eggs are larger, fewer in number, and embryonic development is considerably lengthened.

BIOGEOGRAPHY

Biogeography deals with the distribution of organisms and the broad patterns that occur over large regions. The area covered by this book ranges from the the polar northern Aleutian province and cold temperate Oregonian province through the California transition zone (CTZ; Monterey Bay to Los Angeles) to the warm temperate California, Cortez (Gulf of California), and tropical Panamanian (Panamic) provinces. These provinces have recently been defined using an endemism rate of 10%. Point Conception in southern California has historically been the division of the Oregonian and Californian provinces, but the recent CTZ has been added within the southern range or the Oregonian province so the Californian province now begins in Los Angeles and extends to Magdalena Bay, México. There is another transition zone along the outer coast of Baja California where there is not only a mix of tropical Panamic species and more temperate Californian fauna, but species abundances shift with periodic oceanic climatic events such as El Niños. The Gulf of California is now considered the Cortez province. The Panamic province begins near the southern tip of Baja California and extends to the border of Ecuador and Peru. Water temperatures clearly differ between these regions. Generally speaking, a species' geographic range is related to the water temperatures they tolerate; species with ranges spanning more than one province typically occur in much deeper (and therefore colder) water at the southern end of their distributions.

It is important to know what ecological role a species plays within a locality. Some idea of its abundance and prey/predator relationships helps ascertain the importance of a single species in a particular area. Distributions are not fixed; one must determine whether a species is present in a locality year-round or whether it only periodically or seasonally influences that habitat. Whether or not a species reproduces in a given habitat is very important, as this drastically affects its impact over a prolonged period of time. Like any study of living organisms in their natural environment, biogeographical data must be painstakingly accumulated over many years, in order to accurately assess the long-term situation.

For some species like *Dirona albolineata* defined faunal provinces have not limited their distribution. In these instances, the ability to tolerate wide ranges in water temperature and to feed on a diversity of prey organisms allows them to survive and flourish across boundaries and in areas which have excluded others. Phenomena such as El Niño events can provide the mechanisms for northward transport of a species, and depending upon its thermal requirements, it may remain in the fauna only while increased water temperature persists. Many have been observed to come and go from local habitats, disappearing for years at a time where they were once abundant, and then reappearing once again, e.g., *Flabellinopsis iodinea* and *Polycerella glandulosa* in central California or *Samla telja* in central Mexico. Certainly, biogeography is one of the most speculative aspects of the biology of organisms. Our understanding of the geographical affinities of the marine fauna of this coast continues to grow. It is interesting to note that no group is represented to a greater or lesser degree in one faunal province over the others, e.g., the number of species of dorids and sacoglossids is equally distributed between the temperate and the tropical provinces.

For additional reading, see Bertsch (2010; 2019), Ferreira & Bertsch (1975), Bertsch and Hermosillo (2007), and Hermosillo & Behrens (2005) for discussion of the distribution of the various groups of heterobranchs within these provinces.

Another factor that must be considered when studying the biogeography of organisms is whether a species' presence in an area is a result of natural dispersal or whether man's influence has altered its distributional pattern. For example, the aeolid nudibranch *Leostyletus misakiensis,* the dendronotid *Pseudobornella orientalis,* and the dorid nudibranch *Okenia plana* from Japan have been found on this coast, but only on the pilings and floating boat docks of San Francisco Bay, suggesting importation. The prey of opisthobranchs are frequently colonial organisms that foul ship bottoms, so the slugs (and their food and eggs) can be transported long distances on the hulls of ships. Ships' ballast tanks can serve as giant aquariums, transferring planktonic larvae from one side of the globe to another when water taken on in port in Japan is discharged into San Francisco Bay, for example. This was likely the means by which *Philine auriformis* and *Haloa japonica* were introduced to California bays and estuaries.

FINDING AND OBSERVING HETEROBRANCHS

Larger species of heterobranchs are easily found by scuba divers or tidepoolers, while smaller, more cryptic species generally require patience and laborious searching. Finding the specialized habitats of various species is challenging; patience and a keen eye (or magnifying glass) are necessary to find some species such as *Acteocina* and *Diaphana*, which reach a maximum length of 4 mm. The undersides of ledges and rocks are good places to look for heterobranchs because they afford good protection.

Careful examination of prey favored by nudibranchs, such as hydroids, sponges, tunicates, or algae, is often fruitful. Another very good clue is the occurrence of egg masses, which can indicate the recent visit of an adult. Different methods must be employed in different environments. For example, in order to find small cephalaspideans it is necessary to sift fine sand with a sieve.

When turning rocks, one must remember to carefully return them to their original position. It is no accident that the organisms living under rocks are different from the ones living on the surface, as it is the only place where they can survive. If left exposed to the air, sun, and predators they will not be there for future study and observation, or propagating their species.

The vast majority of heterobranchs are found just beyond the lower fringes of the intertidal, in the shallow subtidal. Thus the way to observe the greatest number of species is by scuba diving, snorkeling, or by examining the fouling organisms on the sides of floating docks. The colonial animals on which nudibranchs feed are most abundant on vertical surfaces and in caves. On a single dive or dock exploration, the inexperienced observer should be able to find 6-12 species of heterobranchs without too much difficulty.

The most productive observations are obtained with living animals in the field. Certainly, the greatest satisfaction is gained from simple morphological and ecological observations made without capturing or killing the animals. The easiest means of achieving this is by photography. If this is not possible, and collection is required, be responsible and take no more than your immediate purpose requires and, of course, abide by the laws regulating scientific collecting in your area.

J. Kocian

PICTORIAL GLOSSARY

The following terms used in this manual are defined and, where applicable, illustrated. Composite terms can be derived from the roots, if not otherwise given. Many nontechnical descriptive adjectives are illustrated to show their applications to heterobranch morphology.

aeolid (eolid) – type of nudibranch possessing cerata rather than a plume-like gill on the back and lacking a rhinophoral sheath.

annulate – referring to a type of rhinophore having a series of rings or bands along its stalk.
anterior – towards the head or front, situated in front.
aperture – the opening or gape of a shell.
apex – the peak of a shell, or high point of a shell.
arborescent – many branches, tree like.
bifurcate – branched, forming a fork.
bilabiate – having two lips.
bipinnate – referring to a gill that branches twice from the central axis.
branchial plume – respiratory structure or gill, usually situated posteriorly on the dorsum.

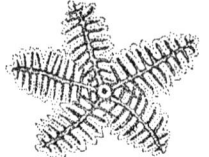  

buccal – mouth cavity.
caryophyllidia (-ium) – a specialized tubercle, surrounded by spicules, which has a sensory function.

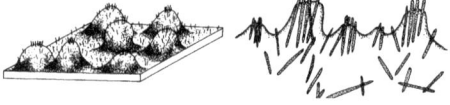

cephalic – of or on the head.
cephalic shield – the fleshy plate, free at the edges, which covers the anterior part of the head.
ceras (pl. cerata) – fingerlike respiratory structure bearing extensions of the digestive gland and occurring in groups of parallel series along dorsum.

     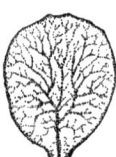   

chitin – a hard material, made of polysaccharides.
clavate – gradually thickening near distal end.
clavus – the expanded or club shaped terminus of the rhinophore, above the stalk.

columella – inner margin of the aperture of a gastropod shell.
cnidosac – the sac at the tip of each ceras, where nematocysts are stored.
cryptic species – species that are visibly indistinguishable from each other.
digitiform – fingerlike.
distal – near the tip or end of a structure.
dorsal – referring to the back or upper surface; the notum.
dorsal slit – in anaspideans, the dorsal opening between the right and left parapodia.
foot corners – anterior lateral projections of the foot.
gill – a respiratory structure.
head shield (see cephalic shield) – anterior fleshy portion of notum covering the head in Cephalaspidea.
hydranth – the terminal end of a hydroid polyp, containing the tentacles.
hyponotal – underneath the notum, on the side of the foot.
inflated – swollen, usually referring to the cerata.
jaw – chitinous structure used to grasp prey while feeding.
labial – lips, around the mouth.
lamellate – referring to a type of rhinophore having a series of plates or lamellae.
mantle – in molluscs: the portion of the integumental fold which secretes the shell; forms the dorsal surface (notum) of nudibranchs
mantle cavity – cavity housing the gill in primitive heterobranchs.
median, medial – toward the center or middle.

nematocyst – a microscopic stinging organelle produced by anemones, corals, and hydroids.
notum – the back surface of a heterobranch, the dorsum.
nudibranch – a suborder of molluscs lacking a shell in the adult and having external respiratory appendages, usually on the dorsal surface.
operculum – a plate serving to close the aperture when a snail retreats into its shell. Present in a few primitive heterobranchs.

palmate – resembling a hand with fingers outstretched, referring to a type of cerata.
papilla (pl. papillae)– a fingerlike extension with a basal diameter much smaller than its length and not containing digestive gland diverticulum.

parapodia – flap-like lateral body extensions which arise ventrally.

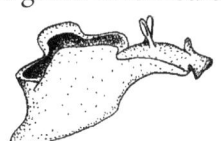

perfoliate – referring to a rhinophore whose central shaft seems to pass through leaf-like extensions. See *lamellate*.
pelagic – oceanic, occurring in the open ocean.
periostracum – the external, chitinous covering of the shell of certain molluscs.
phanerobranch – referring to the type of dorid nudibranchs whose gill is not retractable into a gill cavity, and usually has a long, narrow body.

pinnate – referring to the gill; feather-like, having equal branches extending from both sides of an axis.
posterior – to the rear, behind, tail end.
proximal – nearest to the center of the body or to the point of origin or attachment.
pseudocryptic species – species morphologically recognized as distinct only after other methods (e.g., DNA analysis) revealed their presence.
pulpit – elevated platform, referring to a rhinophore resembling a clergyman's pulpit.
radula (pl. radulae) – a file-like extensible feeding structure found in most heterobranchs, it bears numerous chitinous teeth.
rhinophore – paired sensory apparatus found on the head.
rosette – a flower-shaped cluster, usually referring to a type of gill.
shaft – basal portion of the rhinophore. See stalk.
siphon – a tube-like extension of the mantle for the passage of water currents.
spicule – glass-like supporting needle or rod found in tissue. 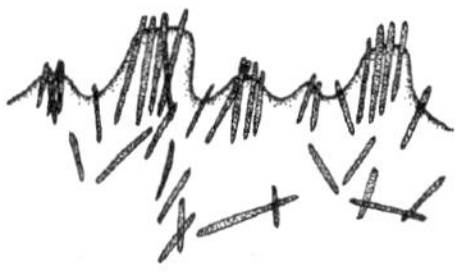
spire – the portion of a gastropod shell above the lowest whorl.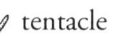
spiral – whorled or twisted in helical fashion. 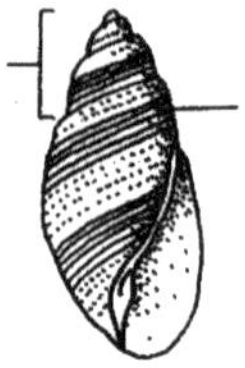
stalk – the basal attachment of the rhinophore.
striae – fine sculptural grooves or lines on the surface of the shell.
subapical – just below the apex or end.
subterminal – just prior to, or below, the distal end of an appendage.
suture – the line marking the junctions between whorls of a spiral shell. 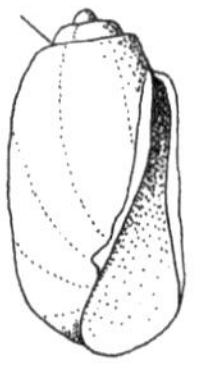
tentacle – an elongate sensory process, usually on the head.

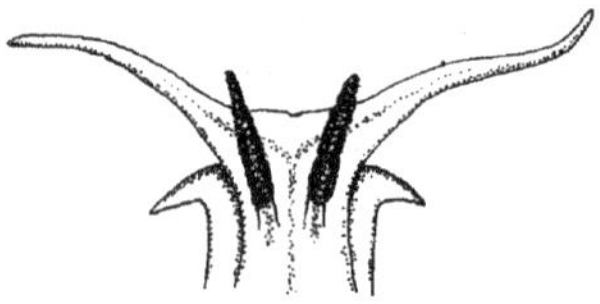

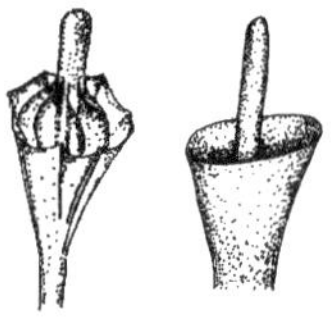

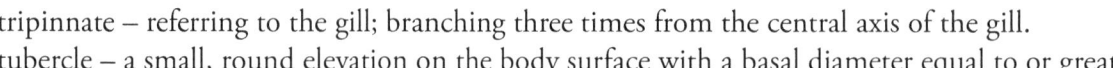

tripinnate – referring to the gill; branching three times from the central axis of the gill.
tubercle – a small, round elevation on the body surface with a basal diameter equal to or greater than its height.
veil – a membranous extension of the head.

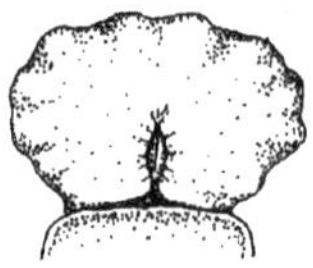

veliger – the larval stage of a mollusc which is furnished with a velum or ciliated swimming membrane. When hatched, veligers are usually free-swimming but they may also be seen rotating within the egg capsule just prior to hatching.
ventral – of, near, or on the underside.
verrucose – covered with warty elevations, referring to a type of rhinophores; wrinkled.
villous – covered with villi or short hair-like processes.

The order in which species accounts have been placed largely mirrors the layout of Behrens & Hermosillo (2005). It does **not** reflect any sort of proposed evolutionary pattern. Within genera, species are listed in alphabetical order. Due to the extensive amount of name changes, the reader may find many familiar species have been moved to unfamiliar genera and may have to refer to the index, which includes the older names.

Superfamily Acteonoidea

Rictaxis punctocaelatus (Carpenter, 1864) — striped barrel shell

Very often mistaken for a regular marine snail. The solid, spiral-sculptured shell has two revolving bands of white and black alternating stripes. There is no operculum and the body is opaque white.
Similar species: Snails in our area with similar banding have much more angular shells and an operculum.
Size: To 20 mm (0.8 in).
Range: Ketchikan, Alaska to Bahía Magdalena, Baja California, Mexico and the Gulf of California.
Habitat: Low intertidal to 230 m (755 ft.), on sand and mud. Rarely to 305 m (1000 ft).

K. Lee

Remarks: Glides along just under the surface of the sediment, where it is believed to feed on small worms. It lays slinky-like egg coils.

Order Runcinida

Recent molecular studies have shown that these little worm-like slugs are a distinct basal lineage that is characteristically distinct from other heterobranchs. They all have gizzard plates to mash their food and an internal shell. They seem to be very rare, possibly due to their seasonal and localized population occurrences. Although we know very little about our tiny species, it is probably an herbivore.

Rfemsia macfarlandi (Gosliner, 1991) (previously *Runcina macfarlandi*) — MacFarland's runcina

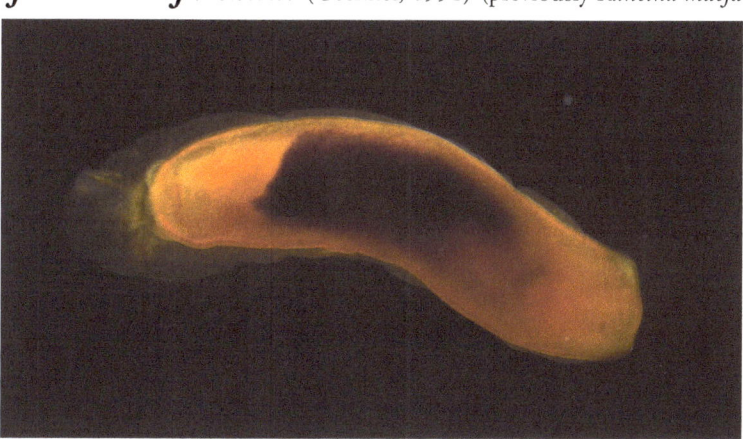

Body varies in color from dark maroon to yellowish brown with darker to brown or black pigment on the central portion. The head is flattened and there are no head appendages. There is a single paddle-shaped gill on either side of the anus.
Similar species: None.
Size: Tiny: to 5 mm (0.2 in).
Range: Lincoln County, Oregon to Long Beach, California.
Habitat: High intertidal, in rock pools.
Remarks: Has been found on the alga *Cladomorpha*.

E. Sanford

Order Cephalaspidea

The cephalaspids, or "headshield slugs," are characterized by the presence of a cephalic shield, and many can be recognized by their bubble-shaped shell. In some species it is internal and in others entirely lacking. Members of the headshield slugs occupy different marine habitats. Many are burrowers in muddy and sandy bottoms, while others live on rocky and hard substrates. The use of bright coloration in this group is not completely understood as the colorful species lack typical heterobranch defensive secretions. The diets of members vary widely from herbivores such as the haminoeids and *Bulla*, to carnivores such as the aglajids, *Philine* and *Navanax*. Some are cannibalistic and even specialized slug-o-vores, feeding on other species of heterobranchs.

Bulla gouldiana with its eggs
M. Passage

Acteocina cerealis (Gould, 1853) — grain barrel bubble

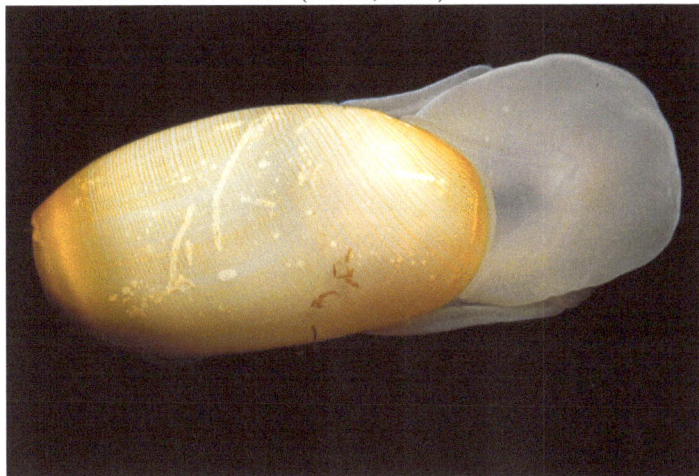

The animal is opaque white with a broad, flat, rounded head with a wide "V"-shaped notch in the back of the cephalic shield. The white shell is covered by light yellowish-tan periostracum with weak brown spiral striations, and has an almost flat spire.
Similar species: *Cylichna diegensis* has a much more elongate head.
Size: Shell to 14 mm (0.5 in).
Range: Kodiak Island, Alaska to central Baja California.
Habitat: Found on sand and mud, from the intertidal to 250 m (820 ft).

G. McDonald

Acteocina culcitella (Gould, 1853)

The shell is oblong, whitish, with a brown periostracum showing fine spiral lines or striae. The apex is high and the suture or crease between the spirals is deep. Body opaque white with white spots; the head is rounded with a central cleft.
Similar species: *Acteocina inculta* has a shorter shell without spiral lines and a much deeper cleft in the cephalic shield.
Size: Shell to 22 mm (0.8 in).
Range: Kodiak Island, Alaska to Laguna San Ignacio, Baja California Sur, Mexico.
Habitat: Lives intertidally to 70 m (230 ft) on sand and mud bottoms.
Remarks: Sporadically common.

R. Roller

Acteocina harpa (Dall, 1871)

This shelled heterobranch has a small white shell with a strong keeled shoulder, deep, flattened whorls, and axial, or lengthwise, striations on its body whorl.
Similar species: *Acteocina inculta* and *Retusa obtusa* lack the lengthwise grooves.
Size: Shell to 9 mm (0.35 in).
Range: Kenai, Alaska to Rocas Alijos, Mexico.
Habitat: Intertidal to 230 m (755 ft).
Remarks: Reportedly common on sand, gravel and mud.

G. Jensen

Acteocina inculta (Gould, 1855) **shouldered acteocina**

The shell is slightly oval with a spire that has deep, flattened (tabulate) whorls; the foot is white and the posterior of the cephalic shield has a deep cleft.
Similar species: *Acteocina harpa* has lengthwise striations on the body whorl.
Size: To 10 mm (0.4 in).
Range: Morro Bay, California to Peru.
Habitat: Intertidal to 30 m (98 ft).
Remarks: Intertidal specimens found in fine mud.

R. Roller

Retusa obtusa (Montagu, 1803)

Shell fragile, oval; apex truncated or slightly elevated; aperture slightly shorter than shell, wider anteriorly an narrowing abruptly at about 1/2 of length. Sculpture with faint growth lines; color uniformly dirty white, often with thin, brown periostracum.
Similar species: The aperture of *Diaphana californica* is as long as the shell, and it has a more southerly range.
Size: Shell to 5 mm (0.2 in).
Range: Arctic Ocean to the Gulf of Alaska and Vancouver Island, British Columbia, Canada.
Habitat: Intertidal to 360 m (1181 ft).
Remarks: Feeds on Foraminifera.

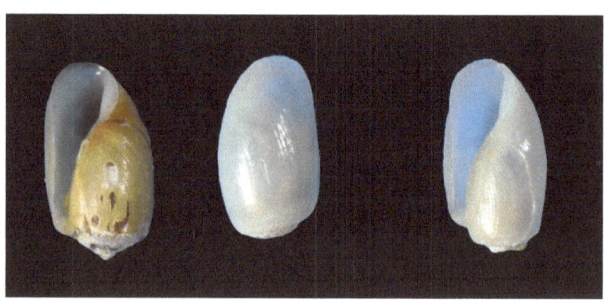

R. Harbo

Cylichna cf. *alba*

R. Long

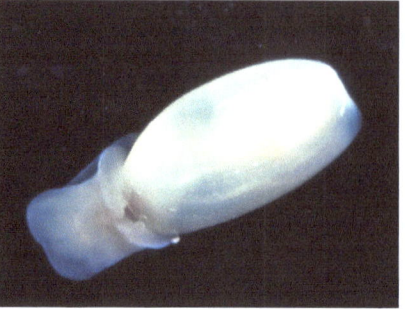

T. Gosliner

The two northeastern Pacific specimens shown here were identified as *C. alba*, but the presence of a periostracum on one suggests they are different species. *Cylichna alba* was originally described from Europe and appears to be a species complex, as Atlantic specimens do not all align with each other. No specimens have been sequenced from our region. Eastern Pacific specimens have been found from the Aleutian Islands and Bering Sea, Alaska to Boundary Bay, British Columbia, on estuarine mud flats and hidden in drying mats of drift eelgrass.

Cylichna cf. *attonsa*

The Puget Sound specimen shown is very similar to *Cylichna attonsa*, but the shell is not as elongate and has a much paler (or thinner) periostracum. *Cylichna attonsa* is primarily a deepwater species, reported from Kodiak Island, Alaska to the San Benito Islands, Baja California.

G. Paulay

Cylichna diegensis Dall, 1919   San Diego bubble

Shell fairly broad (about twice as long as wide) with spire completely sunken; anterior and posterior ends of the white shell with brown striations. Head is elongate, with shield broadening posteriorly.
Similar species: *Cylichna attonsa* and *Cylichna* cf. *attonsa* have longer, narrower shells; *Acteocina cerealis* has a broad, rounded head.
Size: Shell to 10 mm (0.4 in).
Range: Haida Gwaii, British Columbia to Bahía Todos Los Santos, Baja California.
Habitat: Subtidal from 37-353 m (121-1158 ft).
Remarks: Densities greater than 40/m² have been reported in the southern part of its range.

G. McDonald

Volvulella cylindrica (Carpenter, 1864)   cylindrical spindle-bubble

The shell is uniformly shiny and whitish, elongate and spindle shaped, with a tapered apex. The body is white.
Similar species: *Cylichna* cf. *attonsa* does not have a projecting apex.
Size: Shell to 5 mm (0.2 in); living animal to 11 mm (0.4 in).
Range: Vancouver Island, British Columbia, Canada to Panama and the Galapagos Islands.
Habitat: Intertidal to 55 m (180 ft); rarely to 230 m (755 ft).

R. Long

Diaphana californica Dall, 1919   California diaphana

The barely calcified shell is somewhat pentagonal and uniformly translucent white to light brown, with an aperture that runs the length of the shell. The body and foot are translucent white, with opaque white dots on the cephalic shield which is anteriorly divided.
Similar species: *Retusa obtusa* has a more northern distribution (southern British Columbia to the Arctic) and the aperture is a little shorter than the shell.
Size: Tiny; shell to 4.3 mm (0.17 in).
Range: Port Orchard, Washington to Islas Los Coronados, Baja California, Mexico.
Habitat: Intertidal to 353 m (1158 ft).
Remarks: Occurs in subtidal kelp holdfasts and on sand and algae.

K. Fletcher

Bulla gouldiana Pilsbry, 1895 — Gould's bubble snail

The thin shell of this bubble snail is reddish to greyish-brown with dark and light spots. The columella is thick and white. The apex of the shell lies in a pit. The body is orange to brown with light blue to pink-white spots.
Similar species: *Bulla punctulata* has a much smaller and thicker shell, and is found further south.
Size: Shell to 55 mm (2.1 in).
Range: Morro Bay, California to Mazatlan, Mexico.
Habitat: Intertidal to 10 m (33 ft) on mud and sand in bays and lagoons.
Remarks: Burrows just beneath the surface of the sediment, feeding on diatoms and detritus.

G. Jensen

Bulla punctulata A. Adams, 1850 — spotted bubble snail

The thick, squat to pear-shaped shell is brownish to pinkish with scattered dark and white spots and blotches, occasionally merging to form either a zigzag or two spiral bands, one posteriorly and another between the middle and anterior area of shell. Body is light brown to pale pink and covered with tiny bright yellowish-white spots.
Similar species: *Bulla gouldiana* has a much thinner and larger shell.
Size: Shell to 38.4 mm (1.5 in).
Range: Mazatlan, Mexico to Peru.
Habitat: Intertidal to 25 m (82 ft), on sand and mud.
Remarks: Primarily nocturnal.

A. Hermosillo

Haloa japonica (Pilsbry, 1895) (previously *Haminoea japonica*) — Japanese bubble snail

Thin, translucent white, oval to quadrangular shell with a relatively broad apical end and the anterior end covered by a short parapodia. Body elongate, pale to dark greenish-grey with opaque white mottling, dark patches and a pale gray area around the small eyes; viscera grey and black with conspicuous orange-red dots. A deep notch divides the cephalic shield.
Similar species: *Haminoea vesicula* and *H. virescens* do not have the deep cleft in the cephalic shield.
Size: Shell to 22 mm (0.8 in); overall to 40 mm (1.6 in).
Range: British Columbia, Canada to San Francisco Bay, California; Europe. Native to Japan and Korea.
Habitat: Intertidal and shallow subtidal sheltered bays.
Remarks: An introduced species that has displaced the native *Haminoea vesicula* in some areas.

D. Behrens

Haminoea cf. *ovalis* (previously *Haminoea ovalis*)

The body is pale green and densely dotted with orange and purple; the portion seen through the shell has larger yellowish blotches. There is a diffuse cream-white "Y" on the head.
Similar species: Our other species of *Haminoea* lack the orange spotting.
Size: To 12 mm (0.5 in).
Range: Bahía de Banderas, Mexico to Costa Rica, Panama and Peru.
Habitat: Intertidal and subtidal.
Remarks: *Haminoea ovalis* (now *Lamprohaminoea ovalis*) was described from Tahiti and differs in color.

A. Hermosillo

Haminoea vesicula (Gould, 1855)

glassy bubble shell

The thin, oval, translucent white to beige or pale green shell is exposed with a sunken spire; width of the opening half or less the length of the shell. The shell surface is covered with a thin brown to yellow orange-speckled periostracum. The elongate body is translucent grey with opaque white mottling and a pale gray area around the small eyes; distance between the eyes less than the distance from the eye to the side of the head. Cephalic shield sometimes has a central white stripe.
Similar species: *Haminoea virescens* has much more widely-spaced eyes. *Haloa japonica* has a deep notch in the cephalic shield.
Size: Shell to 24 mm (0.9 in); total length to 50 mm (2 in).
Range: Ketchikan, Alaska to Mazatlan, Sinaloa, Mexico.
Habitat: Intertidal to 10 m (33 ft) in muddy bays and eelgrass, and on floating structures.
Remarks: Probably feeds on *Ulva* and *Polysiphonia*.

G. Jensen

Haminoea virescens (Sowerby, 1833)

green bubble shell

Thin, semi-translucent, yellowish to pale brown shell with an aperture that is larger than half the length of the shell. Wide, short, brownish-green body with opaque white mottling and a broad pale grey area around the large eyes; cephalic shield with central white stripe and lacking a notch. Distance between eyes greater than from eye to edge of head.
Similar species: The distance between the eyes of *Haminoea vesicula* is less than from the eye to the side of the head.
Size: Shell to 24 mm (0.9 in); living animal to 45 mm (1.8 in).
Range: Prince William Sound, Alaska to Mazatlan, Mexico.
Habitat: Intertidal.
Remarks: Occurs seasonally in outer coast rocky intertidal pools, and in bays and lagoons.

A. Hermosillo

Gastropteron pacificum Bergh, 1893 — winged sea slug

The body has two wide flaps, resembling wings when it is swimming. Its color may be translucent gray with or without a yellowish tinge with varying amounts of red spots, and occasionally scattered yellow spots.
Similar species: Pteropods like *Clione elegantissima* have proportionately much smaller wings.
Size: To 40 mm (1.6 in).
Range: Aleutian Islands, Alaska to San Diego, California.
Habitat: Low intertidal to 425 m (1400 ft), on sand or mud.

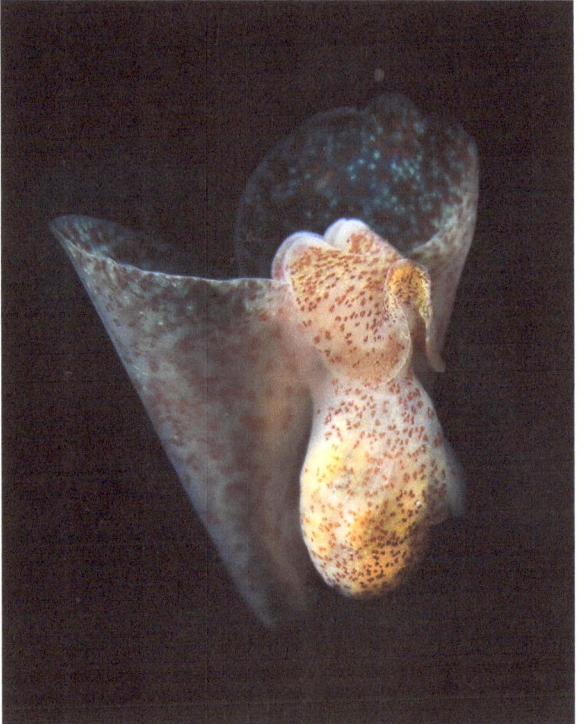
J. Kocian

G. Jensen

Remarks: Lays grape-like gelatinous egg masses considerably larger than itself.

Aglaja ocelligera (Bergh, 1894) — spotted aglaja

Body may be brown-black with yellow and white spots, sometimes with a blue sheen along the sides, or brown with white and yellow spots. The head is short with a white to yellow mark on the lateral lobes. The paired tails are long, with the left tail longer than the right, and there is an internal shell.
Similar species: *Melanchlamys diomedea* lacks the pair of long tails and the spots.

G. Jensen

Size: To 40 mm (1.6 in).
Range: Sitka, Alaska to San Diego Bay, California.
Habitat: Intertidal to 218 m (715 ft), on sand and mud.
Remarks: Feeds on the bubble snail *Haminoea vesicula*, and capable of swimming.
G. Jensen

Melanochlamys diomedea (Bergh, 1894) (previously *Aglaja diomedea*)   **Albatross aglaja**

The body is translucent pale gray with varying amounts of brown to black mottling which, when dense, gives the animal a dark brownish-gray to inky black appearance. Brownish-yellow internal organs may show through the body wall. The head is rounded without lateral processes. The lobes of the tail are short and of equal length, and there is a small internal shell.
Similar species: *Aglaja ocelligera* has a pair of long tails and conspicuous spotting. *Melanochlamys ezoensis* has a longer head shield, reaching over half the length of the body, and white spots.
Size: To 15 mm (0.6 in).
Range: Fairmount Island, Alaska to Carlsbad, California.
Habitat: Intertidal to 100 m (328 ft), on the sand and mud of bays and estuaries and on the open coast.
Remarks: Feeds on nematodes.

K. Fletcher

Melanochlamys ezoensis (Baba, 1957)

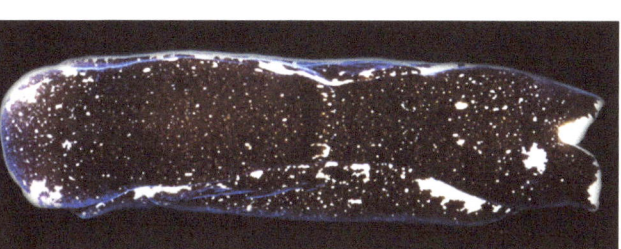

Body elongate, narrow; cephalic shield occupies more than half of body; color brownish grey, mottled with dark pigment; opaque white spots all over body, with larger white patches anteriorly, along the sides, and at the tails.
Similar species: The cephalic shield of *Melanochlamys diomedea* is half or less of the body length, and it lacks the white spots.

H. Tachikawa

Size: To 13 mm (0.5 in).
Range: Introduced in San Francisco Bay. Native range from Hokkaido, Japan and Peter the Great Bay, Russia to Katsuura, Japan.
Habitat: Intertidal, on sand and mud in bays and estuaries.
Remarks: This species was first detected in San Francisco Bay in 2001.

Navanax aenigmaticus (Bergh, 1893)   **riddle navanax**

Color varies from brown to pink, red, purple or olive, mottled with cream-white blotches. There is a series of turquoise blue spots along the inner parapodial border. The shell of this species is internal.
Similar species: *Navanax inermis* has much longer tails and longitudinal stripes.
Size: To 75 mm (3 in).
Range: Bahía Vizcaino, Baja California, Mexico to Chile.
Habitat: Intertidal to 18 m (59 ft).
Remarks: A voracious carnivore that feeds on other sea slugs.

R. Agarwal

A. Hermosillo

K. Lee

Navanax inermis (Cooper, 1863)
California navanax

Color highly variable, but always with parapodia bordered by an orange-yellow stripe and electric blue spots or streaks. Ground color fleshy tan to black; variable yellow, white, or orange striping or streaks over remainder of body. Two long, triangular tails.
Similar species: *Navanax polyalphos* is dark with a uniform covering of tiny light spots; *N. aenigmaticus* has short tails and lacks the longitudinal stripes.
Size: To 225 mm (8.8 in).
Range: Bolinas Lagoon, California to Nayarit, Mexico.
Habitat: Intertidal to 30 m (98 ft), on mud and sand.
Remarks: Feeds on *Haminoea* and other heterobranchs.

K. Lee

K. Lee

P. Garner

Navanax polyalphos (Gosliner & Williams, 1972)
white-spotted navanax

Body color rusty brown to black and covered with fine white to yellow specks. These specks are concentrated into dense white aggregates on each side of the head, across the anterior edge of the mantle, and at the fork in the tail. The internal shell of this species is completely calcified.
Similar species: *Navanax inermis* is striped rather than spotted, and attains a much larger size.
Size: To 45 mm (1.8 in).
Range: Santa Cruz Island, California to Costa Rica; Gulf of California.
Habitat: Intertidal mud flats.
Remarks: Feeds on *Haminoea virescens*.

K. Lee

Philinopsis cf. *speciosa* (previously *Philinopsis cyanea*)

Color variable, from deep blue to translucent cream with minute tan and yellow spots on the dorsum. Parapodia, cephalic shield and tail with elongated black spots, some orange spots and tiny yellow spots; cephalic shield more than half length of body and characteristically held in an elevated position.
Similar species: None.
Size: To 15 mm (0.6 in).
Range: Manzanillo, Mexico to Panama and the Galapagos Islands.
Habitat: Found on sand and mud.
Remarks: Nocturnal.

A. Hermosillo

Philinorbis albus (Mattox, 1958) (previously *Philine alba*)   **white philine**

A nondescript, broad, flat, aglajid-like animal. Overall color creamy white to pale brown; the mantle is smooth and there is a flat, smooth, internal shell.
Similar species: *Philine auriformis* tends to be much whiter, more elongate, and usually found in much shallower water.
Size: To 60 mm (2.3 in).
Range: Monterey Bay, California to central Baja California; also the Galapagos Islands.
Habitat: From 36-274 m (118-899 ft).
Remarks: Typically dredged from sand bottoms in deep water.

D. Behrens

Philine auriformis Suter, 1909   **ear-shaped philine**

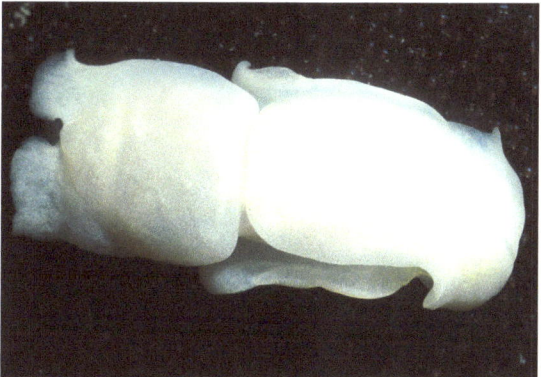

T. Gosliner

Transparent white to yellow in color. The anterior shield is longer than the posterior shield; the latter is notched and conceals the broad shell.
Similar species: *Philinorbis albus* is creamy white, stouter, and found in very deep water.
Size: To 50 mm (2 in).
Range: Vancouver Island, British Columbia to San Diego, California; native to New Zealand.
Habitat: Intertidal to 300 m (984 ft), on sand and mud.
Remarks: Introduced from New Zealand, this species feeds on the small clams *Gemma gemma* and *Transennella*. It is sometimes referred to as the New Zealand tortellini snail.

Several externally-identical species of *Philine* occur in our region. See Valdés (2019) for information on this difficult group.

Order Aplysiida

Members of Aplysiida are called "sea hares" due to their rabbit-like ears, formed by their rhinophores. Most of the species covered in this guide have an internal shell. All are herbivores, feeding on various species of algae. Many are very large; in fact, one of our species, the black sea hare *Aplysia vaccaria*, is considered the largest gastropod in the world. Specimens have been known to reach 99 cm (39 in) in length and weigh up to 15.9 kilograms (35 lbs).

Juvenile *Aplysia californica*

K. Lee

Aplysia californica Cooper, 1863   **California seahare**

G. Jensen

Color varies from reddish brown or tan to a dull green, with fine reticulating patterns and dark blotches and spots. The parapodia are joined about halfway between the exhalent siphon and the end of the tail. The body is quite soft.
Similar species: Parapodia of *Aplysia vaccaria* and *A. juliana* join right behind the exhalant siphon.
Size: To 750 mm (27.5 in).
Range: Yaquina Bay, Oregon to Guaymas, Sonora, Mexico; records from Central America and Japan need verification.
Habitat: Low intertidal to 33 m (100 ft), on both hard and soft bottoms.
Remarks: Feeds on red and green algae and exudes purple ink when disturbed. It is a model organism for neuroscience research.

Aplysia hooveri Golestani et al., 2019
(previously *Aplysia parvula*)   **Hoover's seahare**

Body is greenish-tan to reddish-brown with scattered tiny white spots often forming patches. The parapodia are very large relative to the small size of the animal and have bluish or greenish to black edges.
Similar species: None.
Size: To 60 mm (2.3 in).
Range: Baja California, Mexico and Gulf of California to Peru and the Galapagos Islands. Sighted at San Clemente Island, California during an El Niño event.
Habitat: Shallow subtidal to at least 18 m (59 ft), often among red algae.
Remarks: Named for sea slug enthusiast Craig Hoover.

B. Wight

Aplysia juliana Quoy & Gaimard, 1832   **Juliana's seahare**

Color is highly variable; the most common forms are brownish ones with pale spots or uniformly black specimens. The parapodia join high in the posterior midline. The posterior part of the foot can form a sucker that enables the seahare to move like an inchworm, rather than glide like a typical sea slug.
Similar species: *Aplysia vaccaria* is much darker in color.
Size: To 80 mm (3.1 in) in the eastern Pacific.
Range: Sonora, Mexico to Peru; cosmopolitan in tropics.
Habitat: Intertidal and shallow subtidal.
Remarks: Produces a milky white secretion rather than the usual purple ink released by *Aplysia*. It is a nocturnal species.

A. Hermosillo

Aplysia vaccaria Winkler, 1955   **black seahare**

The firm body is a uniform dark brown to black, rarely with fine grey or white markings. The parapodial junction is immediately behind the exhalent siphon. The foot sole is a deep purple-black.
Similar species: The parapodia of *Aplysia californica* join halfway between the exhalent siphon and the end of the foot, and the body is much softer.
Size: Huge, to 1 m (39 in).
Range: Elkhorn Slough, California to the Gulf of California.
Habitat: Low intertidal to 8 m (26 ft).
Remarks: The largest gastropod in the world, it can weigh up to 15.9 kg (35 lbs). It feeds primarily, if not exclusively, on feather boa kelp (*Egregia menziesii*). *Aplysia cedrosensis*, described from the Gulf of California, is likely a synonym, and that name would have priority if they are determined to be the same.

G. Jensen

G. Jensen

D. Behrens

Dolabella cf. *auricularia*

Color variable but it is usually mottled shades of green and brown which make it extremely well camouflaged among algae. The body has a sloping disc-like shield concealing a heavy, calcified shell with papillae around the edge. The mantle cavity is almost completely enclosed, with one large exhalant siphon in the middle and a blunt back end.
Similar species: In *Dolabrifera nicaraguana* the exhalant siphon is posterior rather than in the middle of the body.
Size: To 500 mm (19.6 in).
Range: Circumtropical, but see Remarks.
Habitat: Intertidal to 15 m (49 ft) in sheltered bays and lagoons; often found burrowing into bottom sediments.
Remarks: There is molecular evidence that this name is currently applied to more than one species. When disturbed, it releases a purple ink.

M. Chamberlain

Dolabrifera nicaraguana Pilsbry, 1896 (previously *Dolabrifera dolabrifera*)   **Nicaragua seahare**

Body color varies from a mottled green to light brown, and even pink to dark brown. The body is relatively flattened and covered in low tubercles and papillae. Animals taper in shape with the posterior half broad and rounded, gradually narrowing towards the small head. The parapodia are fused except for a short region in the posterior midline.
Similar species: *Dolabella* cf. *auricularia* has a centrally-located exhalant siphon.
Size: Small, to 40 mm (1.5 in).
Range: Gulf of California, Mexico to Tumbes, Peru.
Habitat: Intertidal, under rocks.
Remarks: It crawls with an inchworm-like movement, and produces a milky white secretion when disturbed.

A. Hermosillo

Notarchus indicus Schweigger, 1820   **Indian seahare**

Body color varies from yellow to brown with white or yellow specks sprinkled over the surface and is covered in tubercles. The parapodia are almost completely fused, creating a chamber that is used for jet propulsion. This species changes shape as it crawls.
Similar species: None.
Size: To 40 mm (1.5 in).
Range: Circumtropical.
Habitat: Subtidal among algae.
Remarks: When disturbed, this species can inflate its respiratory cavity with water and forcefully expel it, awkwardly swimming by jet propulsion.

A. Hermosillo

A. Hermosillo

Phyllaplysia padinae Williams & Gosliner, 1973
padina seahare

The flattened, elongate-oval body is olive-green to brownish green with random white spotting on the dorsal surface. Some specimens have a few variably shaped papillae, with multiple tips.
Similar species: None.
Size: To 45 mm (1.8 in).
Range: Gulf of California to Panama.
Habitat: Intertidal to at least 7 m (25 ft), usually on the alga *Padina*. Also reported on eelgrass.
Remarks: This well-camouflaged species also crawls with an inchworm-like movement.

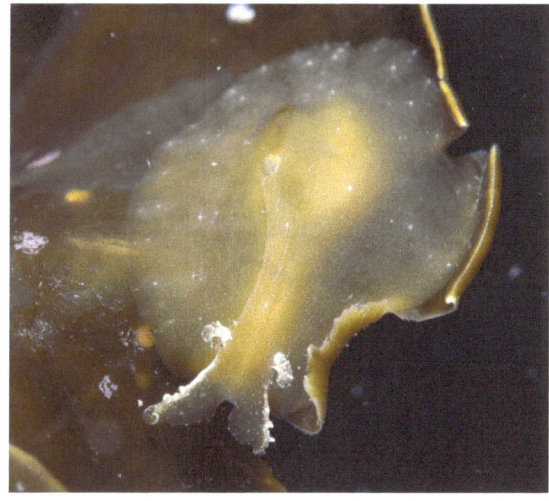

A. Hermosillo

Phyllaplysia taylori Dall, 1900 — Taylor's seahare

The body color is typically bright green, (rarely yellow-orange) with distinct black and white longitudinal stripes. Some (particularly from the southern part of the range) can be boldly marked with many transverse black stripes. The parapodia of this species are poorly developed and the body is dorsally flattened.

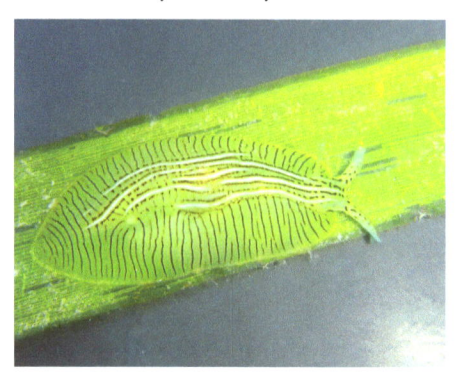

Similar species: Could be confused with the eelgrass flatworm *Triplana viridis*, which lacks longitudinal lines and rhinophores.
Size: To 80 mm (3.1 in).
Range: Vancouver Island, British Columbia to San Diego, California.
Habitat: Low intertidal and shallow subtidal, on eelgrass.
Remarks: Superbly camouflaged when aligned along a blade of eelgrass. Genetic sequencing may reveal cryptic species in this group.

R. Agarwal

M. Chamberlain

Stylocheilus rickettsi (MacFarland, 1966)
(previously *Stylocheilus striatus*) **Rickett's lined seahare**

This is a small elongate sea hare with dark, irregular longitudinal lines interrupted by scattered bright blue spots. The body is adorned with numerous branching appendages and has a prominent dorsal hump and a long tail.
Similar species: None.
Size: To 65 mm (2.5 in).
Range: Baja California, Mexico to the Galapagos Islands.
Habitat: Low intertidal to 12 m (39 ft).
Remarks: Difficult to spot amongst the algae of its preferred benthic rocky habitat.

A. Hermosillo

Order Pleurobranchida

Commonly referred to as "side-gilled slugs" this group is actually very closely related to nudibranchs. The gill leaves are easily seen on the right side of the body under the mantle. All members are carnivorous, feeding on a wide menu of species from sponges to burrowing anemones and even other opisthobranchs. Large *Pleurobranchaea californica* have been collected with a dozen or more small specimens of the same species in their gut. Most species have a reduced internal shell. The defense arsenal of side-gilled slugs includes acidic secretions and the ability to shed (autotomize) portions of their mantle along distinct fracture lines, much like a lizard can drop its tail when attacked.

R. McMunn

Berthella cf. *agassizii*

Body is pink to reddish-brown, sometimes with scattered opaque white spots. The rhinophores are rolled and the dorsal surface has a wrinkled appearance.
Similar species: *Berthella grovesi* has tubercles rather than wrinkles.
Size: To 12 mm (0.5 in).
Range: Punta Eugenia, Baja California to Panama.
Habitat: Intertidal to subtidal, on colonial tunicates.
Remarks: *Berthella agassizii* was described from Brazil; given the separation and differences in size, color, and the reproductive tract between specimens from the Atlantic and Pacific, they are undoubtedly different species.

K. Lee

Berthella andromeda Ghanimi, et al., 2020 (previously *Berthella stellata*) — galaxy sidegill

Body color is translucent white to honey-brown. The smooth notum is covered with a scattering of opaque white markings. An opaque, white transverse bar or cross is generally situated near the middle of the notum, but may be absent in some specimens.
Similar species: *Berthella strongi* has small dorsal tubercles and lacks the transverse white bar or cross.
Size: To at least 6 mm (0.2 in).
Range: Baja California to Mazatlan, Mexico, possibly to Costa Rica.
Habitat: Intertidal to 7 m (23 ft).
Remarks: Feeds on a plankinid sponge, *Oscarella* sp.

B. Green

Berthella californica (Dall, 1900) — California sidegill

Body color varies from white to tan in shallow water specimens to brown in deeper water animals. The mantle is smooth, with a uniform covering of tiny white spots; there is usually a white stripe dorsally on the rolled rhinophores. The mantle and foot have a white margin.
Similar species: *Berthella chacei* has dorsal tubercles and white spots on the rhinophores.
Size: To 127 mm (5 in).
Range: Ventura County, California to the Pacific Coast of Panama and the Galapagos Islands.
Habitat: Intertidal to 86 m (282 ft).
Remarks: Believed to prey on sponges.

G. Jensen

Berthella chacei (Burch, 1944)   Chace's sidegill

Body is white, with randomly-spaced white spots of various sizes on tubercles, oral veil, rhinophores, and foot. Mantle, foot, and oral veil with opaque white margins.
Similar species: *Berthella californica* is smooth with a more uniform covering of tiny white spots; *B. strongi* lacks the white margins on the foot and mantle.
Size: To 70 mm (2.7 in).
Range: Alaska to San Diego, California; Sea of Japan.
Habitat: Intertidal to 33 m (108 ft).
Remarks: Feeds on plakinid sponges, including *Oscarella carmela*. This species was recently resurrected, having long been considered a variation of *B. californica*.

D. Behrens

Berthella grovesi Hermosillo & Valdés 2008 (previously *Berthellina* sp. 1)   Groves' sidegill

Color varies from off-white to pink-brown; body covered with large, irregular tubercles. A few of the larger tubercles have a dark spot surrounded by an opaque white ring on the tubercle tip. Rhinophores are short and rolled and the oral veil is rounded and small. The internal shell is not visible through the mantle.
Similar species: *Berthella* cf. *agassizii* has wrinkles instead of tubercles.
Size: To 30 mm (1.2 in).
Range: Isla Isabel, Nayarit, Mexico to Panama.
Habitat: Shallow subtidal.
Remarks: Found underneath rocks.

A. Hermosillo

Berthella martensi (Pilsbry, 1896)   Martens' sidegill

Color highly variable, ranging from off-white in the Eastern Pacific to orange and deep maroon in the tropical Western Pacific. This species always has characteristic large spots which are dark on lighter specimens and light on dark ones, and there is often a band along the edge of the mantle and foot. The gill is sometimes visible under the mantle on the right side.
Similar species: None.
Size: To 70 mm (2.7 in), but eastern Pacific specimens to only 15 mm (0.6 in).
Range: Baja California Sur to Panama; also found in the Indo-West Pacific.
Habitat: Intertidal to subtidal.
Remarks: May jettison large pieces of its mantle when disturbed.

C. Hoover

Berthella strongi (MacFarland, 1966)   **Strong's sidegill**

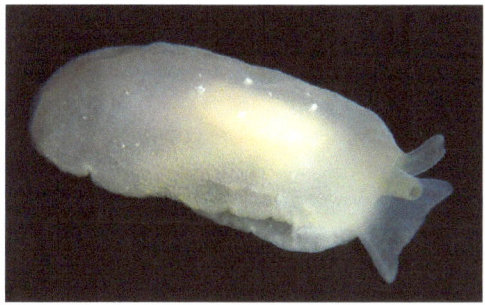

Body very pale yellow to beige with very small ridges and scattered tubercles with apical opaque white spots. Trapezoidal oral veil; no white margin around the mantle, oral veil or foot.
Similar species: *Berthella andromeda* is smooth and usually has a white dorsal bar or cross; *B. chacei* has white margins on the mantle and foot.
Size: To 25 mm (1 in).
Range: Moss Beach, California to Punta Rosarito and El Tomatal, Baja California.
Habitat: Intertidal.
Remarks: Found on compound ascidians.

R. Agarwal

Berthellina ilisima Marcus & Marcus, 1967

orange blob

The dorsum is very smooth, and the entire body apricot to orange-red. The dark internal disc-shaped shell can be seen through the notum.
Similar species: None.
Size: To 100 mm (3.9 in).
Range: Santa Barbara, California to Panama, including the Gulf of California and Galapagos Islands.
Habitat: Intertidal and subtidal.
Remarks: Feeds on the sponge, *Oscarella*, and is active at night.
A. Hermosillo

Pleurobranchus digueti Rochebrune, 1895
(previously *Pleurobranchus areolatus*)   **Diguet's pleurobranchus**

The dorsal surface is covered with different-sized, smooth tubercles with a tiny white apical nipple. The largest tubercles tend to be darker than the small ones. The rolled rhinophores are tan to orange.
Similar species: *Pleurobranchus* sp. 1 has low, smooth tubercles.
Size: To 106 mm (4.1 in).
Range: Santa Barbara, California to Columbia and the Galapagos Islands.
Habitat: Intertidal to subtidal.
Remarks: Found under rocks during the day, active at night.

A. Hermosillo

Pleurobranchus sp.

A large pleurobranch having a notal surface covered with large smooth tubercles, the largest ones brown and the smaller golden brown. In juveniles the border between the tubercules is white; in larger specimens light tan to peach. The rolled rhinophores are tan to orange; the foot is wide and orange in color.
Similar species: *Pleurobranchus digueti* has taller tubercles tipped with white nipples.
Size: To 190 mm (7.5 in).
Range: Anacapa and Catalina Islands, California to Isla Revillagigedos and San Benitos Island, Mexico.

D. Behrens

Pleurobranchaea californica MacFarland, 1966 — California pleurobranchus

Color is a mottled brown to gray, with areas of irregular, colorless patches. The dorsum is covered with low tubercles and the oral veil is fringed with short processes. The rhinophores are long and dark-tipped.
Similar species: *Berthella californica* and *B. chacei* lack the anterior processes on the oral veil.
Size: To 250 mm (9.8 in).
Range: Nootka Sound, BC to San Diego, CA; rarely reported north of Oregon.
Habitat: From 9-400 m (30-1200 ft) on soft bottoms.
Remarks: Preys on a wide variety of smaller invertebrates and fish, and can be cannibalistic.

R. Boerema

Tylodina fungina Gabb, 1865 — mushroom sidegill

This species is quite unique, with its external, cap-shaped shell. The shell is covered with a thick periostracum and the body is bright yellow. The rhinophores are rolled and the gill emerges from the body on the right side.
Similar species: Could be mistaken for a limpet, but easily distinguished by the yellow body and covered shell. A much smaller, flatter species, *Tylodina spongotheras*, is known only from deep water in British Columbia, so does not overlap in range.
Size: To 40 mm (1.5 in).
Range: Morro Bay, California to Costa Rica and the Galapagos.
Habitat: Low intertidal to 20 m (60 ft).
Remarks: Found on the yellow sponges *Aiolochroia thiona* and *Aplysina gerardogreeni*.

A. Hermosillo

Umbraculum umbraculum (Lightfoot, 1786) — umbrella sidegill

The shell is a flat disc with a slightly elevated center, that is usually covered with encrusting plants and animals. The body is covered with large pustules.
Similar species: None.
Size: To 120 mm (4.7 in).
Range: Circumtropical.
Habitat: Intertidal to 100 m (328 ft).
Remarks: The "description" of this species is a listing in a catalog of specimens being sold in an estate sale.

A. Hermosillo

Superorder Sacoglossa

Hermaea vancouverensis, showing the rolled rhinophores characteristic of most sacoglossids.

G. Jensen

Sacoglossids are commonly referred to as "sap-sucking slugs." An interesting characteristic of this group is their habit of storing their used, worn-out radular teeth in a sack below the head, saving their dental history. The nickname "sapsucker" came later, after biologists noted their feeding behavior – stabbing algal cells with their single, long, pointed rachidian tooth, then sucking the algal sap out.

Molecular evidence suggests that that sacoglossans are closely related to air-breathing marine pulmonates such as *Onchidella*. A few of the more primitive genera, such as *Oxynoe* and *Lobiger*, have a shell, while the more derived (advanced) species lack a shell as adults. These have dorsal appendages (e.g., *Placida* and *Stiliger*) or paired elongate parapodia, as in *Elysia*.

Berthelinia chloris (Dall, 1918)
green sapsucker

The body is enclosed between two clam-like shells. The body and shell are green with white markings at the edge of the shell and on the rhinophores.
Similar species: None.
Size: To 18 mm (0.7 in).
Range: Bahía Magdalena, Baja California Sur and Gulf of California to the Galapagos.
Habitat: Subtidal.
Remarks: Feeds and lives on the toxic green alga, *Caulerpa*.

A. Hermosillo

Oxynoe aliciae Krug et al., 2018 (previously *Oxynoe panamensis*)
Alicia's sapsucker

The shell is enclosed by two large parapodia bearing off-white colored papillae and blue spots. The small and blunt head is not retractile; the rolled rhinophores are horizontal and have off-white blotches at the tips.
Similar species: None.
Size: To 28 mm (1.1 in).
Range: Bahía Magdalena, Baja California Sur and the Gulf of California to Panama and the Galapagos.
Habitat: Intertidal.
Remarks: Feeds on the toxic green alga *Caulerpa scalpelliformis*, and secretes a milky substance when disturbed. Named for co-author Alicia Hermosillo.

C. Hoover

Lobiger cf. *souverbii*

The shell and body are green, and there are four long, knobby, parapodial lobes. The shell has fine striations and a few thin bluish lines. The rhinophores are rolled, and small black eye spots are visible.
Similar species: None.
Size: To 15 mm (0.6 in).
Range: Baja California Sur to the Galapagos Islands.
Habitat: Subtidal, from 11-44 m (36-144 ft).
Remarks: Feeds, lives, and lays its flattened, green egg mass on the toxic green alga, *Caulerpa racemosa*. *Lobiger souverbii* was described from the Caribbean, so it's likely that the eastern Pacific harbors a different species.

A. Hermosillo

Elysia cf. *cornigera*

Color a dirty or opaque white with tiny red or dark spots. Body with warty papillations and parapodia that form tall lobes. The rhinophores taper to a smooth point and have undulate edges, making them look like horns.
Similar species: None.
Size: To 15 mm (0.6 in).
Range: Reported from Isla Cerralvo, Gulf of California and Isla Revillagigedos.
Habitat: Intertidal to 3 m (10 ft).
Remarks: *Elysia cornigera* was described from Florida, and is likely a different species from those in the eastern Pacific.

M. Poddubetskaia

Elysia diomedea (Bergh, 1894) — Mexican dancer

Color is highly variable, ranging from green to purple and turquoise with orange, black, white, and blue accents. There are white or blue lines on the sides of the body. The mantle edges are highly ruffled and the appearance can greatly differ depending on whether they are extended or not. The rhinophores are rolled, and have characteristic black and yellow lines which do not vary and are a good character to identify this species.
Similar species: None.
Size: To 100 mm (3.9 in).
Range: Gulf of California and possibly along the Pacific coast of Mexico.
Habitat: Intertidal to 30 m (98 ft), on *Padina* and *Codium*.
Remarks: Specimens from Costa Rica to Peru are genetically different from those in Mexico.

A. Hermosillo

A. Hermosillo

Elysia hedgpethi Marcus, 1961 — Hedgpeth's sapsucker

The body is encompassed by two dorsal parapodia; color is usually a rich green, occasionally a yellowish brown or tan. Under close observation, the entire body is covered with minute yellow, red, and blue metallic spots.
Similar species: *Aplysia* spp. have large oral tentacles that are lacking in this species.
Size: To 25 mm (1 in).
Range: Calvert Island, BC to Puerto Vallarta, Mexico.
Habitat: Intertidal to 10 m (33 ft).
Remarks: Feeds on the green algae *Codium fragile* and *Bryopsis corticulans*.

J. Kocian

Elysia cf. *pusilla*

This extremely cryptic *Elysia* is broadly flattened posteriorly, closely matching the shape and deep green color of the algae upon which it lives and feeds.
Similar species: None.
Size: To 30 mm (1.2 in).
Range: Mexico to Costa Rica.
Habitat: This species lives on the calcareous green alga Halimeda, on which it is nearly impossible to see.
Remarks: Included here as a "cf." since *Elysia pusilla* was described from Palau and Hawaiian specimens are genetically distinct from those in the eastern Pacific. When irritated, this species secretes a defensive mucus containing a toxic diterpenoid metabolite derived from its algal food.

A. Hermosillo

A. Hermosillo

Elysia sp.

Body green with tiny white spots; rhinophores pink with pink color converging into a broad band that runs between the eyes. Parapodia pink with ruffled tan edges.
Similar species: None.
Size: To 20 mm (0.8 in).
Range: Islas Revillagigedos and Bahía de Banderas, Mexico to Costa Rica.
Habitat: Subtidal.
Remarks: Nocturnal.

A. Hermosillo

Cyerce orteai Valdés and Camacho-García, 2000

The color varies from pale cream with some white encrustations to dark olive green with lighter spots. The rhinophores are bifurcated and covered with numerous small tubercles. The cerata are covered with small rounded tubercles and the digestive gland does not extend into the cerata.
Similar species: *Polybranchia mexicana* has thinner, frillier cerata with digestive gland extensions.
Size: To 20 mm (0.8 in).
Range: La Paz, Baja California Sur to Costa Rica.
Habitat: Intertidal and shallow subtidal.
Remarks: Feeds on algae.

A. Hermosillo

A. Hermosillo

Polybranchia mexicana Medrano et al., 2018 (previously *Polybranchia viridis*)

Body translucent yellowish-green to tan or gold, covered in small white specks. The bifurcated rhinophores point forward. Cerata with one or two larger black spots and scattered small black spots; branched extensions of the digestive gland are visible within them. There is an opaque white patch on the back and no papillae on the rhinophores.
Similar species: *Cyerce orteai* has thicker cerata that lack digestive gland extensions.
Size: To 12 mm (0.5 in).
Range: Southern Baja California, Mexico to the Galapagos Islands.
Habitat: Associated with *Caulerpa* spp.
Remarks: A nocturnal species that automizes its cerata when disturbed.

A. Hermosillo

Olea hansineensis Agersborg, 1923

Hansine's egg eater

This sacoglossid has very few cerata. The short, blunt rhinophores are rolled and a black eyespot is visible behind the rhinophore on each side of the head. Body and cerata are a mottled greenish-brown and the tips of the cerata are lighter.
Similar species: None.
Size: To 13 mm (0.5 in).
Range: Prince William Sound, Alaska to San Clemente Island, California.
Habitat: intertidal to 5 m (16 ft).
Remarks: Feeds on heterobranch eggs.

D. Mulliner

R. Roller

Alderia modesta (Loven, 1844)

Alder's sea slug

Body is greenish to yellow, with brown, black and white spots, sometimes with an opaque white dorsal patch; cerata with black spots or reticulations. There are no rhinophores, only rounded lobes on either side of the head, which is bluntly truncated.
Similar species: *Alderia willowi* has larger and fewer cerata, and they are a uniform dark color rather than having black spots or lines.
Size: To 8 mm (0.3 in).
Range: Prince William Sound, Alaska to San Francisco Bay, California; British Isles to France; Nova Scotia to Virginia, and Peter the Great Bay, Russia.
Habitat: High intertidal in brackish water.
Remarks: Feeds on the yellow-green alga, *Vaucheria*. Based on limited genetic information to date, it appears that *Alderia modesta* is a species complex.

R. Roller

Alderia willowi Krug et al., 2007

willow sea slug

There are no rhinophores, only small rounded lobes on either side of the head. Body base coloration is yellow with an overlay of brown coloration; the dorsum is humped anteriorly with a yellow stripe. In large specimens the cerata droop over the edge of the body like willow branches, hence the species name.
Similar species: *Alderia modesta* has scattered black spots or reticulations on its cerata, which are proportionately smaller and more numerous than those of *A. willowi*.
Size: To 6 mm (0.2 in).
Range: Bodega Bay Harbor, California to Baja California, Mexico.
Habitat: Intertidal mudflats, in association with the alga *Vaucheria*.
Remarks: This species can reproduce both by producing planktonic larvae or by direct egg development.

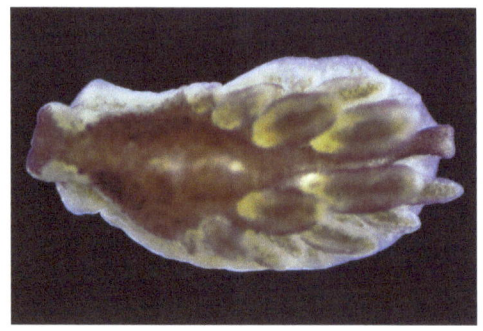

M. Silberstein

Aplysiopsis enteromorphae (Cockerell & Eliot, 1905)

enteromorpha sapsucker

Color varies with size and diet. Body color of animals 15-30 mm is yellowish-white with patches of greenish black; those between 5-10 mm are much darker. Specimens feeding on *Chaetomorpha* are browner than those feeding on *Cladophora*, and in fact shimmer with a golden-reddish reflectance. Cerata often with brownish vertical stripes.
Similar species: *Hermaea oliviae* and *Stiliger fuscovittatus* both have much more obvious white spotting on the cerata.
Size: To 30 mm (1.2 in).
Range: Ketchikan, Alaska to Puerto Vallarta, Mexico.
Habitat: Mid-intertidal.
Remarks: Feeds on filamentous green algae *Chaetomorpha* sp., *Cladophora*, *Urospora*, and *Rhizoclonium*.

J. Hamann

Hermaea oliviae (MacFarland, 1966)

Olivia's sapsucker

Head and sides of body boldly marked with reddish-brown to pale purple streaks on a yellowish to cream background, one line forming a large "U" just above the eyes. Distal third of rhinophores with dense opaque white spotting; small opaque white spots also on the cerata, especially near the tips. The cerata are large with brown to olive cores.
Similar species: *Stiliger fuscovittatus* lacks the "U"-shaped line extending up between and behind the eyes.
Size: To 12 mm (0.5 in).
Range: Seymour Inlet, British Columbia to Isla Cedros, Mexico.
Habitat: Intertidal to 9 m (29 ft).
Remarks: Feeds on red filamentous algae.

B. Horist

Hermaea vancouverensis O'Donoghue, 1924   **Vancouver sapsucker**

Overall color dark brown to almost black. There is a triangular patch forward of the rhinophores and a brown line beginning at the rhinophores curves inward to a brown collar just ahead of the cerata. The cerata are large with brown cores and tiny white surface spots.
Similar species: *Aplysiopsis enteromorphae* lacks the numerous white spots; *Hermaea oliviae* is a dull to bright pink.
Size: To 8 mm (0.3 in).
Range: Shumagin Islands, Alaska to Duxbury Reef, Marin County, California; South Kuril Islands, Russia.
Habitat: Shallow subtidal to 4 m (13 ft).
Remarks: Feeds on diatoms, including *Isthmia nervosa*. Abundant in the spring; hundreds can occur in areas coated with diatoms.
G. Jensen

Ercolania cf. *boodleae*

Shaped like an aeolid, this sacoglossid has a grayish-green body and head. Cerata are wide and bulbous, translucent grayish-green, and covered with scattered white spots and tipped in pinkish-white. Rhinophores are long, smooth and without an external groove. The white on the rhinophores creates a line which extends onto the head, so the eyes are visible within the surrounding grayish-green coloration of the head.
Similar species: None.
Size: To 24 mm (1 in).
Range: San Diego, California, and in the Gulf of California.
Habitat: Intertidal.
Remarks: Feeds on green algae (*Chaetomorpha* and *Cladophora* spp.). Coloration differs from *Ercolania boodleae*, which is found in the Western Pacific and is black with brownish-orange tipped cerata.

J. Hamann

Placida brookae McCarthy et al., 2017 (previously *Placida cremoniana*)   **California bonfire**

The body is yellowish-orange, the color extending halfway up the elongate, cylindrical cerata that cover most of the dorsum; the top halves of the cerata are black. The rhinophores are cylindrical and enrolled, and black except for a posterior white stripe from base to half way up.
Similar species: None.
Size: To 6 mm (0.2 in).
Range: Santa Catalina Island, California to Costa Rica and the Galapagos Islands.
Habitat: Found on an unidentified filamentous green alga.
Remarks: Named after underwater photographer Brook Peterson, who first collected this species from Catalina Island.
B. Peterson

Placida cf. *dendritica*

Color is a pale yellow to green, with head, body, cerata and rolled rhinophores marked by a distinct branching network of olive to green lines of digestive gland. Cerata and tail are quite long.
Similar species: None. The branching green network of digestive gland extending into the rhinophores is unique.
Size: One of our species to 8 mm (0.3 in), the other to 22 mm (0.8 in) (see Remarks).
Range: Alaska to Puerto Vallarta, Mexico, including the Gulf of California.
Habitat: Intertidal to 7 m (23 ft), associated with *Bryopsis*.
Remarks: *Placida dendritica* was described from Great Britain; there appears to be two separate species on our coast that are genetically distinct from each other and almost certainly differ from those in the Atlantic. The larger of these two is likely to be the form named *Placida ornata* by MacFarland in 1966.

K. Fletcher

Stiliger fuscovittatus Lance, 1962

brown-streaked sapsucker

Color is white to greyish white, with reddish brown spots, irregular lines and sometimes with white spots on its cerata and rhinophores tips. Single large extensions of the digestive gland are apparent in the cerata, and parallel, reddish-brown streaks run posteriorly from the smooth, unrolled rhinophores, connecting many of the bases of the cerata.
Similar species: *Hermaea oliviae* has a much larger and denser white area at tips of the rhinophores, and a distinct "U"-shaped line above the eyes.
Size: To 15 mm (0.6 in).
Range: Ketchikan, Alaska to the Gulf of California, Mexico.
Habitat: Intertidal to at least 3 m (10 ft).
Remarks: Feeds on the red algae *Polysiphonia pacifica*, *Dasya* sp., and *Callithamnion* sp.

M. Passage

Stiliger sp.

This species has a cream-colored head with obvious black eyes. The green cerata begin well back from the head and are covered with white specks and have white tips. The distal half of the long, smooth rhinophores are also white.
Similar species: None.
Size: To 15 mm (0.6 in).
Range: Known only from Bahía San Quintin, Baja California, Mexico.
Habitat: Intertidal.
Remarks: Feeds on the green alga *Codium magnum*.

J. Lance

Order Systellommatophora

These air-breathing heterobranchs are often mistaken for dorid nudibranchs, but are more closely related to land snails and slugs. They lack gills altogether and are active at low tide.

Onchidella carpenteri (Binney, 1861) — leather limpet

Color variable, from black, gray, or brown to red; mottled with white and yellow. Dorsal surface (a leathery, limpet-like "shell") with variously-sized low tubercles and margin with regularly-spaced lateral projections. Eye on the tip of a short stalk.
Similar species: *Onchidella hansi* has a smooth margin; *O. binneyi* has a much denser covering of dorsal tubercles.
Size: To 12 mm (0.5 in).
Range: Bering Sea to San Luis Obispo, California.
Habitat: Upper intertidal, on rocks or algae.
Remarks: Formerly *Onchidella borealis*. Feeds on the diatom film on rocks and algae. Genetic sequencing indicates that more than one species is currently lumped under this name.

G. Jensen

Onchidella binneyi Stearns, 1894

Body very thick, broad, and rounded; dorsal surface densely covered with rounded tubercles of various sizes. Color brown or blackish-brown.
Similar species: *Onchidella hansi* has a much smoother, flatter dorsal surface; *O. carpenteri* has a much flatter body with fewer tubercles.
Size: To at least 24 mm (1 in).
Range: Gulf of California to Ecuador.
Habitat: Intertidal.
Remarks: Produces an acetylcholinesterase inhibitor that has been used in pharmacological research. *Onchidella hildae* is a synonym.

S. Vanderplank

Onchidella hansi (Marcus & Marcus, 1967)

Background color brown to black, with lighter areas surrounding the equally-distributed low tubercles that cover the dorsal surface. Eyes on long stalks.
Similar species: *Onchidella carpenteri* has lateral projections; *O. binneyi* has a dense covering of large tubercles.
Size: To 48 mm (1.9 in).
Range: Gulf of California through southern Mexico.
Habitat: Intertidal.
Remarks: Previously in the genus *Hoffmannola*. Releases a viscous fluid from marginal glands.

J. Stauffer

Order Nudibranchia
Suborder Doridina

Dorids make up the majority of the over 6000 species of nudibranchs known worldwide. In most species the gill forms a circlet around the anus; however, in several genera the gill is found beneath the edge of the mantle (e.g., *Phyllidiopsis*) or the posterior end of the mantle (*Corambe* and *Loy*).

Dorids are characterized into three distinct groups: cryptobranchs, whose gill can be retracted into the notum; phanerobranchs, whose rigid gill cannot be retracted, and the porostome dorids. The porostome gill is retractable, but unlike other dorids they have a reduced head with no cephalic tentacles, jaws, or radula. Most dorids are sponge eaters, but different families feed on many other organisms including bryozoans, entoprocts, and barnacles. Each type of predator has a characteristic radular morphology depending on its food preference.

Dorid egg masses are quite characteristic, and can not only alert you to the presence of adult slugs but also be used to differentiate species. This was recently shown to be valuable in separating several white-spotted yellow porostome species.

Peltodoris nobilis   G. Jensen

Corambe pacifica MacFarland & O'Donoghue, 1929 — Pacific corambe

A minute dorid that it is often mistaken for the bryozoan upon which it feeds. Color white to grey, with the dorsum marked by reticulate lines that resemble the surface of a bryozoan. There is a notch in the rear of the dorsum through which the hyponotal gill may be seen. The rhinophore shaft is enclosed in several envelopes.

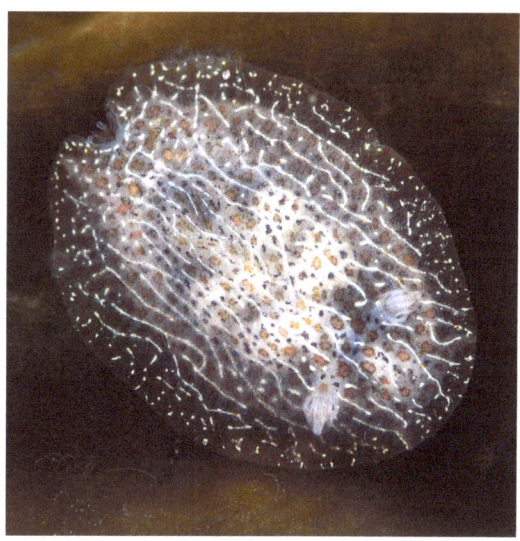

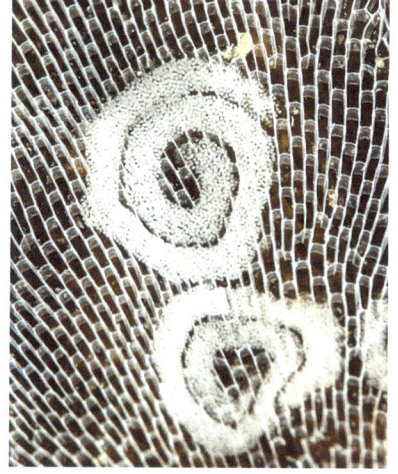

Similar species: *Corambe steinbergae* lacks the posterior notch. *Loy thompsoni* has a posterior notch, but has brown coloration and no reticulated pattern.
Size: To 15 mm (0.6 in).
Range: Alaska to Bahía de Banderas, Mexico.
Habitat: Low intertidal to 60 m (197 ft).
Remarks: Found (and feeds on) the bryozoan *Membranipora*, which typically grows on large flat kelps like *Laminaria*. The eggs are laid in a flat spiral ribbon.

M. Passage

K. Lee

Corambe steinbergae (Lance, 1962) — Steinberg's corambe

Cryptically colored with a reticulate white pattern offset with brown specks matching the encrusting bryozoan on which it feeds. Oral tentacles long and extend beyond notal margin. Rhinophores are simple and tapering. No posterior mantle notch. Gill is located posteriorly under the body. Eggs are laid in an upright "C-" or "S-" shaped ribbon.
Similar species: *Corambe pacifica* has a posterior mantle notch.
Size: To 17 mm (0.7 in).
Range: Katmai National Park, Alaska to Estero del Coyote, Baja California, Mexico.
Habitat: Intertidal to 10 m (33 ft), on *Membranipora*-encrusted kelps such as *Laminaria*.
Remarks: Eggs are laid in upright "C-" or "S-" shaped masses, unlike the flat spiral of *C. pacifica*.

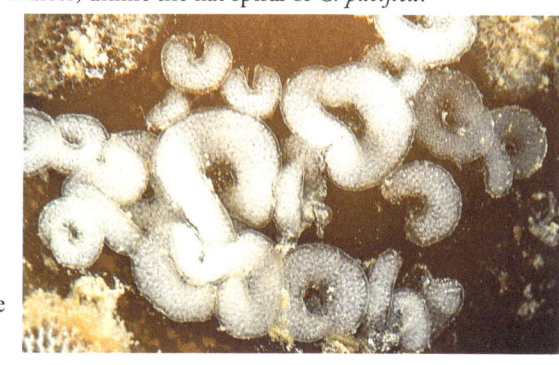

K. Lee

M. Passage

Loy thompsoni (Millen & Nybakken, 1991)

Thompson's corambid

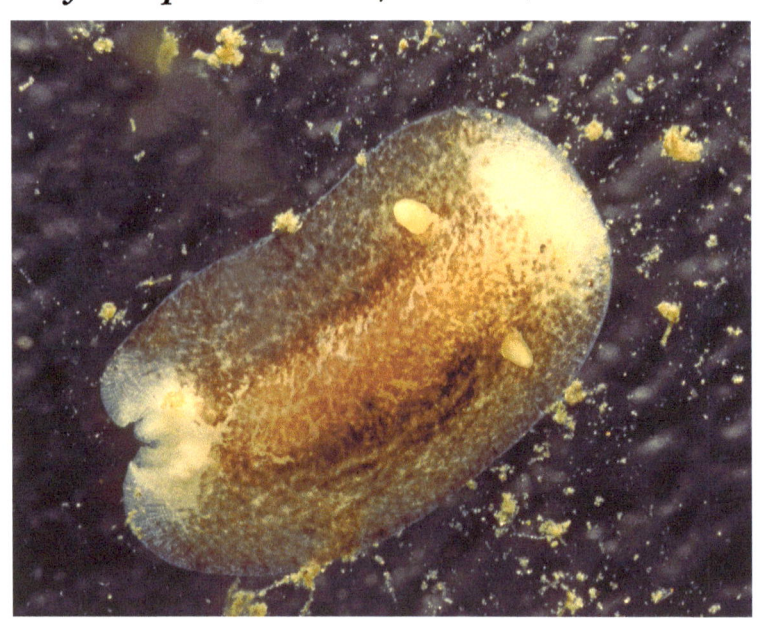

Body white and covered with dense chocolate brown spots on the dorsum except for the front and back ends. Density of spotting increases with age, juveniles may have few spots. Body appears smooth but has spicules over the entire notum except the midline. Rhinophores pale yellow, gills white. Gill located within an obvious posterior notch.
Similar species: Our other species with a posterior notch, *Corambe pacifica*, is white or gray with a reticulated pattern.
Size: A tiny species, to 6.5 mm (0.2 in).
Range: Valdez, Alaska to Monterey, California.
Habitat: Subtidal to 144 m (472 ft), on muddy sand.
Remarks: Rarely seen due to its habitat, size, and drab appearance.

R. Shimek

Ancula lentiginosa Farmer, 1964

freckled ancula

Body is translucent tan to off-white with reddish-brown flecks and patches on the head, tail and sides of body. It has both two extra-branchial and two extra-rhinophoral appendages.
Similar species: *Trapania goddardi* has only single extra-branchial and rhinophoral appendages. *Okenia angelensis* has a series of fingerlike papillae on the dorsum.
Size: To 21 mm (0.8 in).
Range: Marin County, California to Ecuador.
Habitat: Intertidal and shallow subtidal.
Remarks: This species was first described from specimens found in the seawater system at the Scripps Institution of Oceanography in La Jolla, California.

Lower right: detail of rhinophore appendages

A. Hermosillo

J. Hamann

Ancula pacifica MacFarland, 1905   **Pacific ancula**

M. Passage

Body translucent whitish gray with three orange lines along the length of the body. Gill is in the center of the body, and rhinophores and gills tipped in orange. Three to four pairs of extra-branchial appendages can be tipped in orange.
Size: To 24 mm (1 in).
Range: Humboldt County to San Diego, California; possibly Japan. Occasional records as far north as the San Juan Islands, Washington in warm-water years.
Habitat: Intertidal to subtidal, usually in shallow bays.
Remarks: Feeds on the entoproct, *Berentsia*.

G. Jensen   C. Gibbs

Ancula spp.? (previously *Ancula gibbosa*)

Spotted and unspotted specimens lacking the orange lines are also encountered, but it is not known if these are color variations or unnamed species. Neither have been reported from southern California, suggesting the latter.

Okenia angelensis Lance, 1966 — Los Angeles okenia

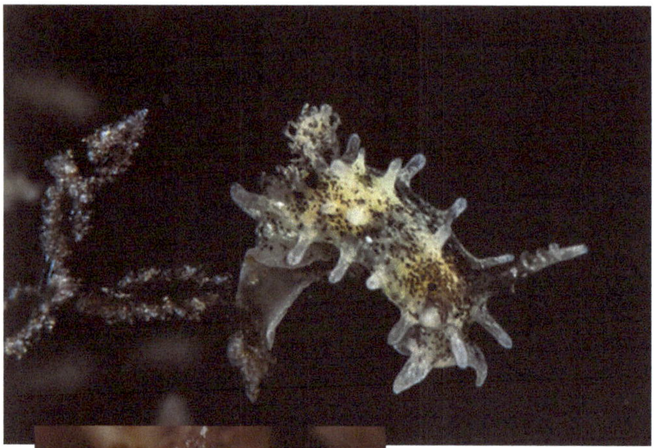

The dorsum of this species bears a series of short, fingerlike papillae. Six to nine are found along each side, two anterior to the rhinophores and four or five medially between the rhinophores and branchial plumes. The ground color is translucent white with spots and patches of brown and green; the darker colors rarely extend onto the papillae. The branchial plumes are arranged in a semicircle and bear yellow and brown flecks, and the rhinophores have few, if any, leaves. The front foot corners are elongated into triangular lobes.
Similar species: *Ancula lentiginosa* and *Trapania goddardi* lack the fingerlike papillae.
Size: To 12 mm (0.5 in).
Range: Miwok Beach, Sonoma County, California to Chile.
Habitat: Low intertidal and subtidal, often on floating docks and pilings.
Remarks: Known from *Sargassum* beds in the Gulf of California.

M. Passage

M. Passage

Okenia angelica Gosliner & Bertsch, 2004 — angelic okenia

Body with varying amounts of purplish brown; center of the dorsum opaque white with dark purple and orange blotches. The elongated rhinophores have purple bases and a translucent yellow to white tip, as do the 7-9 curved papillae on each side of the body. The branchial plume is purple and yellow and the tail is yellow in the center.
Similar species: None.
Size: To 20 mm (0.8 in).
Range: Bahía de los Ángeles to Bahía de Banderas, Mexico and Ixtapa, Guerrero, Mexico.
Habitat: Intertidal and very shallow subtidal, on small rocks.
Remarks: Found in association with bryozoans.

A. Hermosillo

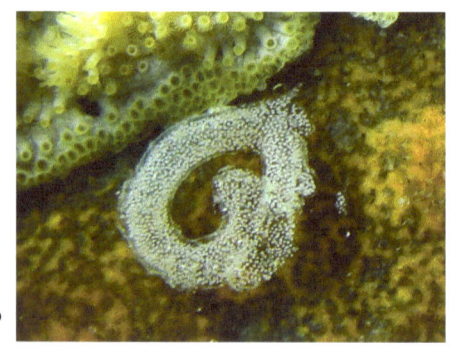

A. Hermosillo

Okenia cochimi Gosliner & Bertsch, 2004   Cochimi's okenia

Body is uniformly yellow. The lamellate rhinophores are very long, and there are five elongate processes along the edge of the notum and several more surrounding the branchial plume.
Similar species: None.
Size: An extremely tiny slug, only 3-4 mm (0.1 in).
Range: Isla Cedros, Baja California to Puerto Vallarta, Mexico.
Habitat: Subtidal from 10-15 m (33-49 ft).
Remarks: Diet is unknown. It was named for the Cochimí tribe of native Americans in Baja California.

A. Hermosillo

Okenia felis Gosliner, 2010   cat okenia

The body is white with granules of opaque white scattered over the surface but more concentrated on the rhinophores and notal appendages. Along the edges of the notum are six pairs of elongate and pointed papillae. There is a single, sharply-pointed papilla just in front of the gill, arising from a sail-like membranous base that extends to the rhinophores. The rhinophores are elongate with lamellae on the posterior part. The gill plume is opaque white, with branches. The foot is thickened anteriorly and there is a pair of short, rounded tentacles on either side of the mouth.
Similar species: The single dorsal papilla of *Okenia plana* has a blunt tip.
Size: To at least 8 mm (0.3 in).
Range: So far only known from the type locality, Point Lobos, Monterey, California.
Habitat: Found at 37-40 m (121-131 ft)
Remarks: Found on a brown ctenostomatous bryozoan.

R. Lee

Okenia plana Baba, 1960   flat okenia

A flattened, round or oval dorid with a single, elongate, blunt tipped papilla in the center of the dorsum. Five similarly-shaped papillae occur along each side of the dorsum, the first being in front of the rhinophores. The foot extends out from the body as a thin layer. Color is whitish with small brown spots, sometimes forming a reticulated pattern.
Similar species: Easily confused with an aeolid at first glance, but for the single papilla in the center of the dorsum. The single median papilla of *Okenia felis* is sharply pointed.
Size: To 15 mm (0.6 in).
Range: On our coast, only known from San Francisco Bay. Widespread in the western Pacific.
Habitat: To at least 6 m (20 ft) in its native range. California specimens and their eggs typically associated with bryozoan colonies that are growing on algae.
Remarks: An introduced species first reported in 1963 in San Francisco; although often common it has apparently not spread.

T. Gosliner

Okenia mexicorum Gosliner & Bertsch, 2004 — Ali & Orso's okenia

The body has an opaque white dorsum with six brick red elongate processes along each side, and more half-white half-red surrounding the branchial plume. There is a single long, median papilla in front of the gill that arises from a median ridge. The rhinophores are white, lamellated in the back and smooth in the front, the oral veil processes are brick red. The branchial plume is transparent white with brick red spots.
Similar species: *Okenia felis* also has a single papilla arising from the posterior end of a median ridge, but it is all white.
Size: To 8 mm (0.3 in).
Range: La Paz, Baja California Sur to Bahía de Banderas, Mexico.
Habitat: Very low intertidal to 20 m (66 ft).
Remarks: The diet of this species is still unknown.

A. Hermosillo

Okenia rosacea (MacFarland, 1905) — Hopkins' rose

The entire animal is rose pink. The rhinophores and branchial plume are usually darker pink to red. Tall, simple papillae cover the entire dorsum and extend in front of the rhinophores.
Similar species: Might be mistaken for the aeolids *Edmundsella vansyoci* or *Bajaeolis bertschi* if the dense dorsal papillae obscure the branchial plume.
Size: To 30 mm (1.2 in).
Range: Cape Arago, Oregon to Isla Cedros, Baja California, Mexico.
Habitat: Low intertidal to 27 m (90 ft).
Remarks: Feeds on the rose-colored bryozoan, *Integripelta bilabiata*.

G. Jensen

R. Agarwal

Okenia vancouverensis (O'Donoghue, 1921) — Vancouver okenia

Body translucent gray with few to many brown spots and speckled with opaque white dots. There is a low pallial ridge that separates the dorsum from the sides and all around its edge are fingerlike papillae. Similar papillae are found in front of and between the rhinophores and the gills. Rhinophores are long, and in lighter-colored animals appear tipped in dark brown. Gill is brown, which is more evident in pale specimens. There is an opaque white line down the center of the tail.
Similar species: None.
Size: To 22 mm (0.8 in).
Range: Haida Gwaii, British Columbia to Waldron Island, Washington.
Habitat: Subtidal to 27 m (88 ft).
Remarks: Rarely reported.

K. Fletcher

Okenia sp. 1

Body translucent white with brown spots. Rhinophores and gill with brown band.
Specimens have been found subtidally on worm tubes on soft bottoms at Huntington Beach, Newport Beach, San Onofre, and Redondo Beach, California.

S. Douglas

Okenia sp. 2

Body is translucent grayish white with maroon-brownish spots. Tall, lamellate rhinophores are translucent purplish at their bases with scattered brownish spots along their length, and anterior yellow spots near their white tips. Top half of gill is speckled brown with yellow near their white tips. One long papilla on either side of the rhinophores, the oral tentacles and the margin papillae along the notum edge have yellow bands below white tips.
This undescribed species was sighted at La Jolla Shores, California.

J. Shephard

Trapania goddardi Hermosillo & Valdés, 2004 — Goddard's trapania

Body varies from off-white with irregular little brown spots to tan with dark blotches, both forms with bigger diamond-shaped markings on the sides of the body. It has one extra-rhinophoral appendage lateral to each rhinophore and an extra-branchial appendage flanking either side of the gill. The oral tentacles, rhinophores, gill, tail and appendages are off-white to pale brown with brown spots.
Similar species: *Ancula lentiginosa* has both two extra-branchial and two extra-rhinophoral appendages. *Okenia angelensis* has fingerlike papillae on the dorsum.
Size: To 7 mm (0.3 in).
Range: Bahía de Banderas and Santa Cruz, Mexico.
Habitat: Intertidal to 12 m (39 ft), under rocks.
Remarks: Difficult to find due to its small size and cryptic markings.

A. Hermosillo

Trapania goslineri Millen & Bertsch, 2000 — Gosliner's trapania

Body is white, with large, oval black spots and streaks. There is a black "V" extending from in front of the rhinophores onto the base of the oral tentacles. The oral tentacles, rhinophores, gill, tail and appendages are tipped in bright yellow. There is one extra-rhinophoral appendage lateral to each rhinophore and one extra-branchial appendage flanking either side of the gill.
Similar species: *Trapania velox* has black lines rather than spots, and lacks the black "V" in front of the rhinophores.
Size: To 15 mm (0.6 in).
Range: Isla Cedros to Bahía de Banderas and Gulf of California, Mexico.
Habitat: Intertidal and shallow subtidal.
Remarks: Considered extremely rare. Believed to feed on entoprocts that are growing on orange sponges.

M. Miller

A. Hermosillo

A. Hermosillo

Trapania velox (Cockerell, 1901) — swift trapania

Body is translucent grayish-white with five dark brown to black lines extending on the midline and branching out of the extra-branchial appendages, down the tail, and along the sides. Tail, rhinophores, gill and extra-branchial appendages are tipped with yellow to orange. It has one extra-rhinophoral appendage on the side of each rhinophore and extra-branchial appendages flanking either side of the gill.
Similar species: *Trapania goslineri* has elongate spots and streaks rather than lines, and a "V" shaped mark in front of the rhinophores.
Size: To 20 mm (0.8 in).
Range: Carmel, California to Bahía Tortugas, Baja California, Mexico.
Habitat: intertidal to 6 m (20 ft).
Remarks: Believed to feed on entoprocts associated with sponges.

J. Hamann

Trapania sp.

Body is a translucent white with some reddish-brown concentrations of blotches on the mid-dorsum, around the gill, and the back and sides of the head. The gill plumes are white with some brown mottling. The bases of the rhinophores are white, with a bright orange ring, followed by a brownish-red one, an orange one and a white tip. The extra-rhinophoral and extra-branchial appendages are also white with brown mottling.
Photographed in Puerto Vallarta, Mexico.

A. Hermosillo

Acanthodoris atrogriseata O'Donoghue, 1927 (previously *Acanthodoris pilosa*)   **hairy horned dorid**

Body can be yellowish-white/black/smoky gray/golden/dark brown with numerous conical, yellow-tipped papillae. Can have yellow flecks on body. Rhinophores are long and bend backwards.
Similar species: *Acanthodoris hudsoni* have a yellow line on the margin. Dark colored *Acanthodoris lutea* have proportionately much shorter rhinophores.
Size: To 22 mm (0.8 in).
Range: Southern Alaska to Puget Sound, Washington.
Habitat: Intertidal to at least 18 m (60 ft).
Remarks: Feeds on bryozoans.

K. Fletcher

K. Fletcher

K. Fletcher

Acanthodoris brunnea MacFarland, 1905 — brown horned dorid

A small dorid with exceptionally long rhinophores. Body brown with light patches and tiny yellow spots; numerous conical, blunt, yellow-tipped papillae. Branchial plumes can be yellow tipped.
Similar species: Could be mistaken for *Onchidoris bilamellata*, which has shorter rhinophores and much more rounded papillae.
Size: To 22 mm (0.8 in).
Range: Vancouver Island, British Columbia to La Jolla, California.
Habitat: Low intertidal to 110 m (361 ft), primarily on sandy bottoms.
Remarks: Feeds on bryozoans, and gives off the smell of cedar when handled.

K. Lee

Acanthodoris hudsoni MacFarland, 1905 — Hudson's horned dorid

Rhinophores long. Dorsal surface with numerous short or tall, conical, yellow-tipped papillae; body typically translucent white, sometimes gray or peach. May also have brown spots scattered on mantle and foot. Rhinophores and gill can have yellow-tips; edge of mantle is outlined in pale yellow. There is no gill pocket and the gill is never fully retracted.
Similar species: Species in the *Cadlina luteomarginata* complex have shorter, broader-based papillae and proportionately shorter rhinophores; light-colored *Acanthodoris atrogriseata* lack a yellow margin.
Size: To 40 mm (1.6 in).
Range: Sitka, Alaska to San Diego and Catalina Island, California.
Habitat: Low intertidal to 25 m (82 ft).
Remarks: Diet is unknown, but it likely feeds on encrusting bryozoans.

R. Agarwal

K. Fletcher

K. Fletcher

K. Fletcher

Acanthodoris lutea MacFarland, 1925   **sandalwood dorid**

Dorsal surface densely covered with papillae. Body color pale to bright orange or sometimes rusty brown to black, but always with numerous yellow or white speckles between the papillae. Gill white and rhinophores tipped with orange or red in orange specimens; gill gray in dark ones.
Similar species: The dark forms of *Acanthodoris atrogriseata* and *A. nanaimoensis* have pale yellow on the tips of the papillae.
Size: To 30 mm (1.2 in).
Range: Indian Arm, British Columbia to Cabo Colnett, Baja California, Mexico.
Habitat: Low intertidal to 49 m (161 ft) in rocky areas.
Remarks: Smells like sandalwood when handled. It feeds on the bryozoan *Alcyonidium*.

K. Lee

K. Fletcher

K. Fletcher

Acanthodoris nanaimoensis O'Donoghue, 1921   **Nanaimo dorid**

Body a translucent white, gray, or black with numerous tall, conical, yellow-tipped papillae. The mantle edge is outlined in yellow and the rhinophores and gill plumes are maroon-tipped. Some Puget Sound specimens have green gill plumes (lower left).
Similar species: The red-tipped rhinophores and yellow-tipped papillae readily distinguish this from dark-colored *Acanthodoris hudsoni* and *A. lutea*, respectively.
Size: To 40 mm (1.6 in).
Range: Baranof Island, Alaska to Santa Barbara, California.

M. Passage

G. Jensen

Habitat: Low intertidal to 25 m (82 ft), on rock or cobble bottoms.
Remarks: Feeds on the bryozoan *Alcyonidium polyoum* and on compound ascidians.

G. Jensen

Acanthodoris pina Marcus & Marcus, 1967

pinecone horned dorid

Dorsal surface black with large reddish papillae interspersed with small white ones. Rhinophores reddish with white tips. Foot margin, frontal veil and notum edged with a red stripe.
Similar species: Unlikely to be confused with any other species.
Size: To 21 mm (0.8 in).
Range: Northern Gulf of California, Puerto Peñasco, Sonora, to Bahía de los Ángeles, Baja California, Mexico.
Habitat: Reported both intertidally and subtidally.
Remarks: Diet unknown; probably feeds on bryozoans.

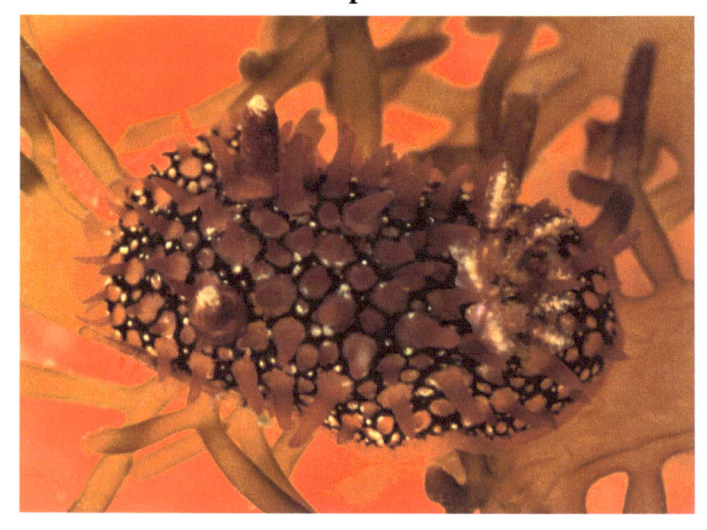

J. Hamann

Acanthodoris rhodoceras Cockerell, 1905

black and white dorid

Dorsal surface is white, gray, or brown (rarely pink) with conical papillae that are usually black. Border of mantle usually with an outer yellow and inner black line. Rhinophores with a middle orange-red band and black tip; gill usually black, sometimes red.
Similar species: Nothing similar in our area.
Size: To 30 mm (1.2 in).
Range: Cape Arago, Oregon to Bahía de los Angeles, Gulf of California, Mexico, but has been found as far north as Barkley Sound, British Columbia in warm-water years.
Habitat: Low intertidal to 24 m (79 ft), in rocky areas.
Remarks: Feeds on the bryozoan *Alcyonidium*.

K. Lee

R. Agarwal

K. Lee

K. Lee

Atalodoris jannae (Millen, 1987) (previously *Adalaria jannae*)   **Janna's dorid**

Body is creamy white, pale yellow or lemon yellow and covered in rounded, spiculated tubercles on short stalks. Large circular gland behind gill.
Similar species: White specimens easily confused with *Onchidoris muricata*, which has a smaller gill with a triangular gland behind it, and is usually conspicuously pink in the middle of the body. White *O. bilamellata* have a unique gill shape.
Size: To 15 mm (0.6 in).
Range: Prince William Sound, Alaska to Lion Rock, San Luis Obispo, California.
Habitat: Low intertidal to 15 m (49 ft).
Remarks: Feeds on the bryozoans *Membranipora*, *Lyrula hippocrepis*, and *Reginella mucronata*.

M. Chamberlain   K. Lee

Adalaria proxima (Alder & Hancock, 1854)   **tuberculate dorid**

A small white dorid with tightly-packed, long, spear-shaped tubercles and star-shaped spicules at the base of each tubercle.
Similar species: *Onchidoris muricata* and *Atalodoris jannae* have much more rounded tubercles. *Diaphorodoris lirulatocauda* has very opaque white areas on the notum between the tubercles, and *Akiodoris salacia* has a row of white glands along the posterior edge of the mantle.
Size: To 20 mm (0.8 in).
Range: Boreo-Arctic; Pribilof Islands, Alaska to Puget Sound, Washington. Also in the Northeast and Northwest Atlantic.
Habitat: Middle intertidal to 60 m (197 ft).
Remarks: Feeds on the bryozoans *Alcyonidium polyoum*, *Electra pilosa*, *Flustrella hispida*, and *Membranipora villosa*.

P. Garner

Akiodoris salacia Millen, 2005   **Salacia's dorid**

A tiny, creamy white and elongate dorid bearing spear-shaped spiculose tubercles with soft pointed tips. There are opaque white, round, granular glands along the posterior edge of the mantle.
Similar species: Our other small, white dorids lack the concentration of white glands behind the gills.
Size: To 6.5 mm (0.25 in).
Range: Hornby Island, British Columbia to Hood Canal, Washington.
Habitat: Subtidal to 25 m (82 ft).
Remarks: Possibly feeds on the bryozoan *Farrela repens*.

R. Long   K. Fletcher

Diaphorodoris lirulatocauda Millen, 1985

ridge-tailed dorid

The elongate, oval body is wider in front than behind, with a ridged tail often trailing behind the mantle edge. Color a dense, opaque white or creamy-white, and there are numerous cylindrical tubercles interspersed with dense, opaque white flecks on the notum. The blunt-tipped rhinophores and gill are creamy-whitish-yellow.

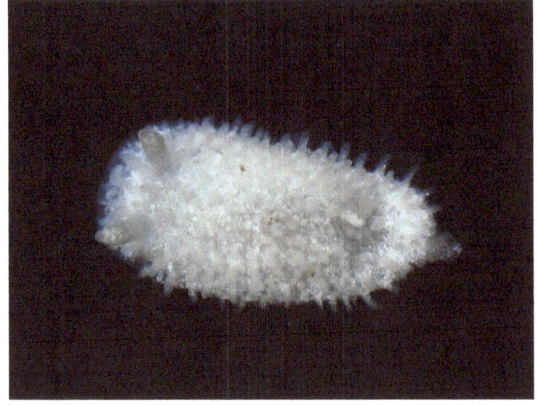

Similar species: *Adalaria proxima* lacks the opaque white dorsal markings. *Acanthodoris atrogriseata* has longer rhinophores that bend backwards, and has yellow-tipped papillae.
Size: To 12 mm (0.5 in).
Range: Ketchikan, Alaska to Ensenada, Baja California, Mexico.
Habitat: Low intertidal to 126 m (413 ft), in sandy or muck-coated areas.
Remarks: Feeds on the bryozoan *Nolella* cf. *stipata*.

K. Fletcher

G. Jensen

Onchidoris bilamellata (Linnaeus, 1767)

barnacle-eating dorid

Mantle covered with spiculated, club-shaped tubercles. Gill forms two semicircles that enclose several tubercles, with an opaque white gland posteriorly. Color varies from a mottled brown and white to all white.
Similar species: The mottled brown form may be mistaken for *Acanthodoris brunnea*, which has pointed papillae and longer rhinophores. Small white ones could be mistaken for *Onchidoris muricata* or *Atalodoris jannae*.
Size: To 40 mm (1.5 in).
Range: Circumboreal; Alaska to Cabo Colnett, Baja California.
Habitat: High intertidal to 250 m (820 ft).
Remarks: Feeds on barnacles, often blending in with their prey. Often seen in large mating aggregations (below, center).

G. Jensen

G. Jensen

G. Jensen

K. Fletcher

Onchidoris evincta (Millen, 2006) (previously *Adalaria* sp. 1) — **crowned dorid**

The white or cream colored, oval elongate body is slightly broader in front and bears small tubercles with a crown of projecting spines. There are 4-7 tubercles at the base of the rhinophore sheath and the gill is circular. Can have a few scattered opaque white spots on body and a small opaque white gland behind gill.
Similar species: The projecting crown of long spines on the tubercles is unique among our small white dorids.
Size: To 16 mm (0.6 in).
Range: Tatitlek, Alaska to Cape Arago, Oregon.

G. Jensen

G. Jensen

Habitat: Low intertidal to 15 m (49 ft).
Remarks: Found on a tan encrusting bryozoan.

Onchidoris muricata (O.F. Müller, 1776) — **fuzzy onchidoris**

Body is white or yellowish, often with reddish-pink area in the center. Knob-shaped tubercles may have spicules projecting beyond the tips. Rhinophores are lamellate and may be yellow-orange tipped with yellow; may have a triangular opaque white gland behind the gill.
Similar species: White specimens of *Atalodoris jannae* have a larger gill, little or no pink color, and a circular gland behind the gill.
Size: To 15 mm (0.6 in).
Range: Circumboreal. Southern Alaska to San Luis Obispo, California.
Habitat: Intertidal to 20 m (65 ft).
Remarks: Feeds on a variety of encrusting bryozoans. The reddish-pink area in the center is the digestive gland showing through the semi-transparent notum.

K. Fletcher

G. Jensen

Aegires albopunctatus MacFarland, 1905 — **white-spotted dorid**

Elongate white to tan body with dark spots (rarely lacking) and cylindrical tubercles. The three brachial plumes are in the middle of the body and each protected anteriorly by fleshy lobes. The rhinophores are white to yellow and closely surrounded by 5-6 tubercles.
Similar species: *Aegires sublaevis* has much fewer and smaller tubercles.
Size: To 23 mm (1 in).
Range: Ketchikan, Alaska to Bahía de los Ángeles, Baja California, Mexico.
Habitat: Low intertidal to 30 m (98 ft).
Remarks: Feeds on calcareous sponges.

M. Passage

Aegires cf. *sublaevis*

Body pale brownish white to yellow, often with large scattered greyish brown spots. A low, rounded median dorsal ridge forms a gill cover posteriorly and splits anteriorly to form a raised rhinophore pocket. There are a few low rounded bumps scattered over the dorsum.
Similar species: *Aegires albopunctatus* is densely covered with large tubercles.
Size: Pacific specimens to at least 8 mm (0.3 in).
Range: Bahía de Banderas, Mexico, and the Galapagos.
Habitat: Probably shallow subtidal.
Remarks: Feeds on bryozoans. *Aegires sublaevis* was described from the Atlantic, where it feeds on sponges and has some subtle differences, suggesting they are different species.

A. Hermosillo

Palio zosterae (O'Donoghue, 1924) (previously *Palio dubia*) — eelgrass palio

Color dark gray to dark brownish fawn with numerous small brown to black dots and a scattering of yellow dots, along with yellow spots on low tubercles. Rhinophores and gill are tipped in yellow. Dorsum is marked off from the sides by a low pallial ridge which bears low tubercles. The ridge in front of the rhinophores bears 5-6 tubercles. There are 3-6 tall, whitish, digitiform processes behind the gill.
Similar species: See *Polycerella glandulosa*.
Size: To 12 mm (0.5 in).
Range: Prince William Sound, Alaska to La Paz, Baja California Sur and Nayarit, Mexico.
Habitat: Intertidal to 20 m (65 ft), on eelgrass or *Laminaria*.
Remarks: Feeds on the bryozoans *Bowerbankia* and *Membranipora*. Sequences of Palio dubia from Europe differ from those in the eastern Pacific.

K. Fletcher

Crimora coneja Er. Marcus, 1961 — rabbit dorid

White body with numerous short, pointed, orange appendages fringing the notum and frontal veil. Most dorsal papillae with black or brown tips. Has orange perfoliate rhinophores and a white tripinnate gill.
Similar species: The white gill and black tips on the papillae readily distinguish this species from *Triopha catalinae*, *T. modesta*, and *Limacia cockerelli*.
Size: To 23 mm (1 in).

C. Hoover

Range: Cape Arago, Oregon to San Diego, California.
Habitat: Intertidal and subtidal in rocky areas.
Remarks: This rarely-seen species feeds exclusively on the encrusting bryozoan *Hincksina minuscula*. Eggs are laid in a white ribbon placed flat against the underside of a rock.

J. Goddard

Limacia cockerelli (MacFarland, 1905) — Cockerell's dorid

Body opaque white, sometimes with large areas of red, and surrounded by 2-3 rows of translucent white to orange slender projections with bright orange spherical to ovoid tips. Gill white to red; rhinophores bright red. Tail may be white or have an orange-red spot on the end.
Similar species: *Limacia mcdonaldi* has a row of orange-red tubercles down the center of the body.

G. Jensen

K. Fletcher

R. Boerema

Size: To 30 mm (1.2 in).
Range: Ketchikan, Alaska to San Diego, California.
Habitat: Low intertidal to 35 m (115 ft) on rocks.
Remarks: Feeds exclusively on the brownish-orange encrusting bryozoan, *Hincksina velata*.

Limacia mcdonaldi Uribe et al., 2017 — McDonald's dorid

Opaque white body surrounded by 2-3 rows of translucent white, slender club-shaped dorso-lateral projections with orange-red spherical to ovoid tips. A single row of orange-red tubercles runs down the center of the back from in front of the rhinophores to the gill, sometimes with orange-red spreading into the area around the tubercles. Gill white with red blotches on the tips. Rhinophores with translucent white base and orange-red tips.
Similar species: *Limacia cockerelli* lacks the line of orange tubercles along the center of the back, and *L. janssi* has shorter and stouter lateral projections on the body.
Size: To 26 mm (1 in).
Range: Salt Point, Sonoma County, California, to Cabo San Lucas, and inside the Gulf of California to Bahía de los Ángeles, Baja California.
Habitat: Low intertidal to subtidal in rocky areas.
Remarks: Long considered a color variation of *L. cockerelli*. It feeds on a species of encrusting bryozoan.

M. Passage

A. Hermosillo

Limacia janssi (Bertsch & Ferreira, 1974) — Janss' dorid

Body opaque white to light yellow with numerous irregular orange dots or patches, surrounded by 2 rows of light orange, often inflated, elongate to oval dorso-lateral papillae which are orange-red towards the tip. Dorsum either completely smooth or with a single row of tubercles running down the back from the rhinophores to the off-white to cream or red-orange gill. Rhinophores with white stalks and orange tips; tail white.
Similar species: The projections on *L. mcdonaldi* and *L. cockerelli* have very slender stalks that give them a "pincushion" look, unlike the stout papillae of *L. janssi*.
Size: To 12 mm (0.5 in).
Range: Northern Gulf of California to Panamá.
Habitat: Intertidal to 9 m (29 ft).
Remarks: Feeds on an encrusting bryozoan.

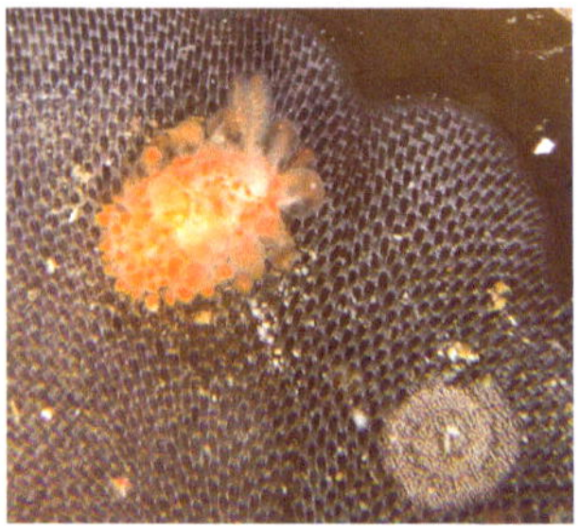

A. Hermosillo

A. Hermosillo

Polycera alabe Collier & Farmer, 1964 — ink stain dorid

A. Hermosillo

A. Hermosillo

The elongate body is blue-black with oval orange spots or lines. There are about 20 black to translucent bluish soft, conical papillae; frontal veil with similarly-colored digitiform processes. Rhinophores are black and gill is pale orange to deep blue or black with orange spots. Foot edge is white.
Similar species: *Polycera anae* has white rhinophores. *Felimare californiensis* and *Polycera atra* both lack the conical papillae.
Size: To 30 mm (1.2 in).
Range: Catalina Island, California to Isla Cedros, the Gulf of California, and Mazatlan, Mexico.
Habitat: Low intertidal and subtidal to at least 12 m (40 ft).
Remarks: It has been suggested that this species is a mimic of the spotted form of *Felimare californiensis*, which releases noxious chemicals when attacked.

A. Hermosillo

Polycera cf. *alabe*

This green nudibranch is similar to *Polycera alabe*. Morphological and molecular work is needed to determine if it is distinct, or yet another color variant of that highly variable species.

A. Hermosillo

Polycera anae Pola et al., 2014 — Ana's dorid

Body is black and densely covered with irregular orange dashes. There are a few translucent white to light green spiky papillae, the same color as the rhinophores, tips of the gill plumes, extra-branchial appendages and velar processes.
Similar species: *Polycera alabe* is a much larger species and has black rhinophores rather than white.
Size: Tiny. Maximum length 5 mm (0.2 in).
Range: Central Mexico to Panama.
Habitat: Intertidal and subtidal to at least 9 m (29 ft).
Remarks: Usually found in clusters of multiple individuals and associated with bryozoans.

M. Pola

Polycera atra MacFarland, 1905 — sorcerer's dorid

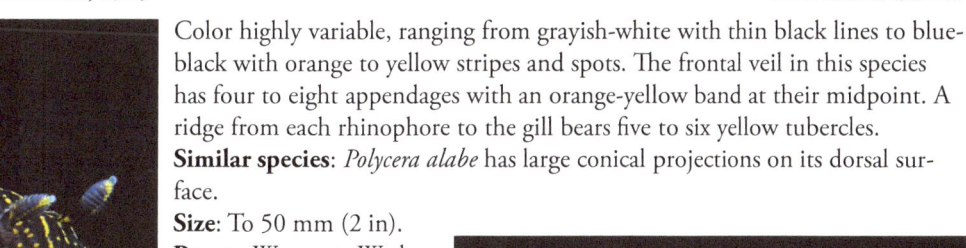

Color highly variable, ranging from grayish-white with thin black lines to blue-black with orange to yellow stripes and spots. The frontal veil in this species has four to eight appendages with an orange-yellow band at their midpoint. A ridge from each rhinophore to the gill bears five to six yellow tubercles.
Similar species: *Polycera alabe* has large conical projections on its dorsal surface.
Size: To 50 mm (2 in).
Range: Westport, Washington to La Paz, Mexico.
Habitat: Low intertidal to 50 m (164 ft); often on kelp, floats, and pilings.

K. Lee

Remarks: Feeds on the bryozoans *Bugula*, *Crisularia pacifica*, and *Membranipora villosa*, and the gorgonian *Leptogorgia chilensis*.

K. Lee

Polycera gnupa (Marcus & Marcus, 1967)

Body is pale greyish-brown. Most of the body is densely stippled with brown pigment, which is a concentrated blackish-brown around the gill and on the head. The two velar processes are long, slender and pointed, white with a bluish and an orange-yellow band around the middle. The perfoliate rhinophores have a dark shaft and a white tip. The two extra-branchial appendages have light tips followed by a bluish and an orange-yellow ring at their midpoint.
Similar species: *Polycera hedgpethi* has more processes on the frontal veil and yellow or white dorsolateral lines.
Size: To 14 mm (0.5 in).
Range: Puerto Peñasco, Mexcio to the Galapagos Islands.
Habitat: Intertidal.
Remarks: Found on branching bryozoans. Confusion currently exists over whether this species is distinct from *Polycera hedgpethi*.

A. Hermosillo

Polycera hedgpethi Er. Marcus, 1964 — **Hedgpeth's dorid**

The body is covered in closely-set dark spots with white or yellow ridges extending between rhinophores and gill, and from gill to tail. Frontal veil bears 4-6 appendages which are white-tipped with lower bands of grey-black and yellow. Rhinophores, gill, and six extra-branchial appendages have a yellow band and a white tip. The tip of the tail is yellow.
Similar species: Dark *Polycera tricolor* have 8-11 frontal processes.
Size: To 25 mm (1 in).
Range: Marin County, CA to Panama; Japan; Australia; New Zealand; South Africa; Atlantic coast of Iberian Peninsula, and the Mediterranean.
Habitat: Intertidal.
Remarks: Feeds on the bryozoan *Crisularia*. This nudibranch has a widespread distribution in ports throughout the world; though first described from California, its origins remain unknown.

A. Hermosillo

Polycera kaiserae Hermosillo & Valdés, 2007 — **Kirsty's dorid**

Color varies from a light to a darker pink. It is sprinkled with numerous irregularly shaped opaque white spots. The gill, extra-branchial processes, rhinophores and velar processes are the same color as the body with a dark blue band in the middle and a white tip.
Similar species: None. The pink color of this species is unique among eastern Pacific *Polycera*.
Size: To 24 mm (1 in).
Range: To date, only known from Bahía de Banderas, Mexico.
Habitat: Subtidal to 30 m (98 ft).
Remarks: Feeds on a transparent, branching bryozoan where it lays its rose-colored ruffled spiral egg mass.

A. Hermosillo

Polycera tricolor Robilliard, 1971 — three-colored dorid

Body is translucent whitish gray often with scattered yellow spots. The 8-11 frontal appendages, 8-12 extra-branchial appendages, gill and rhinophores all have black bands followed by yellow medial bands and white tips. A yellow line runs centrally down the tail, around the edge of the foot and may run along the side ridge between the rhinophores and the gill, but otherwise there are no stripes on the body.
Similar species: Dark specimens can be mistaken for *Polycera hedgpethi*, which have fewer frontal and extra-branchial appendages.
Size: To 36 mm (1.4 in).
Range: Ketchikan, Alaska to Islas San Benito, Baja California, Mexico.
Habitat: Subtidal to 60 m (197 ft) in rocky areas.
Remarks: Feeds on bryozoans.

C. Hoover

M. Passage

Polycerella glandulosa Behrens & Gosliner, 1988 — gland dorid

The body color is dirty white to cream, and the notum is covered with yellow-white and dark brown specks and bears numerous cylindrical papillae. There are two characteristic extra-branchial appendages situated posterolateral to the gill. These structures are branched, and the most distal branch is swollen, yellowish, and glandular.
Similar species: *Palio zosterae* has 3-6 unbranched appendages by the gill.
Size: To 28 mm (1.1 in).
Range: Morro Bay, California to Panama.
Habitat: Intertidal to 20 m (66 ft).
Remarks: Feeds on the bryozoans *Amathia* and *Crisularia*. The function of the unusual swollen glands that give it its name is not known.

J. Hamann

Tyrannodoris tigris (Farmer, 1978) (previously *Roboastra tigris*) — tiger dorid

The body is olive to green with a series of longitudinal black stripes, each edged in white to light blue. The rhinophores and gill are blue-black; the latter with light green central axes.
Similar species: *Tamja abdere* has much more irregular markings, and *T. eliora* has blue lines edged in black rather than black with blue edges.
Size: A very large species, reaching 300 mm (12 in) in length.
Range: Central and Southern Gulf of California to Bahía de Banderas, Mexico.
Habitat: Rocky subtidal areas, to 27 m (88 ft).
Remarks: This species is a voracious predator that feeds on other nudibranchs, particularly *Tambja abdere* and *T. eliora*. When feeding, it everts a large, bright blue buccal hood.

P. Humann

Tambja abdere Farmer, 1978

Body is covered with irregular areas of turquoise and yellow-ochre with a black line between the two colors. The rhinophores and gill have dark tips.
Similar species: *Tyrannodoris tigris* and *Tambja eliora* both have much straighter, uniform lines.
Size: To 80 mm (3.1 in).
Range: Central Gulf of California to Costa Rica; outer Baja California Sur from Bahía Magdalena to Cabo San Lucas, Mexico.
Habitat: Subtidal from 3-60 m (10-197 ft).
Remarks: Feeds on encrusting green bryozoans and erect cream-colored bryozoans. When attacked, it produces defensive secretions.

A. Hermosillo

A. Hermosillo

C. Hoover

Tambja eliora (Marcus & Marcus, 1967)

Varies in color from yellow-ochre to greenish gray, with brilliant blue or turquoise longitudinal stripes that are outlined in black. Foot margin is blue. Gill is black, tipped in bright blue or turquoise and yellow ochre.
Similar species: *Tambja abdere* have much more irregular markings. *Tyrannodoris tigris* has black lines with blue borders, rather than blue lines with black borders.

A. Hermosillo

Size: To 50 mm (2 in).
Range: Central Gulf of California; Ensenada, Baja California to Costa Rica.
Habitat: Intertidal to 45 m (148 ft).
Remarks: Feeds on bryozoans.

A. Hermosillo

Triopha catalinae (Cooper, 1863)

clown dorid

Body is translucent to opaque white (rarely tan) with various numbers of conical or round orange tubercles and 5-7 pairs of long, club shaped appendages each bearing small nodules. The rhinophores and tips of the five white branchial plumes are orange to red. The frontal veil has 8-12 irregular, orange processes.
Similar species: *Triopha modesta* has branching dorsal and dorsolateral structures rather than tubercles. *Crimora coneja* has an all white gill and black-tipped papillae.
Size: Length to at least 84 mm (3.3 in).
Range: Southeastern Alaska to El Tomatal, Baja California and the Gulf of California, Mexico.
Habitat: Mid-intertidal and subtidal in rocky areas, to 450 m (1476 ft).
Remarks: Feeds on several different genera of erect, branching bryozoans.

D. Behrens

M. Passage

D. Behrens

Triopha modesta Bergh, 1880

modest clown dorid

Body is white to gray-tan with branching orange dorsal and dorso-lateral appendages. Rhinophores orange or red; gill orange or red-tipped, and both are lighter in color than the structures on the body. Frontal veil has 8-12 orange appendages.
Similar species: *Triopha catalinae* has orange tubercles rather than branching structures. *Crimora coneja* has an all white gill and black-tipped papillae.
Size: To 180 mm (7 in).
Range: Aleutian Islands, Alaska to La Jolla, California; also Korea, Japan, and Russia.
Habitat: Low intertidal to 40 m (131 ft).
Remarks: Feeds on arborescent bryozoans.

J. Kocian

Dorsal processes of *Triopha modesta* (right) and *T. catalinae* (far right)

G. Jensen

G. Jensen

Triopha maculata McFarland, 1905 — spotted dorid

Color varies from clear, light orange to darker orange or yellow brown with numerous round to oval, pale blue spots and more numerous small, dark brown dots. Lateral ridge with 4-6 orange to vermilion, slightly branched or tuberculate processes. Orange frontal veil with 10-12 stout, slightly tuberculate processes. Lamellate rhinophores with orange tip, paler orange shaft, and thin, smooth sheath margins. The orange branchial plumes are tipped with darker orange to vermilion.
Similar species: *Triopha occidentalis* is nearly identical and considered by many to be a synonym. It has a slightly flared rhinophore sheath, paler gills, and attains a much larger size. See 'Remarks'.

K. Lee

Size: To 90 mm (3.5 in).
Range: Crescent City, California to Ensenada, Baja California, Mexico.
Habitat: Intertidal to 28 m (92 ft).
Remarks: Differences in the egg masses and radulas suggest that *T. maculata* and *T. occidentalis* are separate species, but molecular analysis is needed to address this question.

Triopha occidentalis (Fewkes, 1889) — western dorid

Color varies from pale yellow ochre to dark yellow-brown, most often yellow-orange, with light blue spots which may be almost white or barely visible. Lateral ridge with 4-6 yellow-orange to vermilion long, tuberculate or branched processes. Frontal veil with 7-12 yellow-orange to vermilion or pale burnt sienna tuberculate or branched processes; lamellate rhinophores with yellow-orange to vermilion tips, paler shaft and slightly flared sheath margins. Branchial plumes pale yellow-orange to almost white with yellow-orange to vermilion tips.

K. Lee

Similar species: *Triopha maculata* tends to have a dark gill and the rhinophore sheaths do not flare.
Size: To 180 mm (7 in).
Range: Marin County, California to Punta Rosarito, Baja California; found in Port Hardy, British Columbia during the 2014-2016 warm water event.
Habitat: Intertidal to 30 m (98 ft), usually on kelp far from shore.
Remarks: Feeds on bryozoans. May be a synonym of *T. maculata*; see 'Remarks' for that species.

K. Lee

Hallaxa chani Gosliner & Williams, 1975 — Chan's dorid

Body is dull translucent gray to yellow, usually with a series of dark blotches in the middle of the back and especially in front of the gill; some small dark spots sprinkled around the sides. Tubercles are small, irregular sized bumps concentrated around the sides of the body and practically absent in the center. The large, lamellate rhinophores are pale, often with a dark tip. Gill is retractable inside a sheath which is half the height of the branchial plumes.
Similar species: *Conualevia* spp. have smooth rhinophores.
Size: To 30 mm (1.2 in).
Range: Ketchikan, Alaska to San Diego, California.
Habitat: Intertidal to 20 m (66 ft).
Remarks: Feeds on the slime sponge *Halisarca*, which it resembles.

T. Gosliner

K. Fletcher

Aldisa albomarginata Millen & Gosliner, 1985 — white-lined aldisa

Body is translucent white to greenish-gray with low, conical tubercles. There are white spots on body and a white line around dorsum edge. The gill has green and white spots.
Similar species: Similar to *Doriopsilla spaldingi*, which has an orange gill and rhinophores, and members of the *Cadlina luteomarginata* complex that have a yellow margin.
Size: To 30 mm (1.2 in).
Range: Calvert Island, British Columbia to San Diego, California.
Habitat: Subtidal from 7-27 m (23-88 ft).
Remarks: Feeds on creamy-white and greenish encrusting sponges.

J. Hamann

Aldisa cooperi Robilliard & Baba, 1972 — Cooper's aldisa

Body is yellow to red-orange with a line of small black spots down the center of its back. Rhinophores and gill may be the same color as the body or darker. A yellow form has been seen with no spots down the center line.
Similar species: *Aldisa sanguinea* has just one or two large dark dorsal spots.
Size: To 28 mm (1.1 in).
Range: Hogan Island, AK to Trinidad, CA; also in Japan.
Habitat: Subtidal to 40 m (130 ft).
Remarks: Feeds on the sponges *Antho graceae* and *Hamigera* spp.

R. Green

K. Fletcher

Aldisa sanguinea (Cooper, 1863)   **red aldisa**

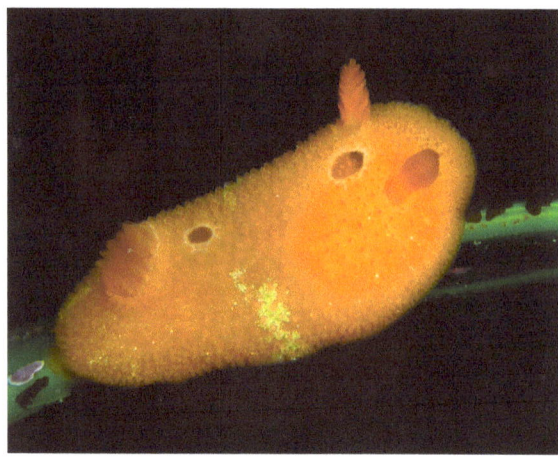

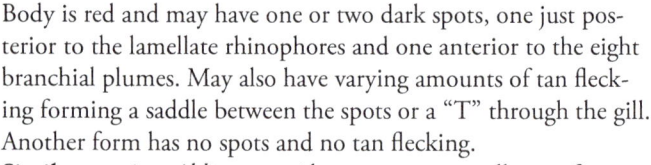

Body is red and may have one or two dark spots, one just posterior to the lamellate rhinophores and one anterior to the eight branchial plumes. May also have varying amounts of tan flecking forming a saddle between the spots or a "T" through the gill. Another form has no spots and no tan flecking.
Similar species: *Aldisa cooperi* has numerous small spots forming a line down the center of the back.
Size: To 20 mm (0.8 in).
Range: British Columbia to the Gulf of California, Mexico.
Habitat: Low intertidal to 10 m (33 ft).
Remarks: Feeds on the sponges *Hymedesmia pennata* and *Clathria brepha*.

R. Agarwal

R. Agarwal

M. Chamberlain

M. Passage

Aldisa tara Milllen & Gosliner, 1985   **kings' aldisa**

Body is translucent white with dull white pigment granules. The numerous and rather uniform conical tubercles have spicules in the middle and can contract, changing the appearance from finely tuberculate to almost smooth. Rhinophores and gill white.
Similar species: Juvenile *Doris odhneri* have much larger tubercles, and small white *Peltodoris lentiginosa* have a mix of large and small tubercles; both have much larger gill plumes and deeper bodies.
Size: To 27 mm (1 in).
Range: Desolation Sound, BC to Howe Sound, BC.
Habitat: Subtidal from 4-24 m (13-79 ft).
Remarks: Feeds on the red sponges *Hamigera* spp. and *Lissodendoryx kyma*, where its contrasting color is quite obvious.
K. Fletcher

Atagema alba (O'Donoghue, 1927)   **hunchback dorid**

Has a distinctive irregular ridge extending along the midline and three blunt extra-branchial lobes anterior to the branchial plumes. Surface of the dorsum is covered with small dark beige papillae giving it a sponge-like appearance. Color is light beige with many brown to black spots.
Similar species: *Atagema notacristata* is darker and lacks the extra-branchial lobes.
Size: To 60 mm (2.3 in).
Range: Monterey, California to Ensenada, Baja California, México.
Habitat: Low intertidal to 27 m (88 ft).
Remarks: Feeds on sponges.

K. Lee

Atagema notacristata Camacho-García & Gosliner, 2008 (previously *Atagema* sp. 1)   **crested dorid**

Body with pronounced mid-dorsal ridge made up of fused tubercles. Ground color cream to reddish-brown with dark brown to reddish-brown spots. Coarse texture due to numerous caryophyllidia-filled tubercles. Apices of rhinophores and gill are cream to light brown with minute white specks. Tubercles, rhinophores and branchial leaves are light brown to reddish-brown.
Similar species: *Doris tanya* has deep pits on the dorsum.
Size: To 30 mm (1.2 in).
Range: Bahía de Banderas, Mexico to Panama.
Habitat: Intertidal to 18 m (59 ft).
Remarks: Named for its prominent crested ridge.

A. Hermosillo

Baptodoris mimetica Gosliner, 1991   **mimic dorid**

Bright lemon yellow dorid with small white spots scattered on the dorsal surface of the rigid, caryophyllidia-covered notum. Perfoliate rhinophores with 14 lamellae uniformly brown. Gill translucent white and always held erect when fully extended.
Similar species: The five white-spotted, yellow species of *Doriopsilla*. *Baptodoris* can be recognized by its tougher, stiffer body and the presence of labial tentacles (right).

K. Lee   K. Lee

Size: To 45 mm (1.8 in).
Range: Salt Point State Park, Sonoma County, California to Isla San Martín, Baja California, Mexico.
Habitat: Low intertidal and subtidal.
Remarks: Feeds on sponges. This species was first recognized when biologists dissecting a "*Doriopsilla*" found a radula, which is not present in *Doriopsilla*.

Diaulula aurila (Marcus & Marcus, 1967)   **salt and pepper dorid**

Body is covered with caryophyllidia; varies in color from light yellow-brown to whitish-tan and is sprinkled with various amounts of tiny black and white spots. There are dusky patches on lighter-colored forms or there may be a dark band in the midline on darker-colored forms. Rhinophore clavus and gill are yellow-orange to brown.
Similar species: *Doris tanya* has a similar overall pattern and color, but with brown rhinophores and gill and deep dorsal pits.
Size: To 50 mm (2 in).
Range: Punto Rosarito, Baja California; Gulf of California to Panama.
Habitat: Intertidal to 6 m (20 ft), under rocks.
Remarks: Named for its light color.

A. Hermosillo

Diaulula nayarita (Ortea & Llera, 1981) (previously *Diaulula greeleyi*)   **Nayarit dorid**

Yellow to red-orange body with long, caryophyllidia-bearing tubercles. There are brown patches on the notum with occasional opaque white patches on the mantle edge. Thick rhinophoral sheaths form a distinctive collar around each rhinophore.
Similar species: Species of *Thordisa* do not have prominent rhinophoral sheaths.
Size: To 30 mm (1.2 in).
Range: Punta Eugenia, Baja California Sur to Costa Rica.
Habitat: Intertidal to 6 m (20 ft), under rocks.
Remarks: Named for the type locality, Nayarit, Mexico.

A. Hermosillo

Diaulula nivosa Valdés & Bertsch 2010   **snowy dorid**

Brownish-orange body with two black patches on either side of the back between the rhinophores and gill. The caryophillidia are white-tipped giving the animal a frosted appearance.
Similar species: *Diaulula sandiegensis* has distinct rings and lacks the "frosted" appearance. *Peltodoris lancei* lacks the large black markings.
Size: To at least 17mm (0.6 in).
Range: Known only from the type locality of Punta la Gringa, Bahía de los Ángeles, Mexico.
Habitat: Intertidal to 2 m (6 ft).
Remarks: The description of this species was based on a single specimen, so additional observations of size and range are welcome.

H. Bertsch

Diaulula odonoghuei (Steinberg, 1963)   **northern leopard dorid**

Body background color white, often overlayed with varying amounts of brown, dark brown or orange-red. Numerous different-sized dark spots are scattered on the notum to the edge of the mantle. Caryophillidia-bearing tubercles give the animal a velvety appearance. Rhinophores and gill are white.
Similar species: *Diaulula sandiegensis* lacks the small spots near the margin and tends to have a deeper, plumper body. The markings on *Dendrodoris nigromaculata* are in clusters and the edge of the mantle is delicate and wavy.

J. Kocian

Size: To 100 mm (3.9 in).
Range: Alaska to Bodega Bay, California; Also, Korea, Japan and Russia
Habitat: Low intertidal and subtidal in rocky areas. Maximum depth not known due to previous confusion with *D. sandiegensis*.
Remarks: Feeds on sponges.

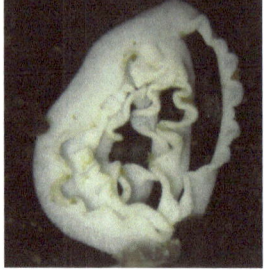

K. Fletcher

J. Kocian

Diaulula sandiegensis (Cooper, 1863)   San Diego dorid

Body pale brown or yellow-white to chalk white with a few usually ring-shaped dark spots scattered on the notum but never extending to the mantle edge. Rhinophores and gill are white.
Similar species: *Diaulula odonoghuei* is flatter and has small spots near its margins; *D. nivosa* does not have rings and has a "frosted" appearance due to white-tipped caryophillidia. *Dendrodoris nigromaculata* has its blotches grouped together and a thin, wavy mantle margin.
Size: To 125 mm (5 in).
Range: Barkley Sound, British Columbia to Cabo San Lucas, Baja California Sur.
Habitat: Low intertidal to 35 m (115 ft); limited to subtidal in the northern part of its range.

P. Garner

M. Chamberlain

G. Jensen

M. Passage

Remarks: Feeds on sponges, particularly *Neopetrosia problematica*.

Discodoris aliciae Dayrat, 2005   Ali's dorid

Body is dull orange to yellow, and covered with long, complexly-branched papillae. Rhinophores, gill, and dorsal papillae darker than the ground color. Underside of foot is bright orange-yellow, with numerous brown spots on the ventral surface of the notum.
Similar species: The long dorsal papillae on *Taringa aivica* are not branched.
Size: To 45 mm (1.8 in).
Range: Puerto Vallarta, Mexico to Panama.
Habitat: Subtidal to 24 m (79 ft), in caves and under rocks.
Remarks: Named for co-author, Alicia Hermosillo.

A. Hermosillo

Discodoris ketos (Marcus & Marcus, 1967)   spotted foot dorid

Body color varies from white-gray to light tan-gray to dark brown with irregularly arranged and various sized spots of different colors which are often larger along the center of the dorsum. Small non-caryophyllid tubercles, small holes, and ciliated tufts are scattered on the dorsum surface.
Similar species: *Atagema notacristata* has a noticeable middorsal crest and larger tubercles.
Size: To 45 mm (1.8 in).
Range: Gulf of California. Mexico to Panama and the Galapagos.
Habitat: Commonly found under rocks in the intertidal and shallow subtidal.
Remarks: Questions remain about whether this species is synonymous with the circumtropical species, *Tayuva lilacina*.

M. Chamberlain

Doris immonda (Risbec, 1928)

Body yellow-orange to pale brown covered with similarly-sized, rounded, slightly conical tubercles, with larger tubercles present in the middle of the body. Some tubercles are dark purple-brown. An opaque white or brown inverted 'Y' or hourglass pattern extends mid-dorsally from between the rhinophores to just in front of the five tripinnate, yellow-orange gill plumes. Some of the gill apices are dark brown. The rhinophores are elongate, pale at the base with a black or purple club.
Similar species: None.
Size: To 25 mm (1 in).
Range: Indo-Pacific and Costa Rica; possibly Mexico.
Habitat: Intertidal to 16 m (52 ft).
Remarks: *Doris immonda* was described from the tropical Indo-Pacific, and that name has been applied to this specimen from Mexico. However, color differences like the lack of black or dark purple tips on the rhinophores and the geographic separation make identification of the Mexican specimen suspect.

A. Hermosillo

Doris montereyensis Cooper, 1863 — Monterey dorid

The arched body is light yellow to dark yellow-orange, sometimes dirty gray-yellow or yellow ochre, with obvious tubercles that tend to be pointed rather than rounded. The number of black tubercles varies and sometimes black tubercles cluster into larger black patches. Gill is the same color as the body, sometimes darker, but generally not lighter; rhinophores may be darker than the body.
Similar species: The black markings on *Peltodoris nobilis* never extend onto the tubercles, while those of *Thordisa bimaculata* are concentrated into two large spots. *Geitodoris heathi* has smaller tubercles, giving it a smoother appearance.
Size: To 150 mm (5.9 in).
Range: Kachemak Bay, Alaska to Punta Banda, Baja California.
Habitat: Middle intertidal to 50 m (164 ft) on rock, cobble, and sandy bottoms; also on pilings.
Remarks: Feeds on a variety of sponges.

K. Lee

K. Fletcher

G. Jensen

Doris odhneri (MacFarland, 1966) — Odhner's dorid

Body usually pure white, occasionally cream yellow to dark tan with primarily large, low, rounded tubercles. No spots or dark markings anywhere on the body. Gill same color as the body and when fully extended appears fluffy and spans nearly the entire width of the body.
Similar species: *Peltodoris lentiginosa* has much smaller tubercles. *Aldisa tara* is a much smaller and flatter species, with conical tubercles.

K. Lee

Size: A large species, reaching 250 mm (9.8 in).
Range: Kenai Peninsula, Alaska to San Diego, California.
Habitat: Low intertidal to 137 m (450 ft) in rocky areas.
Remarks: Feeds on sponges, including *Haliclona edaphus* and the glass sponge *Aphrocallistes vastus*.

G. Jensen

Doris pickensi Marcus & Marcus, 1967 — Pickens' dorid

Body is translucent white to cream, light yellow to yellow-orange with a scattering of tiny brown spots. Foot margin, rhinophores and gill yellow or cream colored; there is one record of a specimen with brick red gill and rhinophores. Small round tubercles and spicules cover the body.
Similar species: Small *Doris odhneri* have no dark markings and a larger gill.
Size: To at least 25 mm (1 in).
Range: Morro Bay, California to Costa Rica, Gulf of California.
Habitat: Found under rocks in the intertidal.
Remarks: Named for Dr. Peter E. Pickens, (1928-2015) Professor of molecular and cellular biology at the University of Arizona.
A. Hermosillo

Doris tanya Ev. Marcus, 1971 — Tanya's dorid

Dorsum has many large, irregular tubercles which may bear smaller papillae and many deep pits. Color beige or tan with irregular dark tan to brown and yellow spots between the tubercles. Tan-brown rhinophores with 40 lamellae. The tan branchial plume has several branches.
Similar species: *Atagema notacristata* lacks pits on its dorsal surface.
Size: To 76 mm (3 in).
Range: Southern California to Panama, including the Gulf of California.
Habitat: Intertidal to 18 m (59 ft), under rocks.
Remarks: The "Tanya" of the species name was the cat belonging to malacologist Gale Sphon (1934-1995).

R. Agarwal

Hoplodoris bramale Fahey & Gosliner, 2003 — truffle dorid

The notum is flat and covered with large, rounded tubercles, which are smaller and denser on the sides. The color is light to dark brown, with a white ring at the base of the tubercles. The rhinophores and branchial plume are light tan and barely visible amongst the tubercles.
Similar species: None.
Size: To 75 mm (2.9 in).
Range: Known from Bahía de Banderas, Mexico, Costa Rica, and Panama.
Habitat: So far only known from the intertidal and shallow subtidal.
Remarks: Feeds on the sponge *Haliclona*.

A. Hermosillo

Geitodoris heathi (MacFarland, 1905) — Heath's dorid

The broad, often flattened body is covered with tiny tubercles which make the animal look gritty to almost smooth. Color varies from white to yellow, dark tan or raw umber and the dorsum may be darker along the midline. Tiny black, red-brown or brown spots are sprinkled over the dorsum and sometimes form a concentrated patch just in front of the gill. Rhinophores may be light yellow to dusky yellow or darker than the body; they are completely retractile within a wavy-margined sheath, as is the gill. Gill can be light yellow, dusky yellow or dark with whitish tips and may be sprinkled with tiny brown flecks.
Similar species: The tubercles of *Doris montereyensis* are more pointed and typically larger and more uniform in size. *Peltodoris nobilis* has larger, mushroom-shaped tubercles; *P. lentiginosa* has a deeper, more rounded body.

G. Jensen

Size: To 90 mm (3.5 in).
Range: Prince William Sound, Alaska to Bahía San Quentín, Baja California, Mexico.
Habitat: Low intertidal to at least 20 m (66 ft) in rocky areas.
Remarks: Feeds on a variety of encrusting sponges. Color and molecular differences indicate that there are two and possibly more cryptic species presently "lumped" under the name *G. heathi*.

D. Behrens

K. Fletcher

Geitodoris mavis (Marcus & Marcus, 1967)

Body is brown, yellowish-brown, or dull orange-pink. The mantle is covered in small tubercles, with a median row of large (sometimes lighter-colored) tubercles on a slight ridge. The lamellate rhinophores are the same color or slightly darker than the body, with a tiny white tip; gill is also the same color as the body.
Similar species: *Taringa aivica* lacks the median row of larger tubercles.
Size: To 24 mm (1 in).

J. Goddard

J. Goddard

Range: El Rosarito, Baja California, Mexico; Gulf of California to Costa Rica and the Galapagos Islands.
Habitat: Intertidal to 7 m (23 ft).
Remarks: As was typical for the Marcus', there was no explanation for the species name.

Jorunna pardus Behrens & Henderson, 1981 — leopard dorid

Color and pattern ranges from white with sparse black speckling to deep yellow with brown to black pigment concentrated into large round leopard-like spots, the largest of which are dorso-medially positioned. The spots do not form rings. Gill and rhinophores are very dark.
Similar species: *Peltodoris mulllineri* has an orange or yellow gill and rhinophores, and *P. rosae* has a grayish-orange gill and white-tipped rhinophores. Discodorididae sp. 1 has marginal white mantle glands, a smoother texture, and the dark areas form large spots.
Size: To 60 mm (2.3 in).
Range: Santa Barbara, California to Isla Cedros, Baja California, Mexico.
Habitat: Low intertidal to 18 m (60 ft).
Remarks: Named for its leopard-like spots. This species is more frequently encountered in the Channel Islands than on the mainland.

D. Behrens

P. Garner

Discodorididae sp.

P. Garner

Body pale yellow to deep yellow-orange with uniform length, villous tubercles covering the dorsum, many of which are covered with brown or black pigment which form various-sized patches. White glands often ring the edge of the mantle. Gill plumes pale yellow with black tips. Upright rhinophores pale yellow with black leaves and a blunt, white tip. No long, thin, black tubercles on rhinophore or gill margin.

It has been found from the Channel Islands, California to South Coronado Island, Mexico.

This may turn out to be an undescribed variation of *Jorunna pardus*, but with no genetic sequences of *Jorunna pardus* as described (nor sequences of this "smooth notum" form) it seems best to list this as "Discodorididae" rather than placing it with *Jorunna pardus* or *Peltodoris mullineri*, a species that it also externally resembles in some respects.

K. Lee

Jorunna osae Camacho-García & Gosliner, 2008 — Osa jorunna

Body pale cream to yellow. The dorsum has light yellow-brown patches or spots, darker in some specimens. The patches on the mantle are homogeneous, composed of minute dark spots. There are some white glandular structures along the mantle edge. Rhinophores are pale cream or yellow and speckled with brown, tipped in a lighter color. Gill is also pale cream to yellow, tipped in a lighter color, and is erect with overlapping branches that form a circle around the anus.

Similar species: *Jorunna tempisquensis* has darker brown spots and the gill spreads wide.
Size: To 13 mm (0.5 in).
Range: Gulf of California to Costa Rica.
Habitat: Intertidal to 13 m (43 ft), under rocks.
Remarks: Named after the Osa Conservation Area in Costa Rica.

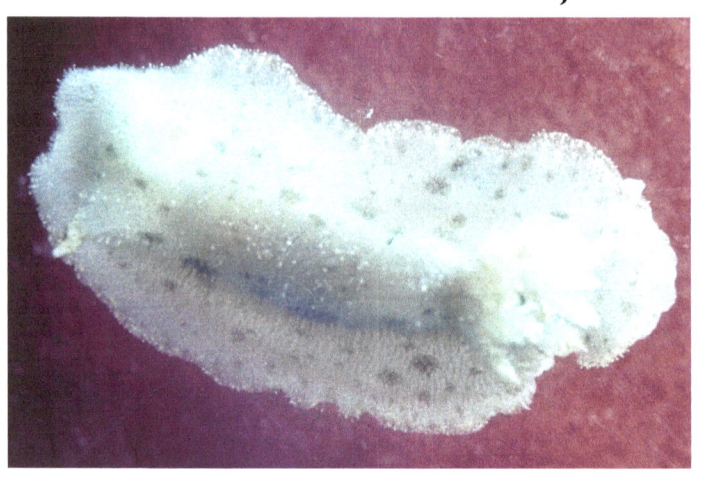

H. Bertsch

Jorunna tempisquensis Camacho-García & Gosliner, 2008 (previously *Jorunna* sp. 1)

Tempisque jorunna

Body color variable, from light cream or light brown to dark purplish black with large light brown or black spots concentrated in the center of the dorsum in darker specimens. Dorsum with even scattering of dark brown spots covering tubercles and caryophyllidia, but no mantle glands. Rhinophores light cream to light brown speckled with minute dark brown spots with yellowish-white tips. Gill is dark brown or purplish at the base with light yellow tips and spreads widely.
Similar species: *Jorunna osae* is lighter in color and has lighter brown spots, and the gill plumes overlap to form a tight, erect circle around the anus.
Size: To 15 mm (0.6 in).
Range: Southern Mexico to Costa Rica.
Habitat: Intertidal to 4 m (13 ft), under rocks.
Remarks: Named after the Tempisque Conservation Area in Costa Rica.

A. Hermosillo

Paradoris lopezi Hermosillo & Valdés, 2004

Lopez's dorid

Body color varies from a light to dark pinkish brown with large, dark reddish-orange tubercles. There is a blotchy tan line around the mantle margin. The gill is clear grayish-tan with darker specks towards the tips.
Similar species: None.
Size: To 32 mm (1.2 in).
Range: Bahía de Banderas, Mexico and La Paz, Baja California Sur, Mexico.
Habitat: Intertidal to 12 m (39 ft), under rocks and coral rubble.
Remarks: Produces a milky substance when disturbed.

A. Hermosillo

Peltodoris lancei Millen & Bertsch, 2000

Lance's dorid

Body dark orange-brown to reddish-orange with a lighter yellowish-orange margin edge; covered with small, conical, white-tipped tubercles and occasionally scattered brownish spots. Rhinophores and gill dusky yellow with lighter yellow tips.
Similar species: *Diaulula nivosa* has two pairs of large dark spots. *Baptodoris mimetica* has a white gill, and white-spotted species of *Doriopsilla* have a white or orange gill and lack oral tentacles and a radula.
Size: To 75 mm (2.9 in).
Range: Bahía de los Angeles, Baja California, Mexico, to Isla de Malpelo, Columbia.
Habitat: Intertidal to 7 m (23 ft).
Remarks: Feeds on a yellow encrusting demosponge on the undersides of rocks.

A. Hermosillo

Peltodoris lentiginosa (Millen, 1982) — **freckled dorid**

A large, loaf-shaped dorid, creamy or translucent white to pale yellow, covered with small, unstalked, dome-shaped and spiculated tubercles. Often the dosum is covered in variously sized dark chocolate brown to pale tan blotches which don't cover the tubercles, but in smaller animals the blotches may be faint or absent. Gill is slightly darker than the body, and the rhinophores bend backwards.
Similar species: *Geitodoris heathi* is a smaller and much flatter species, and *Doris odhneri* have much larger tubercles. *Aldisa tara* are also flatter and have more uniform, pointed tubercles,
Size: To 450 mm (17.7 in).
Range: Kodiak, Alaska to Carmel, California.

M. Passage

Habitat: Low intertidal to 224 m (735 ft).
Remarks: Feeds on encrusting yellow sponges.

M. Chamberlain

G. Jensen

Peltodoris mullineri Millen & Bertsch, 2000 — **Mulliner's dorid**

Body color varies from pale cream to bright yellow or golden-orange, with many irregular dark brown blotches. Dorsal surface covered with small tubercles. Rhinophores with cream base and dark yellow or golden-orange lamellae; gill yellow or golden-orange.

K. Lee

Similar species: *Jorunna pardus* and Discodorididae sp. 1 have dark purple to black rhinophores and gills. *Peltodoris rosae* is flatter and has white spots along the edge of the mantle.
Size: To 70 mm (2.7 in).
Range: Santa Barbara, California to Isla de Malpelo, Columbia.
Habitat: Subtidal to 17 m (56 ft).
Remarks: Thought to feed on sponges.

P. Garner

Peltodoris nobilis (MacFarland, 1905) — noble dorid

The thick, arched body is pale to dark yellow (rarely dark yellow-orange) and covered with various sized, flat-topped, club-shaped tubercles. There are often dark markings on the dorsum, but they do not extend up onto the tubercles. Gill is lighter than the body, often white.
Similar species: *Doris montereyensis* has a yellow gill and black on some dorsal tubercles. *Geitodoris heathi* and *Peltodoris lentiginosa* have much smaller and more widely-spaced tubercles.
Size: A very large dorid, to 250 mm (9.8 in).
Range: Kodiak, Alaska to Punta Banda, Baja California, Mexico.
Habitat: Intertidal to 250 m (820 ft).
Remarks: Found in rocky areas where it feeds on sponges including *Hamacantha hyaloderma* and *Mycale macginitiei*.

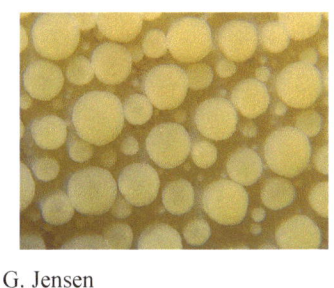

C. Hoover

G. Jensen

M. Passage

Peltodoris rosae Valdés & Bertsch 2010 — Rosa's dorid

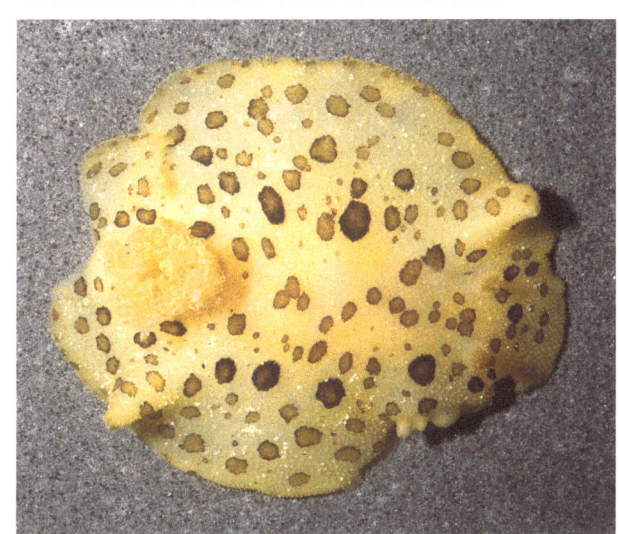

Wide, flattened body is dull yellow with circular solid-colored blackish patches and scattered small, opaque white spots near the margins. Rhinophores are brown with white tips. The 8 tripinnate gill plumes are grayish orange.
Similar species: *Peltodoris mullineri* lacks the white spots along the edge of the mantle; *Jorunna pardus* has dark purple to black rhinophores and gills.
Size: To at least 66 mm (2.6 in).
Range: Punta La Gringa, Bahía de los Angeles, Baja California, Mexico.
Habitat: Found under a rock at a depth of 6 m (20 ft).
Remarks: Known only from the single specimen in the photograph.

H. Bertsch

Platydoris macfarlandi Hanna, 1951 — MacFarland's dorid

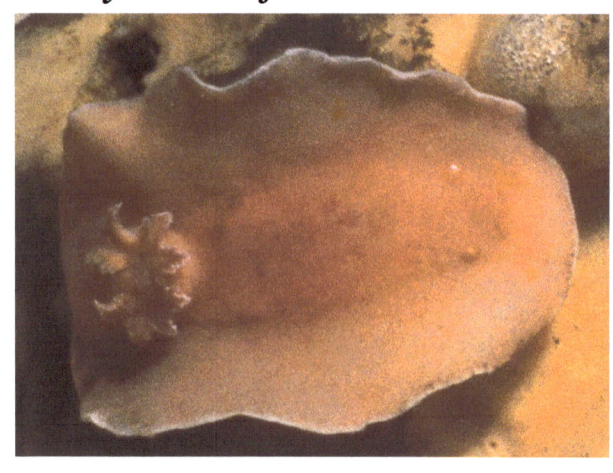

The greatly flattened, dull, velvety body is deep dark red above and almost white below, or pink above with a thin white to light pink margin. The notal margin is flexible and undulating. In the pink form, the rhinophores are white; the base of the gill is pink and the tips are white.
Similar species: None.
Size: To 30 mm (1.2 in).
Range: Pismo Beach, California to Bahía San Cristobal, Baja California, Mexico.
Habitat: Subtidal to 200 m (656 ft).
Remarks: Found on a yellow sponge. Named to honor Frank Mace McFarland (1869-1951) who collapsed and died minutes after discussing this nudibranch with the author.

J. Valle

Rostanga ghiselini Gosliner & Bertsch, 2017 — Ghiselin's dorid

Body bright red or reddish orange with obvious, well-spaced black spots and covered with densely packed caryophyllidia. Rhinophores and gill the same color as the body.
Similar species: *Aldisa sanguinea* only has two large spots. *Rostanga pulchra* has very different and distinctive rhinophores bearing vertical lamellae, while those of *R. ghiselini* have the horizontal lamellae typical of most dorids.
Size: To 30 mm (1.2 in).
Range: Only known from the Gulf of California.
Habitat: Subtidal from 3-10 m (10-33 ft).
Remarks: Of the 24 named species of *Rostanga*, only *R. ghiselini* and *R. pulchra* occur in the eastern Pacific.

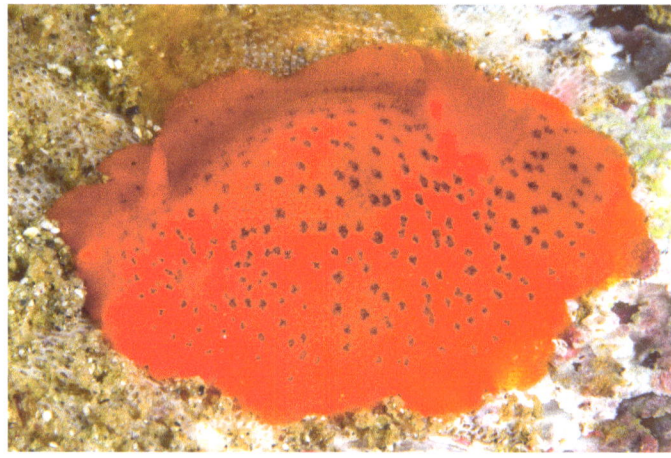

C. Hoover

Rostanga pulchra MacFarland, 1905 — red sponge dorid

Body color typically bright orange or red; occasionally pale tan, pinkish or white; sometimes with some small black spots. The uniquely-shaped rhinophores are best viewed from the side.
Similar species: *Rostanga ghiselini* has typical dorid rhinophores and many black spots; *Aldisa sanguinea* and *A. cooperi* have distinct patterns of black spots and *Thordisa rubescens* has conspicuous gold flecks.
Size: To 33 mm (1.3 in).
Range: Sitka, Alaska to Panama.
Habitat: Low intertidal to 100 m (328 ft).
Remarks: Feeds on sponges, especially *Ophlitaspongia pennata*. Molecular sequencing suggests there are three distinct species in the northeastern Pacific, although it is not known if there are visible external differences.

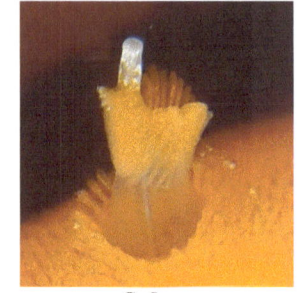

R. Agarwal

G. Jensen

C. Hoover

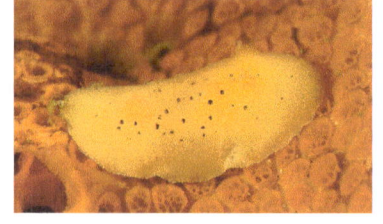

P. Garner

Taringa aivica Marcus & Marcus, 1967

Body color varies from a gray or dusky yellow to orange, brown, pink or purplish. There may be pale patches of white and brown dispersed over the notum, which is covered with minute papillae interspersed with a few larger conical ones. The gill is cream to tan with darker flecks, and the rhinophores dark gray, black, or orange with light tips.
Similar species: *Geitodoris mavis* has a row of tubercles forming a small median crest. *Discodoris aliciae* have long branched dorsal papillae.
Size: To 70 mm (2.7 in).
Range: Palos Verdes, California to Panama.
Habitat: Intertidal and subtidal.
Remarks: Feeds on the sponge *Hamacantha*.

A. Hermosillo

Thordisa bimaculata Lance, 1966

two-spotted dorid

Body whitish to yellow or yellow-orange, typically with two large brown to blackish concentrations of spots on the midline of the dorsum (but pigment may be pale or absent). Dorsum covered with large conspicuous papillae. Rhinophores are perfoliate, darker than the body, and orange to dull brownish-yellow.
Similar species: Specimens lacking the two distinctive spots could be mistaken for *Geitodoris heathi* or *Doris montereyensis*. *Geitodoris heathi* has much smaller and more uniformly-sized tubercles; *Doris montereyensis* invariably has some black lateral or dorsolateral tubercles.
Size: To 32 mm (1.2 in).
Range: Carmel, California to Isla Natividad, Baja California, Mexico. Rare in the northern part of its range.
Habitat: Intertidal to 33 m (108 ft).
Remarks: Feeds on sponges.

D. Behrens

Thordisa rubescens Behrens & Henderson, 1981

red thordisa

The body color is bright red-orange; there may be gold flecks forming a halo around the branchial pit, a line down the middle of the dorsum, and half crescents posterior to the rhinophores. Some specimens bear some black and white spotting as well. The white to yellowish-orange rhinophores and gill are tipped with brown, or can be mostly brown. The notum is covered with inflated papillae of various sizes and shapes.
Similar species: *Rostanga pulchra* has distinctive rhinophores that bear vertical lamellae.
Size: To 90 mm (3.5 in).
Range: Northeast Santa Cruz Island, California to Punta Eugenia, Baja California Sur, Mexico.

D. Behrens

Habitat: Subtidal to 22 m (72 ft).
Remarks: Found on the red-orange sponges *Axinella* spp. and *Lissodendoryx* spp.

M. Passage

Thordisa sp.

The body is brown to orange with a small red or brown spot in the center of the dorsum, surrounded by a smooth area. The rest of the dorsum bears many low papillae with a scattering of long, pointed ones. The rhinophores are heavily perfoliated, dark brown with clear stalks, and the gill is also brown.
Similar species: None.
Size: To 24 mm (1 in).
Range: Bahía de los Angeles and Bahía de Banderas, Mexico.

A. Hermosillo

Habitat: Subtidal.
Remarks: Typically found inside sea caves.

A. Hermosillo

Conualevia alba Collier & Farmer, 1964

white smooth-horn dorid

Opaque white body may be densely covered with minute tubercles and marked with two irregular rows of bright white glands along the dorsal margin. Rhinophores simple, smooth, tapering. The branchial plumes are the same color as the body and completely retractile.
Similar species: *Conualevia marcusi* also has smooth rhinophores, but lacks the conspicuous glands. Other small white dorids have lamellate rhinophores.
Size: To 24 mm (1 in).
Range: Carmel to San Diego, California; throughout the Gulf of California to Panama and the Galapagos.
Habitat: Low intertidal to 21 m (69 ft), under rocks.
Remarks: Lays a flattened egg ribbon.

K. Lee

Conualevia marcusi Collier & Farmer, 1964

Ernst's dorid

Body very light orange to white and the densely papillose dorsal surface has a fine textured appearance. The retractile rhinophores are smooth. The gill plumes are the same color as the body and are also completely retractile.
Similar species: *Conualevia alba* has obvious white glands along its margin, and other light-colored dorids have lamellate rhinophores.
Size: To 20 mm (0.8 in).
Range: Gulf of California, Mexico.
Habitat: Intertidal, under rocks.
Remarks: Named to honor biologist Ernst Marcus (1893-1968).

H. Bertsch

The "yellow margin dorid" complex

Recent molecular work has revealed a number of cryptic species within the genus *Cadlina*. At least four species had been previously lumped under the name *Cadlina luteomarginata*, and it is unclear at present whether these species can be reliably identified by their external characters. Some were described from single specimens, so their size, degree of variability, and full range are unknown. We present images here of specimens that have had their identity confirmed through molecular analysis, but caution the reader that they are not a definitive representation of the species. Since some characters can vary with age, features that appear unique to these single specimens may be misleading. All are sponge predators.

P. Garner

K. Fletcher
Cadlina jannanicholsae Korshunova et al., 2020
To 45 mm (1.8 in). Subtidal; known from British Columbia to Oregon.

K. Fletcher
Cadlina sylviaearleae Korshunova et al., 2020
To at least 25 mm (1 in). Found from Alaska to Puget Sound, Washington.

G. Paulay
Cadlina luteomarginata MacFarland, 1966
Up to 83 mm (3.3 in). Species confirmed from British Columbia to Mendocino, California; possibly to Punta Eugenia, Baja California, Mexico.

K. Fletcher
Cadlina klasmalmbergi Korshunova et al., 2020
To 60 mm (2.3 in). Known from British Columbia to Puget Sound, Washington.

Cadlina flavomaculata MacFarland, 1905   yellow-spotted cadlina

Body whitish, light cream to yellow, with a series of yellow spots along each side; dorsum may be edged with yellow. The lamellate rhinophores dark brown to black, sometimes with a white tip, and the gill white to yellowish.
Similar species: *Cadlina limbaughorum* has a very dark gill and lacks the yellow spots; *C. modesta* has much lighter-colored rhinophores and more yellow spots.
Size: To 25 mm (1 in).
Range: Sonoma County, California to La Paz, Baja California Sur, México; Costa Rica.

K. Lee

Habitat: Low intertidal to 200 m (656 ft).
Remarks: Feeds on the pink slime sponge, *Aplysilla glacialis*. Likely part of a species complex based on wide variation in radular teeth and a 10% genetic difference between specimens collected in Southern California. It is not known if the presence of a yellow margin relates to these differences.

R. Agarwal

Cadlina limbaughorum Lance, 1962   The Limbaughs' cadlina

The white body is liberally sprinkled with opaque subdermal white spots. The rhinophores and branchial plume are dark reddish brown to black.
Similar species: *Cadlina flavomaculata* has a white gill.
Size: To 33 mm (1.3 in).
Range: Monterey, California to Johnson's Sea Mount, Baja California, Mexico.
Habitat: Subtidal, from 15-47 m (49-154 ft).
Remarks: Feeds on the sponges *Axinella*, *Dysidea* and *Leiosella*.

K. Lee

Cadlina luarna (Marcus & Marcus, 1967)

Body color varies from mottled white to pale or purplish-brown with large pale patches on the mantle margin; subdermal bright orange glands may be visible on the mantle margin. There may be scattered dark dots along the elevated center of the dorsum, and there are many large, low, and smooth dorsolateral tubercles. Rhinophores dark; gill dark brown or pale.
Similar species: None.
Size: To 50 mm (2 in).
Range: Gulf of California to Panama.
Habitat: Intertidal and shallow subtidal.
Remarks: A rarely reported species.

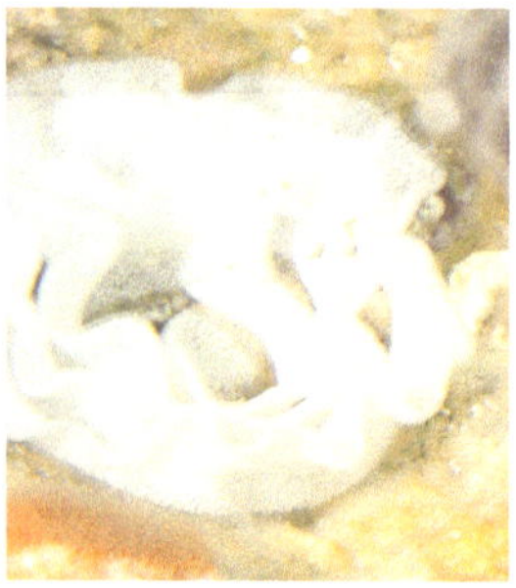

A. Hermosillo

Cadlina modesta MacFarland, 1966   **modest cadlina**

Body color may be milky white, cream colored, or yellow with an orange tint. There is a scattered ring of small bright yellow spots near the mantle margin and extending in front of the rhinophores and behind the gill (and rarely in the center of the dorsum). Rhinophores are pale or dusky tan; gill is pale.
Similar species: Few if any of the series of spots on *Cadlina* cf. *sparsa* extend to the frontal margin or behind the rhinophores. Other similar *Cadlina* spp. are distinguished by their yellowish margins; *C. flavomaculata* that lack a yellow margin still have very dark rhinophores.
Size: To 33 mm (1.3 in).
Range: Point Lena, Alaska to Isla Guadalupe, Baja California, Mexico.
Habitat: Intertidal to 50 m (164 ft).
Remarks: Feeds on the sponges *Aplysilla glacialis* and *Halisarca*.

D. Behrens

K. Fletcher

Cadlina cf. *sparsa*

Dorsum ground color cream, very light yellow or salmon to yellowish-pink and marked with a lateral series of small, often dark dots with yellow or orange centers. Gill and rhinophores are similar in color to the dorsum.
Similar species: *Cadlina modesta* have several yellow spots in front of the rhinophores and behind the gill. Other *Cadlina* with a light-colored gill and rhinophores have a yellow rim on their notum.
Size: To 36 mm (1.4 in).
Range: Marin County, California to Bahía de Banderas, Mexico. May be found as far north as Strathcona, Vancouver Island, Canada during years with warm water events.
Habitat: Intertidal to 40 m (131 ft).
Remarks: Feeds on the sponge, *Aplysilla*. *Cadlina sparsa* was originally described from Chile; morphological and genetic differences between Chilean and California specimens suggest the more northern populations are a separate, unnamed species.

K. Lee

Cadlina sp.

The white body has 4-5 large yellow spots along each side. Rhinophores are white with a reddish-brown medial band.
Similar species: None.
Size: To at least 10 mm (0.4 in).
Range: Bahía de Los Angeles, central Gulf of California to Costa Rica and Panama.
Habitat: Intertidal and shallow subtidal.
Remarks: Feeds on sponges.

A. Hermosillo

Felimida baumanni (Bertsch, 1970)

(previously *Glossodoris baumanni*) **Baumann's chromodorid**

The body color is primarily white, covered with a varying number of red-purple specks. Some specimens may appear completely red due to the density of the specks. The body margin and edge of the foot have a broken band of orange streaks. The bases of the rhinophores and gill are white, with red-purple tips.
Similar species: *Felimida norrisi* has large yellow spots on the dorsum; *F. galexorum* has much larger spots and lacks the marginal band of orange streaks.
Size: To 63 mm (2.5 in).
Range: Central Gulf of California to Ecuador.
Habitat: Intertidal to 18 m (59 ft).
Remarks: A nocturnal species.

A. Hermosillo

G. Jensen

Felimida galexorum (Bertsch, 1978) (previously *Chromodoris galexorum*) **Gale & Alex's chromodorid**

The creamy white body is covered with scarlet spots, many of which are encircled by yellow. The scarlet spots are largest down the midline. There is a yellow band around the margin of the notum, and the rhinophores and gill are red, becoming darker distally.
Similar species: *Felimeda norrisi* and *F. baumanni* have much smaller dorsal spots.
Size: To 24 mm (1 in).
Range: Catalina Island, California; Isla Guadalupe, Baja California and Gulf of California, Mexico.
Habitat: Subtidal, from 3-45 m (10-148 ft).
Remarks: Seasonally abundant during the spring in the shallow subtidal.

C. Hoover

Felimida macfarlandi (Cockerell, 1901) (previously *Chromodoris macfarlandi*)

MacFarland's chromodorid

This species is easily recognized by its pinkish-purple to violet color and three bright yellow longitudinal lines.
Similar species: *Felimare porterae* is dark blue with just two longitudinal orange lines.
Size: To 60 mm (2.3 in).
Range: Monterey, California to Bahía Magdelena, Baja California, Mexico.
Habitat: Low intertidal to 34 m (111 ft).
Remarks: Feeds on sponges in the genus *Aplysilla*.

K. Lee

Felimida marislae (Bertsch et al., 1973) (previously *Chromodoris marislae*) — Marisla's chromodorid

The body is brilliant translucent white with 2-3 irregular rows of orange spots on the sides. These large spots look like bullseyes with orange ringlets, each surrounded or marked centrally with frosty white. The rhinophores and branchial plume are white with an opaque white vertical line.
Similar species: None.
Size: To 80 mm (3.1 in).
Range: Gulf of California to Panama.
Habitat: Subtidal from 5-30 m (16-98 ft).
Remarks: The striking coloration serves as a warning to predators of its unpalatability due to a defensive chemical called marislin, likely derived from its sponge diet.

A. Hermosillo

Felimida norrisi (Farmer, 1963) (previously *Chromodoris norrisi*) — Norris' chromodorid

The background body color is white, sometimes with a sub-epidermal violet coloration in the middle of the dorsum. The notum and sides of the foot have numerous deep cobalt violet spots, small red dots and some large yellow spots. A bright reddish-orange, broken band encircles the edge of the dorsum. The gill and rhinophores are tipped in orange.
Similar species: *Felimida galexorum* and *Felimida baumanni* lack the large yellow spots.
Size: To 61 mm (2.4 in).
Range: Isla Cedros, Baja California and the Gulf of California to Costa Rica.
Habitat: Intertidal to 15 m (49 ft), under rocks.
Remarks: Feeds on the sponges *Aplysilla* and *Dendrilla*. The bright coloration warns predators of its metabolic defense chemical, norrisolide.

A. Hermosillo

Felimida socorroensis (Behrens et al., 2009) (previously *Chromodoris* sp. 1) — Soccoro chromodorid

Ground color is translucent white with large orange-red areas on the dorsum. The gill plumes are white, tipped in pink. There are two distinctive translucent clearings, outlined in white, behind the rhinophores, revealing the eye spots. The frontal part of the dorsum has a dark red patch with varying orange spots, and the clear tail has an orange line in the middle.
Similar species: None.
Size: Small, to 10 mm (0.4 in).
Range: Islas San Benedicto and Soccoro and Isla Revillagigedo, Mexico.
Habitat: Subtidal to 12 m (39 ft).
Remarks: Found under rocks.

A. Hermosillo

Felimida sphoni Ev. Marcus, 1971 (previously *Chromodoris sphoni*) **Sphon's chromodorid**

This species has a distinctive red-cross pattern on its dorsum, along with various bluish-white and yellow streaks and dots. The edge of the mantle has red, cream yellow, and pale blue or mint green bands. The rhinophores and gill are varying shades pink and red with darker tips.
Similar species: None.
Size: To 35 mm (1.4 in).
Range: Central Gulf of California to Ecuador.
Habitat: Intertidal to 18 m (59 ft).
Remarks: Feeds on sponges.

A. Hermosillo

Chromolaichma dalli (Bergh, 1879)

(previously *Glossodoris dalli*) **Dall's chromodorid**

Extremely colorful and varied-- ground color from brown, green, or gray to bluish with scattered black, brown, greenish, yellow and/or blue blotches and black, white, and orange dots; the black dots are also on the sides of the foot. Gill and lamellate rhinophores are white to pale brown with bright red or orange tips. There is an orange and pink band around the mantle margin and foot.

C, Hoover

Similar species: No other species has black spots on the foot.
Size: To 65 mm (2.5 in).
Range: Islas San Benitos, Baja California, Gulf of California and the Mexican Pacific to Panama and the Galápagos.
Habitat: Subtidal from 10-18 m (33-59 ft).
Remarks: Feeds on sponges. Originally described as being from "Puget Sound", an obvious error.

A. Hermosillo

Chromolaichma sedna (Marcus & Marcus, 1967)

(previously *Glossodoris sedna*) **red-tipped sea goddess**

Body is transparent white with an opaque white band, followed by a bright red band and then a yellow band around the often slightly undulating mantle margin. The foot margin may exhibit the same color pattern or be ringed with only yellow. Rhinophores and gill are tipped in red. Gill plumes are often observed vibrating or rotating continuously.
Similar species: None.
Size: To 65 mm (2.5 in).
Range: Gulf of California to Ecuador.
Habitat: Low intertidal to 18 m (59 ft).
Remarks: A common, gregarious species that is often found feeding on sponges.

A. Hermosillo

Felimare agassizii (Bergh, 1894) (previously *Hypselodoris agassizii*) — Agassiz's chromodorid

The body is very dark, sometimes bluish-purple, with light blue patches and yellow spots sprinkled over the notum. A broad dorsolateral band of turquoise, yellow and green runs down each side, with a break in the middle of the body. The rhinophores are black with yellow vertical lines and the gill is light colored with black tips.
Similar species: The southern form of *Felimare californiensis* lacks dorsolateral bands while *Mexichromis tura* has light blue rather than green bands.
Size: To 80 mm (3.1 in).
Range: Gulf of California, Mexico, to Panama and the Galapagos.
Habitat: Intertidal to 18 m (59 ft), on and under rocks.
Remarks: The bright coloration warns predators of its metabolic defense chemical, agassizin.

A. Hermosillo

Felimare amalguae (Gosliner & Bertsch, 1988) (previously *Mexichromis amalguae*) — Cedros chromodorid

Oval body is blue to light purple, sometimes with a diffuse cream line on the midline of dorsum. There is a thin yellow band encircling the entire notal margin, and the rhinophores and gill are navy blue.
Similar species: *Felimare porterae* and *Felimida macfarlandi* have mid-lateral stripes.
Size: To 20 mm (0.8 in).
Range: La Jolla, California to Isla Cedros, Baja California, Mexico.
Habitat: Subtidal to 23 m (75 ft) in rocky areas.
Remarks: This small, attractive dorid is considered very rare.

J. Hamann

Felimare californiensis (Bergh, 1879) (previously *Hypselodoris californiensis*) — California chromodorid

Elongate body is deep blue with either four longitudinal series of yellow spots, one on each side of the foot and the others laterally on the dorsum (northern coloration) or the dorsum is covered with small yellow and whitish-blue spots (southern coloration). A band of cobalt blue may be found along the margin of the dorsum and foot. The rhinophores and branchial plumes are dark blue-black or navy blue with yellow spots.
Similar species: *Felimare agassizii* and *Mexichromis tura* both have multicolored dorsolateral bands.
Size: To 90 mm (3.5 in).
Range: Rarely found as far north as Monterey Bay, California; typically, southern California to Peru and the Galapagos Islands.
Habitat: Low intertidal to 30 m (100 ft) in rocky areas.
Remarks: Feeds on sponges, and releases a noxious substance when attacked. The smaller-spotted southern form was previously considered a separate species, *Hypselodoris ghiselini*.

K. Lee

C. Hoover

Felimare porterae (Cockerell, 1901) (previously *Mexichromis porterae*)   Porter's chromodorid

Body is dark blue, with a white line around the mantle edge. Two yellow-orange lines extend on either side of the dorsum from behind each rhinophore past the branchial plume, and there is a light blue medial line. There is often a yellow-orange curved line in front of the rhinophores.
Similar species: *Felimida macfarlandi* is purple and has a yellow median stripe, while *Felimare amalguae* lacks dorsum stripes.

K. Lee

Size: To 34 mm (1.3 in).
Range: Monterey, California to Bahía Tortugas, Baja California, Mexico.
Habitat: low intertidal to 50 m (164 ft) in rocky areas.
Remarks: Found on the sponge, *Dysidia amblia*.

A. Hermosillo

Mexichromis antonii (Bertsch, 1976)   Ferreira's chromodorid

The body is bluish-white with a broad middorsal magenta band running from the rhinophores to the gill, with a series of elongate white dashes running down the center. The edge of the mantle has a wide black line bordered by a yellow-orange band. The bright pink gill and rhinophores are tipped with black.
Similar species: None.
Size: Small, to 12 mm (0.5 in).
Range: Central Gulf of California to Costa Rica and Panama.
Habitat: Subtidal to 24 m (79 ft).
Remarks: Found on and under rocks.

A. Hermosillo

Mexichromis tura (Marcus & Marcus, 1967)

Body is dark blue-black with orange or yellow-orange spots and dashes. The edge of the mantle has three bands: an outermost yellow, a middle black, and an innermost powder blue. Laterally, the dorsum has larger, whitish-yellow streaks and blotches. The gill plumes are white, with black tips. The rhinophores are completely black.
Similar species: *Felimare agassizii* has green rather than blue lines; the southern form of *F. californiensis* lacks marginal lines.
Size: To 10 mm (0.4 in).
Range: San Carlos Bay, Sonora, Mexico to Panama.
Habitat: intertidal to 20 m (65 ft).
Remarks: This rarely-seen species feeds on sponges.

A. Hermosillo

Tyrinna evelinae (Er. Marcus, 1958)   **Eveline's chromodorid**

Body white to light cream with red to yellow-orange spots on the notum which are larger and more numerous near the edge. Rhinophores and gill are white. The tail is long and projects beyond the notum.
Similar species: *Felimida baumanni* has orange-tipped gills and rhinophores.
Size: To 30 mm (1.2 in).
Range: Bahía Sebastian Viscaino, Baja California to Costa Rica and Peru; also Gulf of California. This species was described from the Atlantic; closer study will probably reveal significant differences.
Habitat: Intertidal and subtidal; maximum depths not known.
Remarks: Feeds on sponges.

A. Hermosillo

Dendrodoris cf. *fumata*

Highly variable in color, including velvety black with a black or red margin and orange, red, or grey forms with white-tipped rhinophores and gill. Notum margin is highly undulate and gill is large.
Similar species: *Doriopsilla janaina* has distinct dorsal tubercles; *Thordisa rubescens* does not have white tips on the gill and rhinophores.
Size: To 30 mm (1.2 in).
Range: Vizcaíno Bay, Baja California Sur, Mexico to Panama and the Galapagos.
Habitat: Intertidal to below 15 m (49 ft).
A. Hermosillo   **Remarks**: True *Dendrodoris fumata* is a widespread Indo-Pacific species that is genetically distinct from Pacific coast specimens. The polyclad flatworm *Pseudobiceros bajae* is believed to be a mimic of this species.

A. Hermosillo

A. Hermosillo

Dendrodoris nigromaculata (Cockerell, 1905) (previously *Dendrodoris behrensi*)   **black spotted dorid**

Smooth translucent white to cream body often with many large chocolate brown to maroon blotches, clustered into three or four groups in front of and behind the rhinophores, in the middle of the body, and in front of the gill, or with only one or two blotches. Smaller brown spots may be scattered near the delicate, wavy mantle edge. Gill and rhinophores are white to cream.
Similar species: The brown blotches of *Diaulula sandiegensis* and *D. odonoghuei* are randomly spaced and the mantle margin is not delicate and wavy.
Size: To 27 mm (1.1 in).
Range: Monterey, California to the San Benitos Islands, Baja California.
Habitat: Intertidal to 46 m (151 ft).
Remarks: Intertidal specimens found under rock rubble.

K. Lee

Dendrodoris stohleri Millen & Bertsch, 2005
Stohler's dorid

Body white to yellow with numerous brown spots of various sizes scattered over the dorsum. The wavy margin is free of spots. Rhinophores and gill are the same color as the body.
Similar species: Other black-spotted, yellow dorids lack the thin, wavy mantle margin.
Size: To 25 mm (1 in).
Range: Known only from Bahía de los Angeles, Gulf of California, Mexico.
Habitat: Intertidal to 12 m (39 ft).
Remarks: Found under rocks.

H. Bertsch

Porostome nudibranchs lack radulas, and feed by spitting digestive enzymes onto their sponge prey and then sucking up the resulting stew. Several of our species are nearly identical in appearance, but the following key derived from Hoover et al. (2015) is very helpful in differentiating them.

Key to yellow pseudocryptic porostomes in the temperate northeastern Pacific

1. White spots found only on top of the tubercles----------*Doriopsilla fulva*
    1' White spots found between tubercles----------2
2. Gill the same color as the dorsal margin----------3
    2' Gill not the same color as the dorsal margin----------4
3. When fully extended, gill less than half the width of the dorsum----------*D. gemela*
    3' When fully extended, gill half the width of the dorsum or greater--------*D. bertschi*
4. With large white spots atop tubercles----------*D. albopunctata*
    4' With only small white spots, surrounding tubercles----------*D. davebehrensi*

The mimic dorid, *Baptodoris mimetica*, is easily mistaken for these species. It has a much tougher, stiffer body and has labial tentacles.

Doriopsilla albopunctata (Cooper, 1863)
white-spotted porostome

Oval body with wide mantle margin. Varies in color from light yellow to dark orange or brown with numerous large white spots on the tubercle tips and smaller white spots ringing the tubercles. Gill often white, sometimes yellow, with five branchial leaves.
Size: To 36 mm (1.4 in).
Range: Mendocino, California to Puerto Viejo, Baja California.
Habitat: Intertidal to 36 m (118 ft).
Remarks: Eggs are laid in an upright coil.

M. Chamberlain

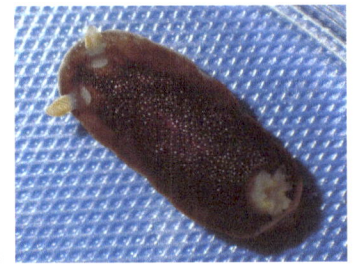

G. Jensen

Doriopsilla bertschi Hoover et al., 2015 — **Bertsch's dorid**

Oval body with narrow mantle margin. Dark yellow to orange with irregularly-scattered small white spots or flecks both on the tubercle tips and between the tubercles. Rhinophores and gill dark yellow to orange. Gill almost as wide as the body with five branchial leaves oriented toward the posterior end of the body.
Size: To 22 mm (0.8 in).
Range: Only known from Bahía de Los Angeles in the upper Gulf of California, Mexico.
Habitat: Shallow subtidal to 6 m (20 ft), usually in association with the sponge *Cliona californiana*.
Remarks: Egg ribbon is a flat coil.

H. Bertsch

Doriopsilla davebehrensi Hoover et al., 2015 — **Behrens' dorid**

Color varies from dark yellow to orange. Body is wide and rounded, with a narrow mantle margin and covered with numerous small tubercles and a few scattered large ones. Small white spots most often between the tubercles but occasionally on the tubercles. Rhinophores are light-tipped and the gill plumes are off-white to yellow.
Size: To 88 mm (3.4 in).
Range: Newport Beach, California to Punta Rosarito, Baja California and the Gulf of California.
Habitat: Low intertidal to at least 6 m (20 ft).
Remarks: Egg ribbon is an upright coil with a wavy free edge. Named for co-author Dave Behrens.

A. Hermosillo

Doriopsilla fulva (MacFarland 1905) — **white-speckled dorid**

Usually yellow, occasionally white, with large white spots on the tips of most tubercles but not in the spaces between them. Gill white. Body is oval with a narrow mantle margin.
Size: To 33 mm (0.7 in).
Range: Northern California to Baja California; may be found in Oregon in El Niño years.
Habitat: Intertidal to at least 18 m (59 ft).
Remarks: Egg ribbon is an upright coil.

P. Garner

Doriopsilla gemela Gosliner et al., 1999 — look-alike dorid

The oval body with a narrow mantle margin is dark yellow to orange with large white spots on the tubercle tips, and numerous small white dots between the tubercles. The dark yellow to orange gill is less than 1/2 the width of the dorsum when fully extended, with small branchial leaves oriented upward.
Size: To 40 mm (1.5 in).
Range: Monterey, California to Bahía Tortugas, Baja California Sur.
Habitat: Intertidal to at least 18 m (59 ft).
Remarks: The egg ribbon is a flat coil.

C. Hoover

M. Passage

Doriopsilla janaina Marcus & Marcus, 1967

Color highly variable: reddish, pink, purple, yellow, or brown, usually with two darker bands running dorsolaterally from the rhinophores to the gill. Dorsum covered with small tubercles, with four large white tubercles forming a rectangle.
Similar species: *Doriopsilla* sp. 1 has four white dorsal streaks rather than tubercles.
Size: To 25 mm (1 in).
Range: Gulf of California to Panama and the Galapagos.
Habitat: Intertidal and subtidal to 21 m (70 ft), on large rocks.
Remarks: This species is very cryptic, and most easily found by searching near its bright orange egg masses.

K. Lee

Doriopsilla sp.

A rather flat, orange species with orange rhinophores and gill. The dorsum is covered with medium tubercles and there are several white markings with black borders. This gregarious, nocturnal species reaches 30 mm (1.2 in).

A. Hermosillo

P. Humann

Doriopsilla rowena Marcus & Marcus, 1967 (previously *Doriopsilla nigromaculata*)

A yellowish-white dorid with a smooth dorsum bearing numerous brown flecks concentrated near the midline. A series of white blotches occur dorsolaterally between the rhinophores and gill.
Similar species: Other yellowish *Doriopsilla* have bright white flecks or a light margin.
Size: To 12 mm (0.5 in).
Range: La Jolla, California to El Campo, near Punta Eugenia, Baja California Sur and northern Gulf of California to Panama, and the Galapagos Islands. May be found on Anacapa Island, California during years with warm water events.
Habitat: Rocky intertidal and shallow subtidal.
Remarks: Based on egg mass types and egg development there may be two species with overlapping ranges along Baja California. *Doriopsilla rowena* has small eggs with planktonic larvae, while the eggs of specimens found in southern California undergo direct development.

C. Hoover

Doriopsilla spaldingi Valdés & Behrens, 1998 — Spalding's dorid

Body creamy white, yellow-orange, or pale orange with evenly distributed low tubercles and a highly undulated white to iridescent bluish margin. Gill and rhinophores yellow-orange.
Similar species: The brilliant, undulating margin is unlike any of the other yellow *Doriopsilla*.
Size: To 83 mm (3.2 in).
Range: Carmel, California to Punta Banda, Baja California and Guaymas, Sonora, México.
Habitat: From 27 m (88 ft) to over 60 m (197 ft).
Remarks: The egg ribbon is a flat coil that hatches planktonic larvae.

M. Miller

Dorid sp.

Body orange with a few random white markings on the mantle and some underlying darker areas. It is covered completely with small tubercles and some larger ones. The margin of the mantle is moderately undulated. The gill plume is the same color as the body with white frosting on the tips. The rhinophores are lamellate and a darker solid orange than the body.
Size: 30 mm (1.2 in).
Range: Known only from Isla Guadalupe in the Mexican Pacific.
Habitat: Found under rocks.
Remarks: Until specimens are available for examination, it cannot even be assigned to a genus.

A. Hermosillo

Phyllidiopsis blanca Gosliner & Behrens, 1988   **white phyllidid**

The body is white to greyish-white. The notum bears numerous soft, low tubercles but no dorsally located branchial plume. Only the anal pore marks the typical location of a gill.
Similar species: Our only other dorid without a dorsal gill is the tiny, bright orange *Vayssierea*.
Size: To 25 mm (1 in).

J. Hamann

J. Hamann

Range: Santa Barbara Island, California to Isla San Benito, Baja California, Mexico.
Habitat: Subtidal to 23 m (75 ft).
Remarks: The gills are located laterally between the notum and the foot. There are approximately 60 gill leaflets along the right side and 70 leaflets along the left side.

Vayssierea sp.

A tiny orange-red, worm-like dorid without an external gill or a gill cavity. *Vayssierea felis* was first described from the South China Sea; preliminary DNA work indicates ours is a distinct species. It has been observed in harbors in Southern California since about 2007, so is undoubtedly introduced.
Similar species: Most likely to be confused with the orange flatworm *Vorticeros praedatorium*. The rhinophores of *Vayssierea* are dorsal and well-separated from each other; the tentacles of the flatworm project from the front and meet at the base.
Size: To 6 mm (0.2 in).
Range: Redondo and San Diego, California.
Habitat: Intertidal.
Remarks: Feeds by drilling into spirorbid tube worms, and lays large eggs (shown). 
J. Goddard

J. Goddard

Suborder Cladobranchia

In the Eastern Pacific, this group contains species of the superfamilies Tritonioidea, Dendronotoidea, Arminoidea, Proctonotoidea, and Aeolidioidea + Fionoidea, often combined as Aeolidida (see Goodheart et al., 2018 and Karmeinski et al., 2021).

Superfamily Tritonioidea

The Tritonioidea are easily recognized by the frill of gills along the margin of the notum. They tend to specialize on sea pens, sea whips, and other soft corals, and some are among our largest nudibranchs. The species pictured here with its eggs, *Tritonia exsulans*, has been extensively used in neurological research.

C. Hoover

Marionia kinoi Angulo-Campillo & Bertsch, 2013 (previously *Marionia* sp. 1) — **Padre Kino's tritonid**

The body has a mesh-like pattern of lighter-colored areas overlying a mid-dorsal orange background and a red background laterally. There are 11 branchial plumes along the side of the body. The sheaths and shafts of the rhinophores are orange, with the apical portions a light brown color.
Similar species: None.
Size: To 80 mm (3.1 in).
Range: Southern end of the Gulf of California to Costa Rica and the Galapagos.
Habitat: Subtidal to 16 m (52 ft).
Remarks: A nocturnal species. It feeds on the octocorals of the genus *Carijoa*.

A. Hermosillo

Marionia sp.

The body is translucent white with opaque tubercles, and the lateral processes, oral veil and rhinophores are white.
Similar species: None.
Size: To 12 mm (0.5 in).
Range: Known only from Isla Isabel, Nayarit, and Manzanillo, Colima, Mexico.
Habitat: Shallow subtidal.
Remarks: A nocturnal species, found feeding on sea pansies and gorgonians.

A. Hermosillo

Tochuina gigantea (Bergh, 1904) (previously *Tochuina tetraquetra*) — **orange-peel nudibranch**

Body is orange to yellow and covered in white-tipped tubercles. A continuous fringe of fluffy white gill tufts extends from the rhinophores back along the length of the undulating body margin, and the oral veil lacks digitiform processes.
Similar species: *Tritonia exsulans* and *T. tetraquetra* have numerous digitiform processes on the frontal veil.
Size: Huge, to 500 mm (19.7 in).
Range: Aleutian Islands, Alaska to San Diego, California; Northern Japan to the Kuril Islands, Russia.
Habitat: Subtidal to 363 m (1191 ft).
Remarks: Feeds on the soft coral *Alcyonium* and gorgonians. It is our largest true nudibranch and one of the largest in the world.

M. Chamberlain

Tritonia exsulans Bergh, 1894 (previously *Tritonia diomedea*)   **pink tritonid**

Body typically light pinkish to dark salmon with a white line marking the edge of the dorsum, the foot margin and the oral veil. Indistinct notal edge fringed with short, branched dorsolateral gills. The bilobed oral veil has 15-30+ white digitiform processes.
Similar species: *Tritonia festiva* and *T. tetraquetra* have fewer digiform processes on the oral veil.
Size: To 300 mm (11.8 in).
Range: Aleutian Islands, Alaska to Panama.
Habitat: On sand and mud bottoms, from 5-100 m (16-328 ft).
Remarks: Feeds on sea pens and sea whips.

G. Jensen

Tritonia festiva (Stearns, 1873)   **festive tritonid**

Body typically translucent whitish gray, but may also appear yellow, burnt sienna or dark pink. A white line runs along the dorsal edge, foot margin, oral veil and across the head between the rhinophores. Dorsum often has a pattern of white lines forming diamonds or ovals. A series of dorsolateral processes line both sides of the notal edge, and the slightly bilobed oral veil has 8-12 white digitiform processes.
Similar species: *Tritonia exsulans* has a conspicuously bilobed oral veil bearing 15-30 processes; *T. tetraquetra* lacks the white markings.
Size: To 100 mm (4 in).
Range: Kachemak Bay, AK to Isla Coronado, Baja California, Mexico; also reported from Japan and Korea.
Habitat: Found on both rocky and soft bottoms, from the low intertidal to 50 m (164 ft).
Remarks: Feeds on sea pens, sea whips, soft corals, and gorgonians. Given the wide variation in radular formulae and the distances between some genetic sequences it's possible there may be separate species with slight external variations.

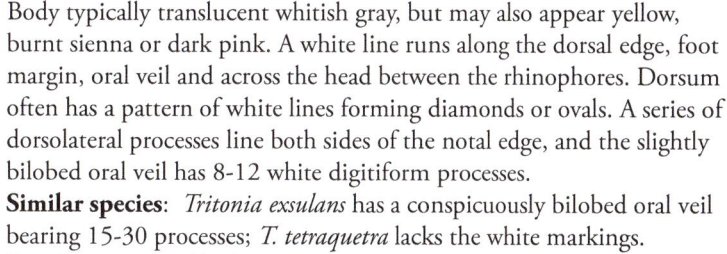

M. Chamberlain   M. Passage    G. Jensen

Tritonia sp. 1

Body of this small tritoniid is translucent pinkish with a light dusting of opaque white which forms faint lines down each side along the branched gill tufts and on the tip of the tail, but not along the foot margin. Dorsum is pebbly. Oral veil with about ten digitiform tentacles.
Similar species: The rougher texture of the dorsum helps distinguish this from small, pink specimens of *Tritonia festiva* that lack dorsal markings.
Range: Found off Langara Island, BC Canada.
Habitat: Subtidal, in rocky areas.
Remarks: Found on the pink soft coral, *Gersemia lambi*.

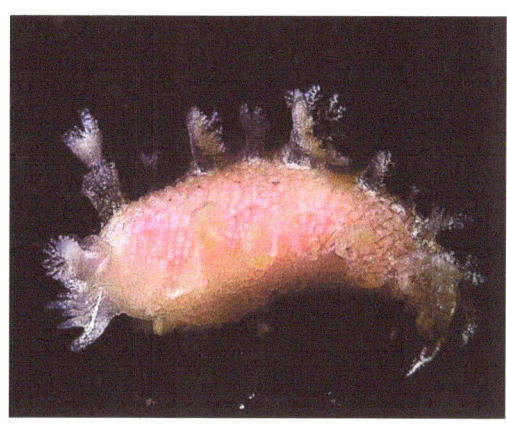

M. Chamberlain

Tritonia sp. 2

Body color yellow, sometimes with brown pigment. Small, rounded tubercles that have an opaque white base and dark brown, purple, or black apex form irregular lines down the body. There are eight pairs of short, delicately branched dorsolateral processes. Rhinophores are pulpit-shaped and the sheaths have tubercles; oral veil with 3-4 digitiform lobes per side.
Similar species: None.
Size: To 20 mm (0.8 in).
Range: Puerto Refugio, Isla Angel de la Guarda, Mexico and the Galapagos Islands.
Habitat: Subtidal, to at least 15 m (49 ft).
Remarks: This is *Tritonia* sp. of Bertsch, 2014 and *Tritonia* sp. 2 of Camacho Garcia et al., 2005. It feeds on a yellow gorgonian in the Galapagos Islands.

C. Hoover

Tritonia tetraquetra (Pallas, 1788)

orange ruffled tritonid

Body typically yellow-orange to dark reddish-orange. Indistinct notal edge with light-colored dorsolateral processes. Bilobed oral veil with 12-16 digitiform processes. No white line along the edge of the foot, dorsum or oral veil.
Similar species: The oral veil of *Tritonia exsulans* has more processes and the oral veil of *Tochuina gigantea* lacks processes; both have white marking the edge of the foot.
Size: To 300 mm (11.8 in).
Range: Bering Sea to Cordell Bank, California; Kamchatka, Russia, and the Sea of Okhotsk.
Habitat: Subtidal from 5-895 m (16-2936 ft).
Remarks: Rarely found within diving depths in the northeastern Pacific.

N. McDaniel

Tritonicula myrakeenae (Bertsch & Mozqueira, 1986)

Keen's tritonid

The thin, delicate body is a pale, dirty orange-brown with one to four (usually two) distinct white patches on the dorsum and a translucent foot. The translucent oral veil has four to seven tentacular processes. Up to nine gill plumes are distributed along the dorsal edges of the body.
Similar species: *Tritonicula pickensi* has most of the dorsum covered in white.
Size: To 18 mm (0.7 in).
Range: Estero Bay, San Luis Obispo County, California to Panama.
Habitat: Intertidal and shallow subtidal.
Remarks: This species feeds on octocorals and gorgonians.

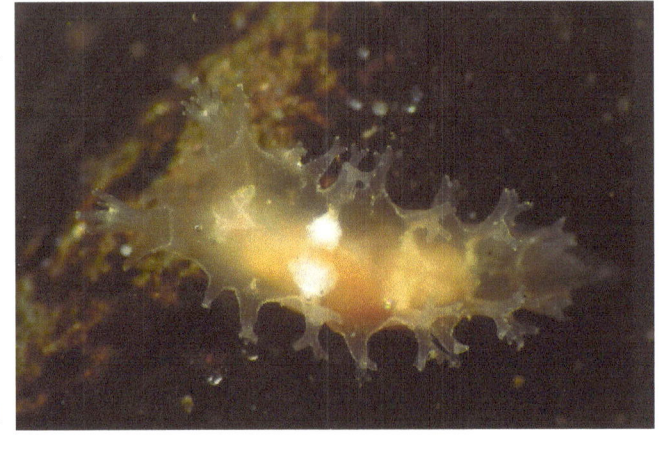

J. Goddard

Tritonicula pickensi (Marcus & Marcus, 1967) — Pickens' tritonid

Body is translucent white to pink or orange with a wide central, opaque white, pink or orange region. This region has scalloped edges which extend out to the gill plumes. There are 7-13 gill plumes which subdivide into 2-3 branches, at least twice on each gill.

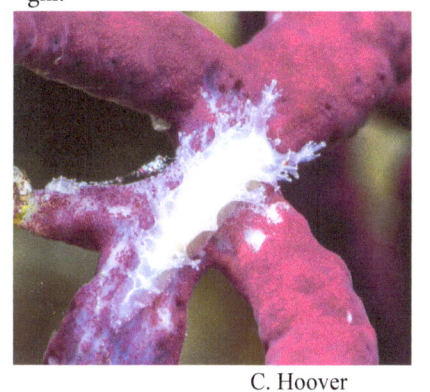

Similar species: *Tritonicula myrakeenae* has two (at most four) discrete white patches; *Tritonia festiva* has lines rather than solid areas of white.
Size: To 25 mm (1 in).
Range: Channel Islands, California to Panama.
Habitat: Intertidal and shallow subtidal.
Remarks: Feeds on gorgonians, especially *Leptogorgia*.

C. Hoover

A. Hermosillo

Trivettea papalotla (Bertsch et al., 2009) (previously *Tritonia* sp. 1) — butterfly tritonid

Body is dark brown to burgundy red with numerous opaque white spots, the foot and sides lighter, sometimes greenish. Several ridges radiate out from the cardiac area with a central ridge down the center of the dorsum. Instead of bearing the typical tritoniid gill-tuft processes, the gills of this species are undulations along the sides of the body.

Similar species: None.
Size: To 12 mm (0.5 in).
Range: Bahía Magdalena to Bahía de Banderas, Mexico.
Habitat: Shallow subtidal.
Remarks: Feeds on a common but undescribed zooanthid, *Epizoanthus* sp., where it is very cryptic. Its pink egg masses are quite visible.

A. Hermosillo

...Nudibranch Day at the Intelligent Design Shop... J. Kocian

Superfamily Dendronotoidea

Swimming *Dendronotus iris*

P. Humann

Members of the Dendronotoidea are most diverse in temperate and cold-water seas. They have a row of cerata-like processes or gills along the margin of the notum, and all have radulas except *Melibe*. With the exception of the genus *Hancockia*, they lack cnidosacs and nematocysts. The rhinophores have a cup-like sheath. This group feeds on a wide variety of prey including soft corals, sea anemones, hydroids, and in the case of *Melibe*, small crustaceans, worms and even juvenile fish.

Bornella sarape Bertsch, 1980
sarape nudibranch
Body is pale yellow-brown, with a dark brown to black reticulate pattern, which sometimes forms dark patches. The rhinophores are exceptionally large, with sheaths bearing several long branches. The oral lobes are hand-like, with several "fingers."
Similar species: None.
Size: To 40 mm (1.5 in).
Range: Bahía de los Ángeles, Mexico to Panama.
Habitat: Subtidal to 21 m (69 ft), under rocks.
Remarks: This species can swim by laterally bending its body.

A. Hermosillo

Dendronotus albopunctatus Robilliard, 1972
white-spotted dendronotid
The wide body is pale pink to red-brown, or yellowish-white with red-brown patches. There are tiny opaque white spots scattered over the entire body with larger white spots on the pale foot edge; an opaque white line runs along the edge of the foot and oral veil. There are 4-5 dorsolateral appendages and no lateral papillae on the rhinophore sheath.
Similar species: *Dendronotus subramosus* lacks the white line along the edge of the foot.
Size: To 60 mm (2.4 in).
Range: Northern British Columbia to southern Oregon.
Habitat: Subtidal in sandy, muddy areas, from 12-40 m (40-131 ft).
Remarks: Feeds on hydroids.
G. Jensen

Dendronotus albus MacFarland, 1966
white dendronotid
Body color ranges from translucent white to dark lilac. Tips of dorsolateral appendages, rhinophores and veil papillae opaque white, or metallic orange with transparent tips. The four pairs of large dorsolateral appendages have only a few secondary branches; there is sometimes a smaller fifth pair. Digestive gland, if visible, only penetrates the rhinophores and first two pairs of dorsolateral appendages. An opaque white line runs from the last pair of doroslateral appendages along the center of the tail to its tip.
Similar species: *Dendronotus dalli* has bushy, branched cerata with white tips; *D. robilliardi* has white stripes on the back of the rhinophore sheaths and oral veil processes. *Dendronotus kamchaticus* has more branched cerata and the digestive gland is visible in all appendages and the rhinophore sheath.
Size: To 70 mm (2.7 in).
Range: Kenai Peninsula, Alaska to Isla Coronado, Mexico.
Habitat: Low intertidal to 30 m (98 ft).
Remarks: Feeds on hydroids. The more colorful variation of this species was previously known as *Dendronotus diversicolor*.

K. Fletcher

K. Lee

Dendronotus dalli Bergh, 1879

Dall's dendronotid

Body translucent grayish-white, light yellow to orange, or brownish to pinkish, with the tips of the cerata, veil papillae and rhinophores tipped in opaque white. The 4-8 pairs of short but extensively branched cerata are arranged in a fan shape; they can appear frosted and lack a visible digestive gland. There are lateral papillae on rhinophore sheaths and 4-5 pairs of short, branched veil papillae.
Similar species: *Dendronotus kamchaticus* cerata have visible digestive gland extensions; *D. robilliardi* has white stripes on the back of the rhinophore sheaths and oral veil processes; *D. albus* cerata have few branches.
Size: To 136 mm (5.3 in).
Range: North Pacific from the Sea of Japan to Washington; also the Chukchi Sea, Russia.
Habitat: Subtidal to 64 m (210 ft).
Remarks: Feeds on hydroids of the genus *Abietinaria*.

G. Jensen

Dendronotus iris Cooper, 1863

giant nudibranch

Sometimes called the "rainbow nudibranch" due to its great variability in color: specimens can be translucent whitish-gray, yellow-brown, dark muddy brown, orange-red, purplish, or maroon. In the gray color form, the tips of the rhinophore crowns and dorsolateral appendages may be opaque white with a band of maroon and yellow or metallic orange. In all color forms there is an opaque white line around the edge of the foot in adult animals. If the digestive gland is visible, it penetrates the rhinophores and dorsolateral appendages, especially in juveniles (< 10 mm). The posterior border of the rhinophore sheath has 4-6 small, branched papillae.
Similar species: *Dendronotus nanus* has much shorter dorsolateral appendages; *D. rufus* and *D. dalli* lack the white edging along the foot.

M. Chamberlain

Size: To 300 mm (11.8 in).
Range: Unalaska Island, Alaska to Isla Los Coronados, Baja California.
Habitat: Low intertidal to 215 m (705 ft), on mud and sand bottoms.
Remarks: This species has a unique method of "pouncing" on the tube-dwelling anemone *Pachycerianthis fimbriatus* to feed, and is also able to swim by laterally bending back and forth. Juveniles feed on hydroids.

M. Chamberlain

P. Garner

Dendronotus kamchaticus Ekimova et al., 2015 — Kamchatka dendronotid

Body semitransparent grayish white, often with brown streaks and spots dorsally and brown spots laterally. Body can be smooth or sprinkled with small white tubercles; the cerata of eastern Pacific specimens are white-tipped. Brown extensions of the digestive gland are visible in the cerata, rhinophore sheaths, and oral veil papillae. The rhinophore sheath has 5-6 appendages plus a lateral papilla.

Similar species: *Dendronotus albus* has fewer branches on the cerata and the digestive gland is only visible in anterior appendages; *D. robilliardi* has a white stripe on the back of the rhinophore. *Dendronotus dalli* has more highly-branched cerata, while those of *D. venustus* lack the white tips.
Size: To 30 mm (1.2 in).
Range: Kamchatka, Russia to Puget Sound, Washington.
Habitat: Subtidal, from 7-17 m (23-56 ft).
Remarks: Feeds on hydroids; can be found with *Dendronotus albus* and *D. robilliardi*.

K. Fletcher

K. Fletcher

Dendronotus nanus Marcus & Marcus, 1967 — dwarf dendronotid

Coloration similar to *Dendronotus iris* but the dorsolateral appendages appear stubby and there may be numerous white spots on the body. In all color forms there is an opaque white line around the foot. Digestive gland not visible in the rhinophores or dorsolateral appendages, even in animals as small as 9 mm.

Similar species: *Dendronotus iris* has much longer appendages.

K. Lee

Size: Maximum size unknown. The original description was from a 13 mm specimen (hence 'nanus' indicating its small size) but suspected specimens much larger.
Range: Described from Puerto Peñasco, Sonora, Mexico, but based on photographs this "stubby" form is found from at least Puget Sound to Baja California
Habitat: Intertidal and subtidal; often found on docks and in sandy eelgrass beds.
Remarks: Some internal differences in the reproductive systems have been noted between *Dendronotus iris* and *D. nanus*, so until genetic analysis is performed on both forms we consider the two species to be separate.

K. Lee

Dendronotus robilliardi Korshunova et al., 2016 — Robilliard's dendronotid

Body translucent grayish-white with opaque white stripes on the oral veil processes, the backs of the rhinophore sheaths, and on tips of dorsolateral processes; orange-copper bands may be present in middle of the dorsolateral and oral processes. Between 5-8 pairs of moderately branched dorsolateral processes, but never less than five pairs. Opaque white line runs from the tip of the tail to between the second and fourth pairs of dorsolateral processes.
Similar species: *Dendronotus albus*, *D. kamchaticus*, and *D. dalli* lack the white lines on the back of the rhinophore sheath.
Size: To 35 mm (1.4 in).
Range: Kamchatka in the northwestern Pacific to Puget Sound; possibly Korea.
Habitat: Intertidal to 30 m (98 ft).
Remarks: Feeds on the hydroid *Sertularia argentea*.

K. Fletcher

K. Fletcher

Dendronotus rufus O'Donoghue, 1921 — red dendronotid

Body translucent grayish-white (occasionally red or pink); with red- to magenta-tipped, highly-branched dorsolateral appendages. The red and pinkish body color forms have a red line around the foot. There are 6-9 dorsolateral appendages, sometimes with small accessory appendages interspersed between the main appendages. Oral veil appendages extensively branched.
Similar species: *Dendronotus iris* does not have as extensively branched appendages, and those with white bodies also have white appendages.
Size: To 280 mm (11 in).
Range: Auk Bay, Alaska to Puget Sound, Washington; also Chukchi Sea, Russia.
Habitat: Low intertidal to 40 m (131 ft), often under overhangs.
Remarks: Feeds on scyphozoan jellyfish polyps. It releases a thick, sticky mucus when disturbed. There is some question whether this extremely large form currently recognized as *D. rufus* is truly the same as that described by O'Donoghue.

J. Kocian

Dendronotus subramosus MacFarland, 1966 — stubby dendronotid

Body usually mottled orange-brown, dark brown or yellow with white, brown, red-brown, gold and green spots and two parallel lines along each side of the dorsum; sometimes white with two pairs of parallel dorsal lines, or solid orange. Rhinophore sheaths lack lateral papillae and are tipped with 3-7 short, blunt papillae. The 3-6 pairs of dorsolateral appendages may be tipped with lemon-yellow or orange spots, and branch in a rosette pattern halfway up the stalk. The digestive gland penetrates the rhinophore stalk and the first pair of dorsolateral appendages.
Similar species: *Dendronotus venustus* has digestive gland extensions in the first 4-5 appendages and a lateral papilla on the rhinophore sheath.

G. Jensen

Size: To 65 mm (2.5 in).
Range: Alaska to Los Coronados Islands, Baja California, Mexico.
Habitat: Intertidal in California; subtidal to 120 m (394 ft) in Washington.
Remarks: Feeds on ostrich plume hydroids (*Aglaophenia* spp.).

Dendronotus venustus MacFarland 1966
(previously *Dendronotus frondosus*) **branched dendronotid**

Narrow body may be translucent gray-white with various amounts of brown, red-brown, yellow, and white pigments, or no pigment at all. Most color forms have yellow or white spots and some have obvious conical tubercles. There are 4-8 pairs of branched, fan-shaped dorsolateral appendages and the digestive gland may be visible within the first 4-5 pairs. Oral veil with 4-8 branched papillae. Rhinophoral sheaths have lateral papillae and are tipped with 4-6 long, stout rhinophore papillae with the posterior one usually the longest.

Similar species: *Dendronotus subramosus* lack lateral papillae on the rhinophore sheaths; *D. kamchaticus* has white-tipped appendages.
Size: To 42 mm (1.6 in).
Range: Alaska to San Diego, California.
Habitat: Intertidal to 40 m (131 ft).
Remarks: Feeds on a variety of hydroids. Some of the color variants may prove to be different species.

Rhinophore showing lateral process

M. Passage

M. Chamberlain

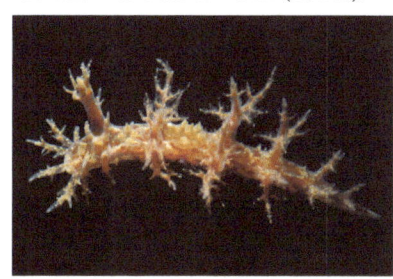

G. Jensen

M. Passage

Dendronotus sp.

Body color orange-red with white tubercles. Dorsolateral processes closely branched; rhinophore sheaths with a large, branched lateral process and white tubercles.
Similar species: The rhinophore sheaths of *Dendronotus venustus* are not covered with white tubercles.
Size: To at least 40 mm (1.6 in).
Range: Anacapa Island and La Jolla, California.

A. Vitsky

Pseudobornella orientalis Baba, 1932   **threaded nudibranch**

Wide translucent grayish-white body with scattered brown spots or patches with yellow lines crisscrossing between and around the spots. The rhinophoral sheath has a long, threadlike posterior appendage which is up to twice the animal's body length. There are four pairs of bushy but simply-branched dorsolateral appendages, and 3-4 appendages on each side of the oral veil.
Similar species: None.
Size: To 30 mm (1.2 in).
Range: South China Sea, Peter the Great Bay, Sea of Japan, Izu Peninsula, Japan and San Francisco Bay, California.
Habitat: Intertidal to 14 m (46 ft).
Remarks: An introduced species, found on the hydroid *Ectopleura crocea* in San Francisco Bay in 2016.

R. Agarwal

Hancockia californica MacFarland, 1923 — Hancock's nudibranch

Body light to dark reddish-brown, occasionally greenish to greenish-brown, with light sprinklings or blotches or scattered encrustations. Broad hand-like lobes on either side of the head, each with at least 6-10 unequal fingerlike processes; 4-7 pairs of palmately-branched cerata topped with fingerlike processes. Rhinophore sheath margins with rounded ridges, rhinophore tips with vertical lamellae.
Similar species: None.
Size: To 21 mm (0.8 in).
Range: Big Lagoon, Humboldt County, California to Costa Rica.
Habitat: Intertidal to 6 m (20 ft). Most often found in rocky areas along open coasts, frequently on brown algae or on drifting kelp mats.
Remarks: Feeds on thecate hydroids.

A. Hermosillo

Doto amyra Er. Marcus, 1961 — hammerhead doto

Body is translucent white with 5-8 pairs of cerata that can be either cream, pinkish, salmon or orange, and each bearing 4-7 rings of white tubercles. Rhinophores and rhinophore sheaths have white encrustations.
Similar species: Two undescribed species are nearly identical in appearance (see below). *Doto columbiana* lacks the white encrustations on the rhinophores.
Size: To 14 mm (0.5 in).
Range: Alaska to Bahia de Banderas, Mexico.
Habitat: Intertidal and subtidal.
Remarks: Feeds on hydroids, including *Abietinaria* sp.

R. Agarwal

K. Fletcher

These two undescribed *Doto* are very similar to *D. amyra*. The "*Doto* form A" of Shipman and Gosliner (2015) is genetically distinct but difficult to differentiate visually. The ceratal cores tend to be a darker orange-pink and the tubercles on the cerata slightly more elevated. At 7 mm (0.2 in), it is only half the size of *D. amyra*, and is most common in southern California. It lays small eggs that release planktotrophic larvae rather than the lecithotrophic young of *D. amyra*; note the relative size difference of the eggs to the adults in the photos.

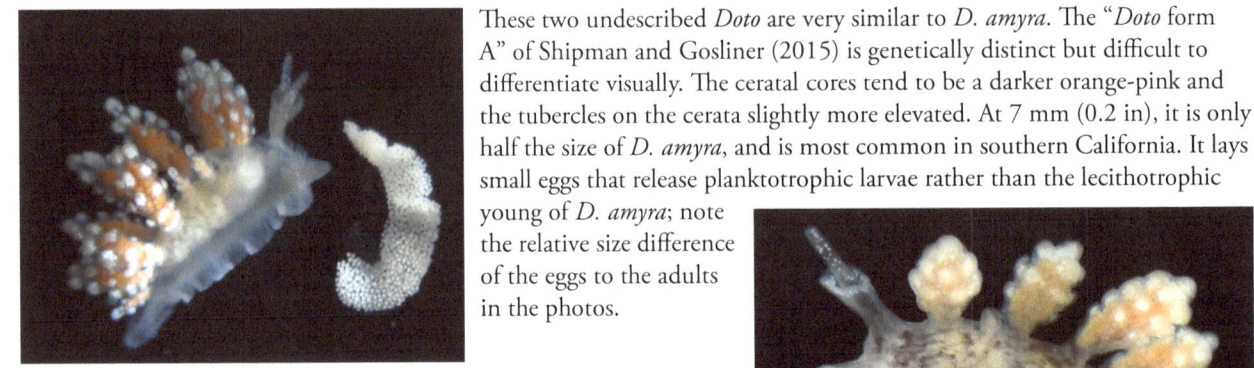

J. Goddard

The second is from Friday Harbor, Washington, and is also genetically distinct. It co-occurs subtidally with *D. amyra*, and is identical in appearance except for dark subcutaneous markings on the body.

G. Paulay

Doto columbiana O'Donoghue, 1921   **British Columbia doto**

Body is whitish to gray-yellow with brown pigment on the top and sides. The cerata can appear inflated and quite smooth, or bear large, flat tubercles which may be surrounded by a black ring. The rhinophores lack white encrustations. There is black pigmentation on the back and sides of the body and foot, but not at the base of the cerata; juveniles may lack pigmentation.
Similar species: *Doto lancei*, *D. amyra*, and its undescribed lookalikes all have white on their rhinophores.
Size: To 12 mm (0.5 in).
Range: Calvert Island, British Columbia to Carpinteria, California.
Habitat: Intertidal to 60 m (197 ft).
Remarks: Feeds on the hydroid *Aglaophenia*. Egg ribbons are tall and flat compared to other *Doto* egg ribbons.

M. Passage

K. Fletcher

Doto kya Er. Marcus, 1961   **seal doto**

Body is yellowish-white and covered with irregular brown-black blotches. Cerata are white to brown with 4-5 rings of oval tubercles. The rhinophore tips and sheaths have white encrustations and the sheaths have scalloped edges.
Similar species: *Doto columbiana* has no white on the rhinophores and a dark foot.
Size: To 10 mm (0.4 in).
Range: Bamfield, British Columbia to Ensenda, Baja California.
Habitat: Intertidal and subtidal.
Remarks: Feeds on hydroids.

K. Lee

Doto lancei Marcus & Marcus, 1967   **Lance's doto**

Body light brown to yellowish with blackish brown or reddish pigment on the notum, oral veil and the rhinophoral sheaths. The oral veil projects laterally beyond the anterior border of the foot and bears a ridge in front of each rhinophore. Many of the tubercles on the cerata have a black subapical ring, and often a black apical spot.
Similar species: *Eubranchus* sp. 2 and 4 have "eye-like" rings, but have simple rhinophores.
Size: To 10 mm (0.4 in).
Range: San Diego, California to Panama, including the Gulf of California.
Habitat: Low intertidal and shallow subtidal.
Remarks: Found on the hydroid *Aglaophenia*.
K. Lee

114

Several species of Doto *remain undescribed.*

Doto sp. 1
Body is orange with minute white specks, and rhinophores encrusted in white pigment. Cerata have brown cores and rounded, white tubercles. It has been found from San Carlos, Sonora to Ixtapa, Guerrero, Mexico in association with hydroids, and lays orange, string-like eggs. It reaches 7 mm (0.2 in) in length.

A. Hermosillo

Doto sp. 2
The body is a dark fuchsia, with pale dorsolateral bands along each side. Cerata are white with bright pink apices. The rhinophores are translucent with opaque white specks and the sheath the same color as the body. It has been recorded from Cabo San Lucas and Bahía de Banderas to Ixtapa, Guerrero, Mexico, and also in Panama, and was "Doto sp. H" in Pola and Gosliner (2010). This 8 mm (0.3 in) species is found on hydroids.

A. Hermosillo

Doto sp. 3
The cerata are reddish with a large green tip, while the foot is dark laterally, sometimes black. Specimens have been found in several locations in Mexico (Bahia de Banderas, Ixtapa-Zihuatanejo) and Panama. It reaches 13 mm (0.5 in) in length.

A. Hermosillo

Doto sp. 4
Body translucent grayish-white with scattered tiny orange tubercles and sometimes with subcutaneous black streaks. The 7-8 pairs of pink cerata have extended white tubercles. Rhinophores lightly frosted with a fluted sheath. Reported from Palos Verdes Peninsula, La Jolla, and Anacapa Island, California.

M. Webb

S. Johnson

Crosslandia daedali Poorman & Mulliner, 1981 — Daedalus' nudibranch

The body is green, brown, or red with fine longitudinal red-brown lines and small, round, bright blue spots along sides and on the dorsum. There are two pairs of lateral mantle lobes; the anterior pair is much larger and located at about mid-body. The dorsal surface of the lobes have irregularly-placed tufts of very fine retractable gills.
Similar species: The mantle lobes of *Notobryon panamicum* are about equal in size.
Size: To 25 mm (1 in).
Range: Outer coast of Baja California, Gulf of Mexico and the Mexican Pacific to Costa Rica.
Habitat: Intertidal and subtidal.
Remarks: Feeds on hydroids which grow on algae. They often rest with just a small portion of the foot attached to a stem and with head and neck elevated, closely resembling a piece of algae.

D. Behrens

Notobryon panamicum Pola et al., 2012 (previously *Notobryon wardi*) — Panama notobryon

Color varies from translucent brown to orange, often with opaque white or bluish patches. Two equally-sized pairs of lateral mantle lobes are held erect when crawling and extended to the sides when at rest. There are four finely branching gills associated with each mantle lobe, and the tail has a sail-like median crest.
Similar species: The anterior mantle lobes of *Crosslandia daedali* are much larger than the posterior ones.
Size: To 20 mm (0.8 in).
Range: Pacific coast of southern Mexico to Costa Rica and Panama; reports from the Caribbean are most likely a separate species.
Habitat: Subtidal to 12 m (39 ft).
Remarks: A nocturnal species that feeds on hydroids of the genus *Macrorhynchia*, and is capable of swimming by bending its body laterally.

D. Behrens

Lomanotus cf. *vermiformis*

(previously *Lomanotus vermiformis*)

Body is greenish-brown with numerous fine white lines. Edge of notum with 22-25 white-tipped branchial lobes; rhinophores and oral tentacles with thick opaque white lines.
Similar species: None.
Size: To 25 mm (1 in).
Range: Isla Magdalena, Baja California Sur; from Bahia de Los Angeles and Loreto, Gulf of California to Panama.
Habitat: Subtidal.
Remarks: Feeds on hydroids. *Lomanotus vermiformis*, described from the Red Sea, is more elongate and has more cerata.

A. Hermosillo

Lomanotus sp. 1

Rhinophores exceptionally large compared to the size of the body, and branched like in *Tritonia*. The three to four lateral processes on each side are simple, pointed projections. It is found on hydroids and only known from Bahía de Banderas, Mexico; it reaches 5 mm (0.2 in) in length.

A. Hermosillo

Lomanotus sp. 2

Also sighted on hydroids at Bahía de Banderas, Mexico, the notum of this species is densely fringed with thick white branchial lobes. The olive green body is marked by numerous thin white lines. This species has been genetically sequenced and differs from all other *Lomanotus* analyzed to date. It was referred to as "*Lomanotus* sp. E" in Pola & Gosliner (2010).

A. Hermosillo

Melibe leonina (Gould, 1852) — hooded nudibranch

Color a translucent yellow-brown to white, sometimes with bright speckles. The large oral hood has two rows of cirri around the edge; cerata are large, flat, and disc-shaped with a visible digestive gland.
Similar species: None.
Size: To 175 mm (6.9 in).
Range: Kodiak, Alaska to Cabo San Lucas, Mexico; Gulf of California.
Habitat: Intertidal to 37 m (121 ft), on eelgrass and algae.
Remarks: Uses its hood as a cast net to capture smaller organisms, primarily crustaceans, which are ingested whole. It can swim by thrashing from side to side.

M. Chamberlain

K. Lee

Superfamily Arminoidea

The Arminoidea is one of the smallest of the heterobranch groups and are often found on soft substrates. Members of this group have a large oral veil and the gills are found under the mantle.

Armina californica (Cooper, 1863) — striped nudibranch

Body is oval with longitudinal wavy ridges and alternating white and pinkish-brown stripes, and a white line edges the foot. The two rhinophores share a thick common stalk. Gills are hidden on both sides under the dorsum.
Similar species: *Armina* sp. (below) is black with orange trim.
Size: To 100 mm (3.9 in).
Range: Aleutian Islands, Alaska to Panama.
Habitat: Low intertidal to 230 m (755 m), on sand bottoms.
Remarks: A burrowing species that feeds on sea pens, sea whips, and the sea pansy, *Renilla*.

G. Jensen

Armina sp.

Body is oval with wavy alternating ridges of white with black space in between. An orange line edges the foot and the black oral veil, and the black rhinophores have tiny white tips. This form has been seen occasionally off San Diego, California. Until a specimen is collected for close examination, it will not be known if it is a distinct species or a rare color variant of *Armina californica*.

A. Baldwin

Histiomena marginata (Mörch, 1859) (previously *Histiomena convolvula*) — convoluted armina

Mottled brown and white dorsum bears a series of convoluted, longitudinal ridges. Oral veil large with an expanded margin; foot is bright pink and bordered with lavender and orange.
Similar species: *Armina* spp. are distinctly striped and their rhinophores are much closer together.
Size: To 75 mm (3 in).
Range: Gulf of California, Mexico, to Panama.
Habitat: Subtidal to 45 m (148 ft).
Remarks: Feeds on gorgonians and sea pens.

M. Miller

Superfamily Proctonotoidea

Members of Proctonotoidea in the eastern Pacific, such as the genus *Dirona*, have dorsal cerata which lack cnidosacs. Two other genera, *Antiopella* and *Janolus*, have numerous cerata extending anterior to the rhinophores. They also have an interesting "cockscomb-like" organ between the rhinophores called a caruncle. The function of this organ is unknown, but thought to be sensory in nature as its cellular morphology is similar to that of the rhinophoral surface.

Dirona albolineata MacFarland, 1905
white-lined dirona

Body usually a translucent grayish-white, sometimes salmon, tannish-orange or pale purple. Cerata smooth and edged in opaque white; opaque white lines around oral veil, along the midline of the tail, and running from one rhinophore to the other across the head.

Similar species: *Dirona pellucida* has an orange body with white spots. *Antiopella gelida* has visible ceratal cores.
Size: To 180 mm (7 in).
Range: Kachemak Bay, Alaska to San Diego, California; also Japan and East Russia.
Habitat: Low intertidal to 37 m (121 ft), on both hard and soft bottoms.
Remarks: Grazes on bryozoans, hydroids, tunicates, sponges, and sea anemones, and uses its strong jaws to crack and eat small snails.
G. Jensen

G. Jensen

Dirona pellucida Volodchenko, 1941
golden dirona

Body pale golden to bright red orange with white spots. Cerata with white edges.
Similar species: *Antiopella gelida* is nearly identical in appearance, but has a single thin black line of digestive gland in the cerata and a small crest between the rhinophores. Orange-colored *Dirona albolineata* have white edging along the front and foot, and a white line across the head.
Size: To 120 mm (4.7 in).

P. Garner

Range: Bering Sea, Alaska to Coos Bay, Oregon, and the Sea of Japan.
Habitat: Low intertidal to 55 m (180 ft).
Remarks: Grazes on the bryozoans *Bugula* and *Dendrobeania*, and has also been found with hydroids in its stomach. 
G. Jensen

Dirona picta MacFarland, 1905   **colorful dirona**

Color highly variable, ranging from a dull grayish-green to a pinkish-orange and usually with a sprinkling of lighter dots. The cerata are plump and covered with tubercles.
Similar species: The cerata of *Janolus anulatus* are much narrower.
Size: To 30 mm (1.2 in).
Range: Typically, Cape Meares, Oregon to Isla Ángel de la Guardia, Gulf of California, Mexico, but has been found as far north as Bamfield, British Columbia during El Niño years. Also occurs in the Sea of Japan and Russia.
Habitat: Intertidal to 10 m (33 ft).

K. Lee

R. Agarwal

Remarks: Feeds primarily on bryozoans and hydroids of the genus *Aglaophenia*.

Antiopella barbarensis (Cooper, 1863) (previously *Janolus barbarensis*)   **cockscomb nudibranch**

Body greyish-white; cerata and rhinophores have supapical yellow-orange bands and light to deep blue tips. The smooth and often inflated cerata begin well in front of the rhinophores, and their brownish unbranched (or branched near the tip) digestive gland extensions are clearly visible. There is an orange-red crest (caruncle) between the rhinophores.
Similar species: *Antiopella fusca* has white-tipped cerata with unbranched digestive gland extensions.
Size: To 50 mm (2 in).
Range: San Francisco Bay, California and throughout the Gulf of California to Costa Rica.
Habitat: Low intertidal to 27 m (90 ft) on both hard and soft bottoms.

K. Lee

K. Lee

Remarks: Feeds on the bryozoan *Bugulina californica* and the hydroid *Corymorpha palma*.

Antiopella fusca (O'Donoghue, 1924)
(previously *Janolus fuscus*)   **white-and-orange-tipped nudibranch**

Body translucent grayish-white with numerous (and often inflated) cerata beginning in front of the rhinophores. The cerata have a subapical yellow-orange band with a white tip and a single unbranched digestive gland extension. A dashed orange line runs from the crest (caruncle) between the rhinophores and down the middle of the body.
Similar species: *Antiopella barbarensis* has blue-tipped cerata and rhinophores; *Hermissenda* spp. cerata begin behind rhinophores.
Size: To 50 mm (2 in).
Range: Homer, Alaska to San Luis Obispo, California; Russia.
Habitat: Low intertidal to 30 m (100 ft) on rocks, kelp, and soft bottoms.
Remarks: Feeds on the bryozoans *Bugulina* and *Tricellaria*.

P. Garner

Antiopella gelida (Millen, 2016) (previously *Janolus* sp. 2) — **frosty-tipped nudibranch**

Body a translucent pale to medium orange with white specks, and there may be a broken white line along the midline of the body. The smooth cerata are white-edged and have an unbranched digestive gland extension. The rhinophores have white tips and a line down the back, and there is a small, dusky yellow crest between the rhinophores.
Similar species: *Dirona pellucida* and *D. albolineata* lack both the digestive gland in the cerata and the crest between the rhinophores.
Size: To 50 mm (2 in).

G. Jensen

E. Gullekson

Range: Quatsino Sound, Vancouver Island, and Narrows Inlet, British Columbia to Des Moines, Washington.
Habitat: Subtidal from 17-30 m (56-98 ft) on mud, sand, and silt; occasionally on rocks.
Remarks: Appears to feed on bryozoans.

Janolus anulatus Camacho-García & Gosliner, 2006 (previously *Janolus* sp. 1) — **annulated nudibranch**

Body is broadest anteriorly, tapering to a pointed tail. The color is translucent grayish-white with brown or reddish-brown blotches and tiny white spots or larger opaque white areas. The bottom half of the cerata are smooth and the top half studded with papillae. The unbranched digestive gland extensions are brown and confined to the lower half of the cerata.
Similar species: *Dirona picta* has much broader cerata.
Size: To 17 mm (0.6 in).
Range: Hazard Reef, San Luis Obispo, California to Costa Rica. May be found as far north as Montana de Oro State Park, Los Osos, California, during years with warm water events.
Habitat: Intertidal to at least 10 m (33 ft).
Remarks: Feeds on the brown bryozoan, *Symnotum aegyptiacum*.

J. Goddard

Embletonia cf. *gracilis*

Body is white and extremely long and narrow, with a single row of plump, pinkish-orange cerata down each side. The tips of the cerata are divided into knobs. The rhinophores are simple and lack rhinophoral sheaths; the oral tentacles are flattened lobes on each side of the mouth.
Similar species: *Limenandra confusa* has double rows of cerata down each side.
Size: Typically less than 8 mm (0.3 in).
Range: Baja California; Bahía de Banderas, Mexico.
Habitat: Unclear due to species confusion (see Remarks).
Remarks: Feeds on campanularid hydroids. Each of the terminal knobs on the cerata contain nematocysts. It has historically been listed as an aeolid. *Embletonia gracilis* was described from New Caledonia and is almost certainly a different species from those in the eastern Pacific.

A. Hermosillo

Superfamily Aeolidida

The aeolid nudibranchs take their name from *Aeolis*, the Greek god of the wind. They lack distinct gills, utilizing cerata for respiration and often also for defense. Their cerata contain branches of the digestive tract. In nearly every aeolid genus, undeveloped stinging cells called cnidoblasts are acquired from the slug's prey (typically hydroids or sea anemones) and transported through the digestive tract to the tips of the cerata. Here they are stored in structures called cnidosacs until they develop into fully functional microscopic harpoons called nematocysts, which the aeolid uses for defense.

Aeolids are characterized by strong jaws which hold onto their prey while the radula rasps away at their polyps. Most have very specific diets; the presence and abundance of those that feed on ephemeral prey like hydroids often reflects the availability of their highly seasonal prey.

Coryphella trilineata

G. Jensen

Apata pricei (MacFarland, 1966)
(previously *Flabellina pricei*) **Price's aeolid**

Body is translucent grayish-white with an opaque white line on the tail only. The cerata may be white, yellowish-white or greenish but always have a brown or maroon band near the white tip, and form 10-12 comb-shaped rows. Perfoliate rhinophores have white near the tip; oral tentacles are frosted white or bluish-white.
Similar species: *Apata* cf. *pricei* lacks the distinct reddish band near the tip of the cerata. The cerata of *Coryphella verrucosa* and *C. trophina* are not clustered into fans or comb-shaped rows.
Size: To 25 mm (1 in).
Range: Crescent City, California to La Jolla, California.
Habitat: Subtidal, from 4-18 m (13-59 ft).
Remarks: Feeds on hydroids.

A. Valdés

Apata cf. *pricei*

Body is translucent gray-white with a white opaque line running from the tip of the tail part way up the sides of the dorsum. The white-tipped cerata have a reddish or brownish-red core and may have a greenish cast, and form up to ten comb-shaped rows. Rhinophores are perfoliate and frosted white along most of their length, and oral tentacles have a white line on their dorsal surface.
Similar species: The rhinophores of *Apata pricei* are only white near the tips, and the cerata have a red band near the tip. The cerata of *Coryphella verrucosa* and *Coryphella trophina* are not clustered into fans or comb-shaped rows.
Size: To 25 mm (1 in).
Range: Ketchikan, Alaska to Sonoma County, California.
Habitat: Subtidal from 4-18 m (13-59 ft).
Remarks: Feeds on hydroids.

K. Fletcher

Coryphella amabilis (Hirano & Kuzirian, 1991) (previously *Flabellina amabilis*) **charming aeolid**

The body is translucent white. The head is long and the foot corners small; rhinophores are smooth or wrinkled and are often frosted white, but may have a white line on the back instead. Oral tentacles are often frosted, but may have a white line down the center of each one instead. Cerata are red or orange with white tips, and form clusters on the notal flange; in the Western Pacific they are often sprinkled with white spots. There is a short, white line on the ridge of the tail.
Similar species: *Pacifia amica* has a white line down the center of the back; the white tail line of *Coryphella verrucosa* extends to the middorsal part of the back.
Size: To 26 mm (1 in).
Range: Vancouver Island, BC, Canada to San Juan Islands, Washington; Sea of Japan.
Habitat: On rocks in the intertidal and shallow subtidal.
Remarks: In Japan, it feeds exclusively on the athecate hydroid *Eudendrium boreale*.

K. Fletcher

Coryphella cooperi (Cockerell, 1901) (previously *Flabellina cooperi*) — Cooper's aeolid

Body translucent grayish-white with a pink tinge and a greenish-blue patch between the first and second rows of cerata. There is a distinct, sometimes wide, sometimes broken, white line down the center of the back and sometimes white lines along the sides of the body. The verrucose rhinophores and oral tentacles may be tipped in orange. Cerata have a greenish-blue color at the base with red, reddish-brown, or green cores, various amounts of tiny white flecks on the surface and large white tips.
Similar species: *Coryphella trilineata* has perfoliate rhinophores and *Pacifia amica* has smooth rhinophores.

R. Agarwal

J. Goddard

Size: To 25 mm (1 in).
Range: Contra Costa County, California to Punta San Andres, Baja California, Mexico.
Habitat: Intertidal mud flats and subtidal.
Remarks: Feeds on the hydroid *Tubularia crocea*.

Coryphella fogata (Hermosillo & Millen 2007) (previously *Flabellina* sp. 1) — bonfire aeolid

Body is semi-transparent red to light pinkish-orange to almost translucent white, with orange organs visible through the dorsum. The orange cerata have a dark fiery-red core and numerous opaque white spots, and the cerata are inserted in clusters along the notal brim. The long oral tentacles and slightly annulate rhinophores are translucent and colorless.
Similar species: *Bajaeolis bertschi* has smooth rhinophores with dark purple near the tips. *Edmundsella vansyoci* is much more pink and has pink or purple rhinophores.
Size: To 15 mm (0.6 in).
Range: Known only from Bahía de Banderas, Mexico.
Habitat: Subtidal, from 15-20 m (49-66 ft).
Remarks: Feeds on one species of *Eudendrium* hydroid.

A. Hermosillo

Coryphella trilineata (O'Donoghue, 1921) (previously *Flabellina trilineata*) — three-lined aeolid

Body is translucent gray to white with a white opaque line running down each side and one down the center of its body. The central line branches at the white-tipped perfoliate rhinophores and continues down the oral tentacles. Ceratal cores are orange to red, occasionally purple, tipped with white, yellow or orange.
Similar species: *Coryphella* cf. *trilineata* has orange-tipped rhinophores and tentacles; *C. cooperi* has slightly verrucose rhinophores rather than perfoliate. *Pacifia amica* lacks the white line on the side of the body.
Size: To 25 mm (1 in).
Range: Alaska to Oregon.
Habitat: Intertidal and subtidal. Maximum depth unclear due to previous "lumping" with *Coryphella* cf. *trilineata*.
Remarks: Eats a variety of hydroids.

G. Jensen

Coryphella cf. *trilineata*

Body is translucent gray to white with a white opaque line running down each side and one down the center of its body. The central line branches at the orange-tipped perfoliate rhinophores and continues down the orange-tipped oral tentacles. Ceratal cores are orange to red, sometimes purple, tipped with white, yellow or orange.
Similar species: *Coryphella trilineata* does not have orange-tipped rhinophores and tentacles; *C. cooperi* has verrucose rhinophores.
Size: To 36 mm (1.4 in).
Range: Cape Arago, Oregon to Isla San Geronimo, Baja California, Mexico; possibly to Puget Sound.
Habitat: Intertidal to 50 m (164 ft).
Remarks: Despite its strong similarity to *C. trilineata*, there is a very large genetic difference between the two species.

M. Chamberlain

Coryphella sp.

The body is a translucent grayish white or milky white and the ceratal cores bright orange or red. The rhinophores are perfoliate and translucent orange; the oral tentacles sometimes have an opaque white line underneath the translucent orange pigment. When present, the opaque white line down the center of the body and white lines along the sides of the body are faint. This form has been found at Catalina Island and Santa Barbara, California, and could possibly be a color variation of *Coryphella* cf. *trilineata*.

S. Thiebaud

K. Lee

Coryphella trophina (Bergh, 1890) (previously *Flabellina trophina*)   **long-mouthed aeolid**

Body is wide, translucent gray to white with a white opaque line running from the tip of the short tail and faintly for a short distance along the sides of the body. Cerata have a pinkish to red or red-purple core, and appear continuous on each side of the body. The head is long and often appears upturned. Rhinophores are annulate and may have a thin white line on the posterior side; oral tentacles have a thin white line.
Similar species: The long mouth and continuous cerata readily distinguish this from the many similar aeolids.
Size: To 120 mm (4.7 in).
Range: Bering Sea to Seal Rocks State Park, Oregon; also Kamchatka, Russia.
Habitat: Subtidal to 115 m (377 ft), usually on sand.
Remarks: Food varies from hydroids to polychaetes, crustaceans, and other nudibranchs.

J. Kocian

Coryphella verrucosa (previously *Flabellina verrucosa*)

warty aeolid

Body is translucent whitish gray. Cerata vary from orange-red to dark red to purple with a subapical white ring and a transparent tip. Cerata cluster in groups rather than forming a single line along each side of the back. The back of the rhinophores and the face of the oral tentacles have either a white line or may be entirely frosted with white pigment. The rhinophores usually have a wrinkled or bumpy appearance. A broken white line begins along the middle of the back and becomes a solid line to the tip of the tail.
Similar species: *Coryphella trophina* has a much longer snout and annulate rhinophores. The white line on the tails of *Coryphella amabilis* and *Apata* cf. *pricei* do not extend middorsally onto the back.
Size: To 22 mm (0.8 in).
Range: Alaska to Tacoma, Washington; north Atlantic.
Habitat: Low intertidal to 300 m (984 ft) in rocky areas.
Remarks: Feeds on hydroids.

K. Fletcher

Coryphellina marcusorum (Gosliner & Kuzirian, 1990)

(previously *Flabellina marcusorum*) **Marcus' aeolid**

The body is a translucent bright pink or orange, and the rhinophores, cephalic tentacles and cerata are tipped with opaque white-yellow, with a wide, purple band mid-length. The rhinophores have a dense patch of up to 100 projections on the posterior surface only.
Similar species: *Kynaria cynara* has much longer cerata.
Size: To 30 mm (1.2 in).
Range: From Isla San Diego, Baja California, Mexico along the west coast of central America to the Galapagos Islands; also from the Caribbean Sea to Brazil.
Habitat: Intertidal to 22 m (72 ft).
Remarks: Preys on hydroids.

C. Hoover

Chlamylla sp. (previously *Flabellina* sp. 2)

Body is transparent gray with peach overtones on dorsum. Cerata cores are peach-pink with white tips and arranged irregularly in a continuous row down both sides of the back. The long, smooth rhinophores and shorter oral tentacles have a faint dusting of opaque white on the tips.
Similar species: None.
Size: To 9 mm (0.3 in).
Range: Strait of Georgia, British Columbia, Canada.
Habitat: From 10-20 m (33-66 ft) in high-current, rocky areas.
Remarks: Found on the solitary hydroid, *Tubularia indivisa*, in March, May and early June.

R. Long

Flabellinopsis iodinea Cooper, 1863
(previously *Flabellina iodinea*) **Spanish shawl**

Body, oral tentacles, and base of cerata are deep purple. Cerata are bright orange past the base to their tips. Rhinophores are deep maroon, often with a white line on their face. The long oral tentacles may have whitish tips.
Similar species: *Hermosita sangria* has red and yellow bands on the oral tentacles.
Size: To 90 mm (3.5 in).
Range: Northern California to the Gulf of California, Mexico. In El Niño years sometimes extends northward to the outer coast of Washington and Vancouver Island, British Columbia.
Habitat: Lower intertidal to at least 56 m (184 ft).
Remarks: Feeds on hydroids and compound ascidians. Can swim by bending its body side to side.

A. Hermosillo

Edmundsella bertschi (Gosliner & Kuzirian, 1990) (previously *Flabellina bertschi*) **Bertsch's aeolid**

Body is translucent white with opaque white pigment covering most of the dorsal surface except for an area behind the smooth rhinophores. The top two-thirds of the rhinophores and oral tentacles are overlayed with opaque white. Ceratal cores red to red-brown with a large, opaque white tip and arranged in obvious clusters inserted into slightly stalked mounds. The elongated foot corners are held perpendicularly when actively crawling, and it has a sharply-pointed tail.
Similar species: None.
Size: To 12 mm (0.5 in).
Range: Santa Barbara, California to Panama; throughout the Gulf of California.
Habitat: Intertidal to at least 13 m (43 ft).
Remarks: Feeds primarily on a species of *Eudendrium* with red-orange polyps. Molecular and morphological evidence indicate it belongs in the genus *Edmundsella*.

A. Hermosillo

Edmundsella vansyoci (Gosliner, 1994) (previously *Flabellina vansyoci*) **Van Syoc's aeolid**

The body and cerata of this striking aeolid are deep pink and the cerata are speckled with white flecks. The cephalic tentacles and verrucose rhinophores are pink to purple; the tentacles are slightly longer than the rhinophores. Some specimens may be pinkish orange.
Similar species: *Bajaeolis bertschi* has perfoliate rhinophores that are much shorter than the oral tentacles. *Coryphella fogata* has clear rhinophores, and the cerata are more clustered and have bright red cores.
Size: To 30 mm (1.2 in).
Range: Gulf of California to Panama.
Habitat: Shallow subtidal, below 3 m (10 ft).
Remarks: Feeds on a bright orange athecate hydroid.

A. Hermosillo

Kynaria cynara (Marcus & Marcus, 1967) (previously *Flabellina cynara*) — swimming cynara

Body color translucent pinkish to orange with scattered opaque white spots. Long cerata are pink to salmon orange with a purple subapical ring, red to orange cores, opaque white tips, and variable amounts of white spotting. The rhinophores have a purple band just below a white tip, and the long oral tentacles have a purple band mid-length and frosted tips.
Similar species: *Coryphellina marcusorum* has much shorter, stouter cerata.
Size: To 60 mm (2.3 in).
Range: Puerto Peñasco, Sonora, Mexico, to Panama; Ecuador.
Habitat: Subtidal to 15 m (49 ft).
Remarks: This species swims by curling its cerata forward and then whipping them backwards.

A. Hermosillo

A. Hermosillo

Pacifia amica Korshunova et al., 2017 — red sparkly aeolid

Body translucent grayish-white. Smooth rhinophores, frosted with opaque white, are the same size as the oral tentacles. There is a white line on each oral tentacle that merges between the rhinophores and extends down the body to the tip of the long, thin tail. Cerata in 4-5 clusters along the dorsal edge with scattered small, opaque white spots and orange-red to light pink cores and large white tips.
Similar species: *Coryphella trilineata* and *C.* cf. *trilineata* have a white line along each side of the body; *C. cooperi* has a wider center stripe.
Size: To 10 mm (0.4 in).
Range: Plumper Islands, British Columbia to Tacoma, Washington.
Habitat: Subtidal to 18 m (59 ft); also on floating docks.
Remarks: Often found with *Coryphella trilineata*.

K. Fletcher

Pacifia goddardi (Gosliner 2010) — Goddard's aeolid

Body is translucent white, occasionally with an opaque white line on the middle of the back and along each side. Elongated cerata can have milky to pale olive cores with bright yellowish-orange tips and a subapical red band, or the subapical red band can blend into bright orange and extend at least halfway down. Cerata are arranged in distinct groups on cushions elevated from the notum. Oral tentacles are thin, elongate, taper to a point and occasionally have opaque lines on their dorsal surface. Smooth rhinophores are shorter than the oral tentacles and may have a white line on the posterior surface.
Similar species: The cerata of *Coryphella cooperi* have white rather than orange/red tips; *C. trilineata* have perfoliate rhinophores.
Size: To 15 mm (0.6 in).
Range: Carpinteria State Beach, Santa Barbara County to Los Angeles, California.
Habitat: Intertidal to at least 18 m (59 ft).
Remarks: Feeds on a *Bougainvillia*-like, filiferan anthomedusan hydroid.

J. Goddard

J. Goddard

Paracoryphella sp. (previously *Flabellina islandica*)

The body is wide and translucent pinkish cream; opaque white spots on body, cerata and tips of oral tentacles and rhinophores. Notal flange has continuous, stubby, dark orange-red cerata 4-5 deep with light tips. Long oral tentacles and foot corners; rhinophores smooth. The penis is non-retractile and posteriorly curved.
Similar species: None.
Size: To 16 mm (0.6 in).
Range: So far only Victoria and Vancouver Harbors, British Columbia, Canada.
Habitat: Subtidal from 5-10 m (16-33 ft) on soft mud bottoms.
Remarks: Appears to eat the athecate hydroid, *Euphysa*.

N. McDaniel

Samla telja (Marcus & Marcus, 1967) (previously *Flabellina telja*) — telja

The pale body has a bluish tinge, and the cerata are pinkish brown to red with white tips. The rhinophores are bulbous, heavily perfoliated and white-tipped, as are the distal two-thirds of the oral tentacles and front corners of the foot; the tail has a white crest and tip.
Similar species: None.
Size: To at least 20 mm (0.7 in); possibly to 40 mm (1.5 in).
Range: Puerto Peñasco, Sonora, Mexico, to Panama and the Galapagos Islands.
Habitat: Low intertidal to 20 m (66 ft).
Remarks: Believed to feed on athecate hydroids. It swims by laterally bending its body, and is active in the daytime.

A. Hermosillo

A translucent pink form (right) covered with opaque white spots that was once named *Flabellina stohleri* has been questionably synonymized with *S. telja*; DNA sequencing is needed to help resolve the issue.

A. Hermosillo

Ziminella japonica (Volodchenko, 1941) (previously *Flabellina japonica*) — Japanese aeolid

Body is cream to pinkish, with abundant cerata; the cerata have cream-colored cores that have a knobby or knotted appearance. Rhinophores and oral tentacles may have white encrustations and there are no cerata in the middle of the back.
Similar species: *Aeolidia papillosa* and *A. loui* have much less obvious cores in their cerata, and the cores do not have a knotted appearance.
Size: To 40 mm (1.5 in).
Range: Entire coast of British Columbia, likely in Alaska; the Sea of Japan.
Habitat: Subtidal to 20 m (66 ft) in British Columbia, in rocky areas with high current.
Remarks: Found with tiny white hydroids, *Similiclava nivea*.

G. Jensen

Cumanotus fernaldi Thompson & Brown, 1984 — **Fernald's aeolid**

The wide body is cream to peach-pink and abruptly tapers to a blunt tail. The rhinophores are smooth and joined at the base. Densely-packed cerata have dark red digestive gland extensions with visible knobs and twists and long, white tips; they begin in front of the rhinophores. Body and appendages can have a sprinkling of opaque white spots.
Similar species: *Cuthona divae* has separate rhinophores and the cores of the cerata are much smoother; *Cumanotus* sp. 1 lacks oral tentacles.
Size: To 29 mm (1.1 in).
Range: Victoria, British Columbia to San Diego, California.
Habitat: Subtidal, from 6-13 m (20-43 ft) on soft bottoms.
Remarks: The cerata move with a rowing motion for swimming or as a means of propulsion when buried in soft sediments. This species feeds on the athecate hydroids *Euphysa* and *Corymorpha* and lays corkscrew-shaped egg masses that are attached by one end to the soft bottom.

K. Lee

Cumanotus sp.

The broad body is translucent whitish-gray or pale pink with an abruptly pointed, short tail. The pale gray rhinophores are smooth and there are no oral tentacles. Cerata are wide and round at their base, long and thin with pink, tan or greenish knobby, branched cores and long, pink tips that make it nearly indistinguishable from the hydranth of its hydroid prey.
Similar species: *Cumanotus fernaldi* has oral tentacles and foot corners, and is in a very different habitat.
Size: To 14 mm (0.5 in).
Range: Saturna Island, British Columbia to San Diego, California.
Habitat: Subtidal to 18 m (59 ft) in rocky areas.
Remarks: Capable of curling its cerata in order to swim. Feeds exclusively on *Tubularia* hydroids, either on docks and floats or subtidally, and lays its corkscrew egg masses on the hydroid stalks.

R. Agarwal

Leostyletus misakiensis (Baba, 1960) (previously *Eubranchus misakiensis*) — **Misaki aeolid**

Body is translucent yellow-white with oval tannish-brown spots which extend onto the cerata. Foot corners are long and pointed. Cerata have subapical constriction giving them an hourglass shape, and a yellow ring.
Similar species: *Eubranchus rupium* and *Eubranchus* cf. *rupium* have rounded foot corners.
Size: To 20 mm (0.8 in).
Range: Bodega Bay to Santa Cruz, California; native to Japan.
Habitat: Intertidal to at least 7 m (23 ft).
Remarks: Feeds on hydroids of the genus *Obelia*. It was likely introduced from Japan in ballast water.

A. Smith

Eubranchus cucullus Behrens, 1985 — hooded aeolid

Body is usually tan, encrusted with white and sometimes with rust-brown specks and spots, while the head, rhinophores, oral tentacles and the top half of the foot margins are rusty brown. Cylindrical and irregularly inflated cerata vary from white, yellow, green, orange to tan or dark brown. The foot is narrow, linear and tapers posteriorly into a short blunt tail. The foot corners are triangular but not elongate. Oral tentacles are cylindrical and short with a blunt tip. The rhinophores are long and smooth, also with a blunt tip.
Similar species: *Tenellia ivetteae* has a white head.
Size: To 10 mm (0.4 in).
Range: Puerto Peñasco, Mexico, Gulf of California, Mexican Pacific and Panama.
Habitat: Intertidal to at least 10 m (33 ft).
Remarks: Lives on a plumularid hydroid.

J. Hamann

Eubranchus cf. *mandapamensis*

The ground color of the body is translucent grayish brown or white with a dense cover of brownish-red spots and some larger patches of the same color. The cerata are large and bulbous with tubercles; with a subapical orange band preceded by a pale blue band. The tubercles on the distal half of the cerata are frosted with opaque white. The rhinophores are annulate and blunt-tipped.
Similar species: None.
Size: 10 mm (0.4 in).
Range: Bahía de Banderas, Bahía de los Angeles, and Ensenada, Mexico.
Habitat: Shallow subtidal.
Remarks: *Eubranchus mandapamensis* was described from India. Color differences and geographic separation make it highly unlikely that Mexican specimens are the same species.

A. Hermosillo

Eubranchus rupium (Møller, 1842) — rocky aeolid

Body is cream or yellowish with irregular reddish-tan streaks and spots, and often opaque white spots. Rhinophores have white encrustations and often have a reddish band in the middle. Cerata can have tan, green or pink cores, sometimes with a pronounced hourglass tip and a broken subterminal reddish-brown band at this constriction; a greenish digestive gland is usually visible through the dorsum. The foot corners are rounded.
Similar species: The subterminal reddish-brown band is a distinct ring and closer to the tip (above the constriction) of the ceras in *Eubranchus* cf. *rupium*. *Leostyletus misakiensis* has long, pointed foot corners.
Size: To 10 mm (0.4 in).
Range: Alaska to Washington; Sea of Japan, Barents Sea, and the northeast and northwest Atlantic.
Habitat: Intertidal to 10 m (33 ft).
Remarks: Feeds on hydroids.

G. Jensen

Eubranchus cf. *rupium*

Body is whitish with few to many scattered oval tan spots and white spots. Rhinophores have white encrustations and often have a red band; foot corners are rounded. Cerata can have tan or olive-green cores, sometimes with an hourglass tip and subterminal yellow-brown bands close to the tip. Sometimes the digestive gland visibly crisscrosses the dorsum.
Similar species: The reddish-brown bands on the cerata of *Eubranchus rupium* are further from the tip, on the subterminal constriction. *Leostyletus misakiensis* has long, pointed foot corners.
Size: To 10 mm (0.4 in).
Range: Oregon to at least San Diego, California.
Habitat: Intertidal and subtidal.
Remarks: Although it has been referred to as *Eubranchus rupium*, this more southern form is genetically distinct from that wide-ranging species. It has also been incorrectly called *Eubranchus olivaceus*.

B. Green

Eubranchus rustyus (Marcus, 1961) — homely aeolid

Body is white with brown or green spots or blotches; the same color forms two lines extending from the front base of the rhinophores to the oral tentacles. Rhinophores and oral tentacles sometimes with faint white specks near their tips and a subterminal brown or green band. Digestive gland may visibly crisscross the dorsum. Cerata have brown, tan or green cores with rings of tubercles and may look inflated.
Similar species: *Eubranchus rupium* and *E.* cf. *rupium* usually have opaque white spots on the body and the cerata lack tubercles; *E. steinbecki* has dark dorsolateral lines connecting the cerata bases.
Size: To 25 mm (1 in).
Range: Ketchikan, Alaska to Punta Abreojos, Baja California, Mexico.
Habitat: Intertidal.
Remarks: Found on colonies of the hydroid *Hydractinia*.

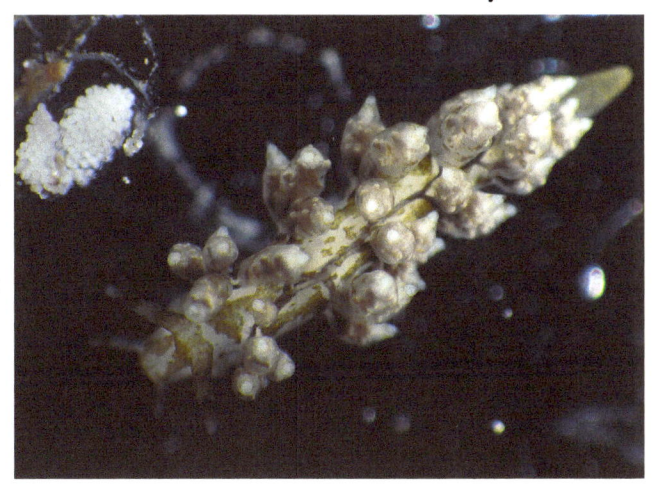

J. Goddard

Eubranchus sanjuanensis Roller, 1972 — San Juan aeolid

Body is translucent whitish-gray and brown jaws may be visible in front of the rhinophores. Rhinophores and oral tentacles are simple and translucent with no white encrustations. Cerata are smooth and often inflated, with bright orange-red cores and white tips.
Similar species: The cores of the cerata of *Eubranchus* cf. *sanjuanensis* are much paler and there is often reddish color near the base of the rhinophores.
Size: To 6 mm (0.2 in).
Range: Nigei Island, British Columbia to the San Juan Islands, Washington.
Habitat: Subtidal.
Remarks: Feeds on the hydroid *Symplectoscyphus tricuspidatus*.

K. Fletcher

Eubranchus cf. *sanjuanensis*

Body is whitish-gray. Rhinophores are simple and translucent and can have a reddish coloration at the base; oral tentacles are also translucent. Cerata have pinkish-white tips with brown to red cores, sometimes with a reddish coloration at the base.
Similar species: *Eubranchus sanjuanensis* has much brighter red ceratal cores.
Size: To 10 mm (0.4 in).
Range: Ketchikan, Alaska to Brookings, Oregon.
Habitat: Subtidal.
Remarks: Previously considered a color variant of *E. sanjuanensis*, but genetic analysis revealed substantial differences.

K. Fletcher

Eubranchus steinbecki Behrens, 1987
Steinbeck's aeolid

Body is tan with dark olive-green mottling, and darker pigment forming two bands that connect the cerata. The head and oral tentacles are speckled with olive-green. The cerata are irregular and nodular with a cream-colored core and the surface is covered with various amounts of dark green specks, some of which form rings around the nodulations.
Similar species: *Eubranchus rustyus* does not have the parallel dark lines connecting the cerata.
Size: To 6 mm (0.2 in).
Range: Palos Verdes, California to La Paz, Mexico.
Habitat: Intertidal.
Remarks: Has also been found on floating docks.

D. Behrens

Eubranchus yolandae Hermosillo & Valdés, 2007
(previously *Eubranchus* sp. 1)
Yolanda's aeolid

Body is translucent grayish-white, with areas of pale blue along the sides below the level of the cerata. The head has two orange triangular patches that begin anterior to the bases of the rhinophores and end at the bases of the oral tentacles. The oral tentacles are shorter than the rhinophores, basally white with a large orange midsection and a white tip. Cerata are long and wine red with a distal orange band and a white tip; some specimens have dark brown cerata. The long, smooth rhinophores are white with a distal orange band and a lighter, blunt tip.
Similar species: None.
Size: To 8 mm (0.3 in).
Range: Loreto, Baja California Sur to Bahía de Banderas, Mexico.
Habitat: Subtidal to at least 17 m (56 ft).
Remarks: Feeds on hydroids.

A. Hermosillo

Several forms suspected to be undescribed species of *Eubranchus* occur in our area.

Eubranchus sp. 1

The body is cream with a white patch on the head and a dark band sub-apically on the rhinophores; body and cerata are spotted with brown. The cerata bear tall irregular nodules, which are arranged in rings. This 7 mm (0.3 in) species lays eggs that hatch into planktotrophic veligers, and has been found at La Jolla and Carpinteria, California.

J. Hamann

Eubranchus sp. 2

The ground color of the body is olive green, with a rose-colored line on both sides of the dorsum. There is a pink opaque band from the base of the oral tentacles to the end of the tail. The cerata are a blotchy green with a thick rose ring and a pink band with a turquoise tip. The rhinophores and oral tentacles are basally dark, with a pink band and a distal green band. It is found under rocks and lays a small, transparent egg coil. It has been found at Puerto Vallarta and Isla Isabel, Mexico, and Costa Rica, and may also occur in the Indo-Pacific. To 7 mm (0.3 in).

A. Hermosillo

Eubranchus sp. 3

Body is translucent gray with oval tan spots and tiny scattered white spots. Rhinophores smooth and long with scattered white and tan spots, sometimes with a red band near the tip. The dark digestive gland often visibly crisscrosses the dorsum. Cerata have a definite hourglass shape and make the animal appear spiky. Top half of cerata frosted in whitish-yellow spots and with a yellow subapical ring near the tip. It has been found from Washington State to San Diego, California, subtidally to 20 m (66 ft). It feeds on a short, delicate hydroid.
K. Fletcher

Eubranchus sp. 4

This small aeolid was photographed with its egg mass on a hydroid at Loreto, Mexico. The habitat and brown color of the head and rhinophores is similar to *Eubranchus cucullus*, but the form of the cerata and body coloring are different.

J. Hamann

Eubranchus sp. 5

This intertidal and subtidal species has been encountered from Palos Verdes to San Diego, California. The body is translucent gray with olive to brown markings on the body and sometimes on the rhinophores. Often a brown to olive line begins at the rhinophores and forms a "V" as it splits to extend to each oral tentacle. Rhinophores also have a brown band near the tip. Cerata form groups and are smooth with yellow-white specks, white or brown subterminal bands and a distinctive iridescent bluish-green near their bases.
K. Lee

Aeolidia loui Kienberger et al., 2016   **warty shag-rug nudibranch**

Body background color ranges from translucent white, to pinkish-grayish-green, to bright orange or brown. The flattened, translucent cerata are the same color as background, usually wider at the base than the light-colored tip. The center of the dorsum is free of cerata. The rhinophores are covered with distinct, wart-like tubercles.
Similar species: The rhinophores of *Aeolidia papillosa* can have wrinkles and some slight bumps, but are not covered with wart-like projections. *Ziminella japonica* has smooth rhinophores and much more obvious cores in the cerata.
Size: To 100 mm (3.9 in).
Range: Port Hardy, British Columbia to Isla de Cedros, Baja California, Mexico.
Habitat: Intertidal and subtidal.
Remarks: Preys on anemones. Those feeding on bright pink *Epiactis* anemones can acquire an overall pink color.

G. Jensen

Rhinophores of *Aeolidia papillosa* (far left) and *A. loui*, showing the difference in surface texture.

Eggs of *A. papillosa* (right)

G. Jensen

G. Jensen

Aeolidia papillosa (Linnaeus, 1761)   **shag-rug nudibranch**

Body background color ranges widely, from light white-beige to dark brown with dark flecks scattered over the notum. There is often a triangular white patch in front of the rhinophores. Rhinophores conical, blunt, and slightly wrinkled; usually with a mottled appearance. Cerata elongate, often thin for most of their length and usually with pinkish or purplish tips; the center of the dorsum is free of cerata.
Similar species: *Aeolidia loui* is virtually identical but genetically distinct; its rhinophores have very discrete wart-like bumps. The cerata of *Ziminella japonica* have obvious cores with a knotted appearance.
Size: To 127 mm (5 in).
Range: Amphiboreal species; Alaska to Washington; both eastern and western Atlantic coasts; Barents Sea.
Habitat: Intertidal and subtidal.
Remarks: Feeds on sea anemones, incorporating nematocysts from their prey into their cerata for defense.

G. Jensen

Bulbaeolidia sulphurea (Caballer & Ortea, 2015) (previously *Aeolidiella alba*) — **sulfur aeolid**

Broad body with chalk-white pigment on notum and head. The translucent rhinophores have two large swellings and a sulfur-yellow pigmentation; there is a conspicuous red band circling the bases. The club-shaped cerata are covered with opaque white or yellowish pigment.
Similar species: None.
Size: To 12 mm (0.5 in).
Range: Puerto Vallarta, Mexico, to Panama and the Galapagos Islands.
Habitat: Found under rocks in the intertidal, and subtidal to at least 10 m (33 ft).
Remarks: This species moves using a jumping motion. It feeds on anemones.

A. Hermosillo

Anteaeolidiella chromosoma (Cockerell & Eliot 1905)
(previously *Aeolidiella chromosoma*) — **colorful aeolid**

Body is translucent white to dull orange with midline bearing irregular small patches of opaque white and clear of cerata. Rhinophores, oral tentacles and foot corners same color as background color; cerata with broken white bands on distal half and light tips. Perfoliate rhinophores also have white or cream pigmentation in the upper third or brown pigmentation on the oblique lamellae, plus a white tip.
Similar species: *Anetarca armata* has very long foot corners.
Size: To 25 mm (1 in).
Range: Monterey, California to Panama; Japan.
Habitat: Intertidal and shallow subtidal.
Remarks: Feeds on anemones. Likely part of a species complex based on sequencing data.

A. Hermosillo

M. Passage

Anteaeolidiella ireneae Carmona et al., 2014 — **Irene's aeolid**

Body is dull to bright orange or red, with an opaque white line running from the head between the rhinophores that widens to a series of diamonds or circles as it trails down the back. Rhinophores are dull or bright orange with white tip. The bright orange or dark gray cerata have a white subapical band and white tip; they are stout and cylindrical.
Similar species: None.
Size: To 12 mm (0.5 in).
Range: Gulf of California to Panama.
Habitat: Subtidal, under dead coral heads and sand from 15-20 m (49-66 ft).
Remarks: Feeds on sea anemones.

A. Hermosillo

Anteaeolidiella oliviae (MacFarland 1966) (previously *Aeolidiella oliviae*) — Olive's aeolid

The body and cerata are bright orange and the head may be completely white. The perfoliate rhinophores are vermilion with a white tip; oral tentacles translucent white with white tips.
Similar species: None.
Size: To 30 mm (1.2 in).
Range: Duxbury Reef, Marin County, California to Bahía Todos Santos, Baja California, Mexico.
Habitat: Intertidal and shallow subtidal.
Remarks: The brightly-colored rhinophores are constantly in motion as the animal crawls. Feeds on anemones.

M. Passage

Baeolidia moebii Bergh, 1888 (previously *Berghia major*) — Moebius' big aeolid

Body commonly greyish white, brown or brownish green overlaid with reticulate ochre pattern with bright white patches on cerata and body. Apex of cerata may also have a bluish band followed by a yellowish band and a white tip. Dark pigmentation on head surrounded by whitish or yellow ring on front edge of head. Rhinophores densely papillose with a white tip.
Similar species: *Baeolidia* cf. *salaamica* has orange bands near the tips of the cerata, and white on the head.
Size: To 40 mm (1.5 in).
Range: Tropical Indo-Pacific; tropical Eastern Pacific; Turkey & Cyprus.
Habitat: Subtidal to at least 20 m (66 ft).
Remarks: Feeds on cnidarians.

A. Hermosillo

O. Angulo Campillo

Baeolidia cf. *salaamica*

Body translucent pale orange with some white patches scattered over the dorsum. White ring on head and a white diamond shape behind rhinophores. Rhinophores studded with minute white knobs. Rhinophores and oral tentacles translucent with white markings and white tips. Cerata purplish with some lighter streaks or spots and a subterminal orange band.
Similar species: *Baeolidia moebii* lacks the white on the head and the orange bands on the cerata.
Size: To 6 mm (0.2 in).
Range: Eastern Pacific specimen from Bahía Kino, Gulf of California; *B. salaamica* found in Tanzania, Papua New Guinea, Philippines, Hong Kong, Japan, Korea, and Hawaii.
Habitat: Subtidal.
Remarks: Although *B. salaamica* has been confirmed to have a widespread circumtropical distribution, the single specimen from the eastern Pacific (shown) differs in color and rhinophore ornamentation.

A. Hermosillo

Cerberilla chavezi Hermosillo & Valdés 2007 (previously *Cerberilla* sp. 1)
Chavez's cerberilla

The center of the dorsum is translucent pink, and the extremely long oral tentacles are purple. The cerata have an opaque dorsal yellow line extending vertically, interrupted by a large reddish-brown patch. There is an opaque yellow margin along the edge of the foot and anterior corners, and the short rhinophores are translucent red with white tips.
Similar species: None.
Size: To 22 mm (0.8 in).
Range: Bahía de Banderas, Jalisco-Nayarit and in Bahía Santiago, Colima, Mexico.
Habitat: Subtidal to at least 10 m (33 ft).
Remarks: Found on sand-mud bottoms at night, and buries when disturbed by lights.

A. Hermosillo

Cerberilla mosslandica McDonald & Nybakken, 1975
Moss Landing aeolid

Translucent grayish-white with whitish, brownish to reddish brown encrustation on the dorsum, dorsal foot margin and head. The cerata are flattened against the dorsum and encrusted with various amounts of brown, reddish brown and white. Short, smooth rhinophores are colored like the cerata. Long oral tentacles and pointed foot corner. A red streak may be present on either side of the head below each eye.
Similar species: *Cerberilla pungoarena* have longer oral tentacles and the cerata are not held against the body.
Size: To 9 mm (0.3 in).
Range: Cook Inlet, Alaska to La Jolla, California.
Habitat: Subtidal, from 4-63 m (13-207 ft) on mud/sand bottoms; occasionally on mixed cobble and sand.
Remarks: Spends much of its time buried in the sediment.

K. Fletcher

Cerberilla pungoarena Collier & Farmer, 1964

Translucent white with light brown or tan on the dorsal surface; cerata light brown with white tips. The oral tentacles are exceptionally long, as are the foot corners; the small eyes are readily visible at the base of the short, smooth rhinophores. The foot is wider than the body.
Similar species: *Cerberilla mosslandica* have shorter oral tentacles and the cerata are flattened against the dorsum.
Size: To 20 mm (0.8 in).
Range: Morro Bay, California to Isla Ángel de la Guardia, Gulf of California, Mexico.
Habitat: Very low intertidal to at least 17 m (55 ft), on sand.
Remarks: When disturbed, this species extends and contracts its cerata while waving them about.

K. Lee

Limenandra confusa Carmona et al., 2014 (previously *Limenandra nodosa*) — confusing aeolid

Body is dull olive greenish-gray to reddish; a series of yellow, red and white concentric circles may be present along the dorsal midline. The rhinophores are shorter than the oral tentacles and the posterior side has elongate papillae. The cerata are dorsoventrally flattened with posterior papillae, in distinct clusters that alternate in size.
Similar species: None.
Size: To 8 mm (0.3 in).
Range: Gulf of California, Mexico to Costa Rica; also Philippines, Midway Islands, and Hawaii.
Habitat: Subtidal, from 3-10 m (10-33 ft).
Remarks: Found under coral rubble feeding on small anemones. A distinctive characteristic to watch for is the jerking motion of its cerata as it crawls.

A. Hermosillo

Anetarca armata Gosliner, 1991 — armed aeolid

The orange-red body is mottled with yellow-gold and opaque white spots. The ceratal cores are dark orange to brown and the cerata tend to curve toward the midline of the body. The foot is broad and the foot corners elongated into tentacles, and the ventral part of the head is deeply cleft.
Similar species: *Anteaeolidiella chromosoma* does not have elongate foot corners.
Size: To 14 mm (0.5 in).
Range: Punta Asunción, Baja California and Gulf of California to Costa Rica.
Habitat: Intertidal and shallow subtidal in sandy areas.
Remarks: Feed on hydroids that envelop snail shells, and lays its eggs on the snails.

J. Lance

Spurilla braziliana MacFarland 1909 (previously *Spurilla neapolitana*) — Brazil spurilla

Body color olive to pale orange with white spots; cerata dark greenish-gray with white spots and lighter tips. The rhinophores are perfoliate with a white tip. The thick, short cerata have strongly inward-curving tips.
Similar species: None.
Size: To 70 mm (2.7 in).
Range: Baja California Sur, Mexico, to Columbia; also widely distributed in the Caribbean, Western Atlantic and Western Pacific.
Habitat: Intertidal to shallow subtidal.
Remarks: One of the few widespread species that has had its distribution confirmed by genetic testing.

A. Hermosillo

Babakina festiva (Roller, 1972)
Baba's festive aeolid

The body and head are pinkish to purplish; head with a broad white anterior stripe. The perfoliate rhinophores have their bases fused for the first third of their length; distal half greatly expanded into a large club. "Candy corn"-like cerata have a prominent orange or yellow subterminal band bounded on each side by white or pale blue.
Similar species: None.
Size: To 32 mm (1.2 in).
Range: Duxbury Reef, Marin County, California to Nayarit, Mexico.
Habitat: Intertidal and shallow subtidal.
Remarks: Previous reports from Japan are now considered to be of a separate species, *B. indopacifica*.

R. Agarwal

Nanuca galaxiana Millen & Hermosillo 2012
(previously *Dondice* sp. 1)
galaxy aeolid

Dorsum cream to gray with darker patches between the cerata. The rest of the body may be covered with a various amount of random small white spots. The cerata are the same color as the body, have scattered white spots, and often have a subterminal brown band. The rhinophores and oral tentacles have a brown band near their base, and the rhinophores have 4-8 dish-shaped rings spaced along their length.
Similar species: None.
Size: To 8 mm (0.3 in).
Range: Bahía de Banderas, Mexico to Costa Rica.
Habitat: Subtidal from 7-90 m (23-295 ft).
Remarks: Found on or under rocks with hydroids.

A. Hermosillo

Bajaeolis bertschi Gosliner & Behrens, 1986
Bertsch's rainbow aeolid

Pink or reddish body densely covered with numerous white spots giving it a frosted appearance; cerata with larger white spots except for the tips. A purple ring encircles the middle of the oral tentacles; the club-shaped rhinophores are translucent with a pink spot near the tip. The rhinophores are much shorter than the oral tentacles.
Similar species: *Edmundsella vansyoci* has verrucose rhinophores that are only slightly shorter than the tentacles. *Okenia rosacea* has numerous cerata in front of the rhinophores.
Size: To 40 mm (1.5 in).
Range: Central Gulf of California to Panama.
Habitat: Subtidal to at least 10 m (33 ft).
Remarks: Feeds on the hydroid *Eudendrium*.

A. Hermosillo

Emarcusia morroensis Roller, 1972   **Morro Bay aeolid**

Body is grayish-white. There are two faint oval orange spots on the head, one in front of and one behind the rhinophores, which are sometimes connected by an orange line. The long oral tentacles and smooth rhinophores are tipped in opaque white, and irregular white specks are on the dorsum. The foot corners are elongate and tentacle-like. Cerata largely greenish-brown, darkest at the base and with translucent to white tips; dark markings on cerata sometimes appearing as three bands.
Similar species: *Sakuraeolis* cf. *enosimensis* has white lines on its much longer oral tentacles, and longer, more slender cerata.
Size: To 16 mm (0.6 in).
Range: Ft. Baker, Marin County to San Diego, California; one record from Seattle, Washington.
Habitat: Intertidal to 19 m (62 ft), usually in bays and on floating docks and pilings.

R. Agarwal

Remarks: Given its use of floating docks, it is possible the Washington record was due to transport on the fouled hull of a ship or barge.

Austraeolis stearnsi (Cockerell, 1901)   **Stearns' aeolid**

Body pale pink or purple; the annulate rhinophores, oral tentacles, and elongate foot corners have an orange to red band and white tips. The long oral tentacles have a white/cream line running from dorsal side across the head to rhinophore bases, and there is a white or orange line from posterior cerata group to the tip of the tail. Cerata with a bright orange subterminal band and very sharply pointed tip.
Similar species: *Phidiana hiltoni* has an orange line across the front, connecting the oral tentacles.
Size: To 30 mm (1.2 in).
Range: Santa Cruz, California to Bahía de Banderas, Mexico.
Habitat: Subtidal to at least 21 m (70 ft) on a wide variety of bottoms, from mud to rock.
Remarks: Typically found on or near hydroids.

M. Passage

Facelina sp.

Body translucent gray, as are the long oral tentacles, pointed foot corners, and the simple, smooth rhinophores. Cerata with tan cores and pointed white tips, grouped in discreet clusters in well-spaced rows that end well before the tip of the finely pointed tail; tail with a thin white dorsal stripe.
Similar species: *Coryphella amabilis* has much shorter oral tentacles.
Size: To 30 mm (1.2 in).
Range: Known from Cuevitas, Bahía de los Angeles, Mexico.
Habitat: Subtidal.

H. Bertsch

Adfacelina medinai Millen & Hermosillo 2012 (previously *Facelina* sp. 1)
Medina's aeolid
Body orange-pink to red with irregular opaque yellow blotches and spots. Rhinophores lamellate, clear yellow with medial deep pink band. Oral tentacles long with a deep pink medial band, spotted with yellow, lighter towards tips. Cerata orange-red and covered with irregular opaque yellow blotches with a deep pink ring just below the clear tips.
Similar species: None.
Size: To 18 mm (0.7 in).
Range: Known only from Bahía de Banderas, Mexico, and Clipperton Island.
Habitat: Subtidal to 93 m (305 ft).
Remarks: Has been found inside sea caves, and produces very large pink eggs.

A. Hermosillo

Favorinus elenalexiarum García F. & Troncoso, 2001
Elena & Alexia's aeolid
Body translucent white with fine opaque white spots which merge as blotches everywhere except the base of the rhinophores and the base of the oral tentacles. Cerata pinkish-red with a white subapical ring and white specks. The rhinophores are brown with three cup-like swellings and white tips.
Similar species: None.
Size: To 15 mm (0.6 in).
Range: Outer coast of Baja California Sur and Gulf of California to Panama and the Galapagos Islands.
Habitat: Intertidal to 31 m (102 ft).
Remarks: Eats heterobranch eggs, especially those of sidegill sea slugs. During the day, it can be found under rocks immersed in the egg masses.

A. Hermosillo

Favorinus sp.
The body color is grayish-white with opaque white spots, some forming large white patches on the notum between the cerata. The rhinophores have a prominent subterminal swelling; cerata have brown bases but are tan on the upper third. This small species (6 mm or 0.2 in) is only known from Bahía de Banderas, Mexico and the Galapagos Islands.

A. Hermosillo

Unidentia angelvaldesi Millen & Hermosillo, 2012 (previously *Facelina* sp. 2)

Valdés' aeolid

The body has an orange, yellow, or pinkish tint, and the orange internal organs can be seen in most specimens. There is a deep purple line down the middle of the dorsum and on both sides of the foot. The oral tentacles are long and partly to fully purple, sometimes with opaque white blotches; rhinophores also with some mix of white and purple. The cerata vary in color among individuals, from light orange to light red, deep red, and purple; tips are white.
Similar species: None.
Size: To 20 mm (0.8 in).
Range: Mexican Pacific to Panama.
Habitat: Subtidal to 21 m (69 ft).
Remarks: Found on the orange gymnoblastic hydroid *Corydendrium parasiticum*.

A. Hermosillo

Glaucilla thompsoni and *G. marginata*

pelagic aeolids

Body color white with silver reflective pigment on top with blue and brownish coloration on the foot sole and white with silver reflective pigment around a large, broad foot. Rhinophores and oral tentacles short and smooth. Four clusters of conical, fan-like cerata on each side of the body which are blue at their bases and white or transparent at their tips. The only way to distinguish between *Glaucilla thompsoni* and *G. marginata* is through internal examination or molecular analysis.
Similar species: None.
Size: To about 40 mm (1.5 in).
Range: Both species occur in the north Pacific subtropical gyre system.
Habitat: Pelagic, open ocean species.
Remarks: *Glaucilla* are pelagic species which live upside down (as pictured) floating on the water surface feeding on siphonophores. They hold an air bubble in their stomach for floatation. The stored nematocysts from their prey can deliver a painful sting.

A. Hermosillo

Noumeaella rubrofasciata Gosliner, 1991

red-headed aeolid

The body, head, oral tentacles, and lamellate-tipped rhinophores are pure white, except for a median red or orange patch on the head. The cerata vary from bright red-orange to brown with orange tips.
Similar species: None. The pure white body and rhinophores with a red-orange head patch are a unique combination.
Size: To 8 mm (0.3 in).
Range: Channel Islands, California to Panama; also the Gulf of California.
Habitat: Subtidal, 3-20 m (10-66 ft).
Remarks: Feeds on hydroids.

A. Hermosillo

A. Hermosillo

Hermissenda crassicornis (Eschscholtz, 1831) — horned nudibranch

Body is whitish-gray with a white to bluish line edging the foot. There is an orange stripe between the rhinophores with whitish-blue lines on either side, and the oral tentacles have a blue-white line on the dorsal surface. Ceratal core colors highly variable and influenced by diet; there is either a subapical orange band with a white tip or a band of white encrustations near the tip. Cerata have either a white line or a series of white dashes.
Similar species: *Hermissenda opalescens* lacks the white lines on the cerata and has white tips. *Sakuraeolis* cf. *enosimensis* lacks the orange stripe between the rhinophores and has opaque white spots on the head, body, and cerata. *Antiopella fusca* has many cerata in front of the rhinophores.
Size: To 80 mm (3.1 in).
Range: Popof Island, Alaska to Los Angeles, California.
Habitat: Intertidal to 37 m (121 ft), on hard and soft bottoms and common on floats.
Remarks: Primarily feeds on hydroids and nudibranchs, but will prey opportunistically on a wide range of organisms.

J. Kocian

Although *Hermissenda crassicornis* typically have lamellate rhinophores (left), these structures can be barely wrinkled or even perfectly smooth (far left).
G. Jensen

G. Paulay

Hermissenda opalescens (Cooper, 1863) — opalescent nudibranch

Body is whitish-gray and usually with a white and blue edge on the foot. There is an orange stripe between the rhinophores with whitish-blue lines on either side. The oral tentacles have a blue-white line on the dorsal surface. Ceratal cores are variable from gray to orange to brown with white tips and sometimes have a subapical orange band. Rhinophores are lamellate and can have an orange hue.
Similar species: The cerata of *Hermissenda crassicornis* have a white stripe but not white tips, and *Sakuraeolis* cf. *enosimensis* lacks the orange between the rhinophores.
Size: To 42 mm (1.6 in).
Range: Oregon to La Paz, Baja California Sur; in El Niño years may be found as far north as Port Hardy, British Columbia.
Habitat: Intertidal and subtidal, often on mud or sand.
Remarks: Feeds on hydroids, crustaceans, and nudibranchs.

M. Passage

P. Garner

Hermosita hakunamatata (Ortea et al., 2003)
hakunamatata aeolid

Body is a deep rose to black and cerata also rose colored; both are covered with minute black and gold specks. The heavily perfoliate rhinophores are rose colored with a white tip; the oral tentacles and cerata also have light tips.
Similar species: None.
Size: To 22 mm (0.8 in).
Range: Puerto Magdelena, Baja California Sur, Mexico to Panama.
Habitat: Subtidal to at least 10 m (33 ft).
Remarks: Feeds on the hydroid *Solanderia* sp., which is dark purple with pink polyps.

A. Hermosillo

Hermosita sangria Gosliner & Behrens, 1986
wine-red aeolid

Body ground color is violet, which deepens to rich vermilion red in the middle of the cerata, foot corners, oral tentacles, and rhinophores. The distal third of these structures is tipped with yellow or white in some animals.
Similar species: *Flabellinopsis iodinea* has no banding on the oral tentacles.
Size: To 70 mm (2.7 in).
Range: Isla Cedros and Gulf of California, Mexico to Costa Rica.
Habitat: Subtidal, from 3-17 m (10-56 ft).
Remarks: Feeds on the hydroid *Solanderia*.

A. Hermosillo

Phidiana hiltoni (O'Donoghue, 1927)
Hilton's aeolid

Body translucent grayish white, occasionally with a pale orange or red hue and scattered white spots. The rhinophores are perfoliate and each has a yellow tip, below which is a red band. The frosted white- to bluish-white-tipped oral tentacles have a red line extending across the front, the frosting sometimes forming a line above the red line. There may be a white line along the foot border and a broken white line along the back. Ceratal cores are brown to black and the cerata are tipped with white or gold, sometimes followed by a rose-pink band which fades proximally.

R. Agarwal

Similar species: *Hermissenda opalescens* and *H. crassicornis* have an orange line between the rhinophores and blue lines.
Size: To 63 mm (2.5 in).
Range: Bodega Bay, California to Isla de Cedros, Baja California, Mexico.
Habitat: Intertidal to 220 m (722 ft), in rocky areas.
Remarks: Feeds on hydroids, stony corals and dendronotid and aeolid nudibranchs.

R. Agarwal

Phidiana lascrucensis Bertsch & Ferreira, 1974   **Las Cruces aeolid**

The body is orange to yellow-orange, with a sprinkling of white. The annulate rhinophores and head tentacles are orange, with a white tip. Ceratal cores are brown to orange depending upon its food, with a faint white band in the middle and white tip.
Similar species: None.
Size: To 25 mm (1 in).
Range: Central Gulf of California to Panama.
Habitat: Intertidal to 20 m (66 ft).
Remarks: Capable of at least limited swimming by thrashing from side to side.

A. Hermosillo

Phidiana sp.

The body is a pale pink with blotches of pink or fushia, darker in the middle of the dorsum. The cerata are brown to pink with a distal gold ring. The oral tentacles are the same color as the body, with a yellow band and the distal two thirds white; the distal half of the annulate rhinophores are also white. Photographed in Puerto Vallarta, Mexico, this specimen was 18 mm (0.7 in) in length.

A. Hermosillo

Sakuraeolis cf. *enosimensis* (previously *Sakuraeolis enosimensis*)

The body is grayish-white to pale orange, with numerous opaque white spots and a broken white line between the rhinophores. There are also opaque white lines on the dorsal surface of each oral tentacle, the midline of the tail, and often continuing as a broken line along the middle of the back. Rhinophores are simple, shorter than the oral tentacles, often orange and tipped in white. The numerous long, densely-set cerata are sprinkled with white and have white tips; ceratal cores range from yellow-orange through reddish-brown and occasionally green.
Similar species: *Hermissenda crassicornis* and *H. opalescens* both have an orange stripe between the rhinophores.
Size: To 40 mm (1.5 in).
Range: San Francisco Bay area, California.
Habitat: Typically found on floats in the bay, where it has become the second-most abundant nudibranch.
Remarks: Assumed to have been introduced from Japan; however, the specimen that was sequenced from San Francisco Bay was genetically distinct from an *S. enosimensis* from Japan. It was first collected in the bay in 1972.

D. Behrens

Catriona columbiana (O'Donoghue, 1922)

British Columbia aeolid

The body and foot are translucent grayish white, and covered with long, cylindrical cerata filled with light vermillion cores and with a broad opaque white stripe extending up the outer side, widening as it approaches the tip. The smooth rhinophores are translucent at their bases with wide, translucent orange bands and opaque white tips. The area in front of the rhinophores and dorsal surface of oral tentacles is densely frosted in opaque white.
Similar species: *Cuthona punicea* does not have orange on the rhinophores.
Size: To 15 mm (0.6 in).
Range: Gambier Bay, Alaska to Cape Arago, Oregon.
Habitat: Intertidal to 30 m (98 ft).
Remarks: It is often found nestled at the base of *Tubularia* or *Ectopleura* hydroids subtidally or on floating docks.

K. Fletcher

A similar form that occurs from Cape Arago, Oregon to San Diego, California has orange oral tentacles and ceratal cores that are dull or dark brown to dull pink or red, rather than shades of reddish-pink. Given these differences and the geographical separation of the two, there is a strong likelihood that they are a different species; DNA sequencing is needed to resolve the question.

K. Lee

Catriona rickettsi Behrens, 1984

Doc's aeolid

Body is translucent white, the area behind the rhinophores sometimes appearing yellow to orange. There is opaque white pigment on the distal 1/3 of the rhinophores, the dorsal surface of the oral tentacles and the cerata tips; there is an orange band below the white rhinophore tips and an orange band may be present on the oral tentacles. The color of the ceratal core varies greatly, from yellow through orange, pink, or brownish-green. In some specimens the color may change from greenish near the base to reddish-brown below the white cap.

Similar species: *Tenellia ivetteae* is shorter with larger cerata; *Eubranchus cucullus* has a brown head, and *Embletonia* cf. *gracilis* has single rows of cerata.
Size: To 20 mm (0.8 in).
Range: Umpqua River, Oregon to Morro Bay, California.
Habitat: Intertidal and in fouling communities on floating docks.
Remarks: Feeds on the hydroid, *Ectopleura crocea*. Lays string-like egg ribbons.

D. Behrens

Catriona **sp. 1** (left) has been reported from the Channel Islands, California to Punta Eugenia, Baja California, Mexico. The ceratal cores are orange-red to dark red, or a combination of orange and red. The distal 2/3 of the rhinophores and oral tentacles are orange, often with white tips.

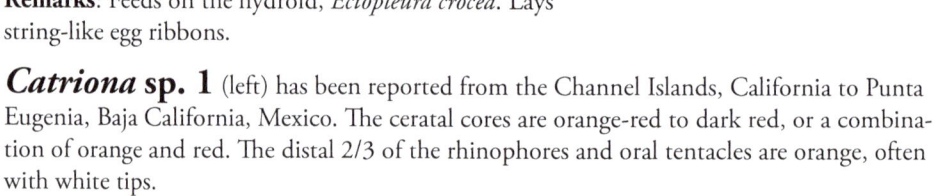

J. Lance

Abronica abronia (MacFarland, 1966) (previously *Cuthona abronia*)
elegant aeolid

Body translucent gray with some opaque yellowish spots; cerata are red at the base, olive green to brown in the middle, and also bearing yellowish spots that sometimes form bands. There is a purple band in the middle of the rhinophores and oral tentacles.
Similar species: *Kynaria cynara* and *Coryphellina marcusorum* also have purple bands on the rhinophores and tentacles, but are much more colorful.
Size: To 13 mm (0.5 in).
Range: Makah Bay, Washington to Islas Coronados, Baja California.
Habitat: Intertidal to 12 m (39 ft).
Remarks: Feeds on hydroids.

K. Lee

Trinchesia albocrusta (MacFarland, 1966) (previously *Cuthona albocrusta*)
white-crusted aeolid

This small species has inflated cerata and is characterized by varying amounts of opaque white encrustations on its head, cerata, and tips of its simple rhinophores. Ceratal core coloration can vary from green to umber to pale pinkish-tan.
Similar species: *Cuthona hamanni* has longer cerata and much less white coloration.
Size: To 12 mm (0.5 in).
Range: Prince William Sound, Alaska through Baja California Sur and the Gulf of California.
Habitat: Intertidal to 30 m (98 ft).
Remarks: Feeds on hydroids.

R. Agarwal

Cuthonella cocoachroma (Williams & Gosliner, 1979) (previously *Cuthona cocoachroma*)
chocolate aeolid

Body is translucent grayish-white. Opaque white encrustations cover the dorsal surface of the oral tentacles, the distal half of the rhinophores and the tips of the cerata. Rhinophores are twice the length of the oral tentacles. Ceratal cores are deep reddish brown to dark chocolate brown.
Similar species: *Cuthonella concinna* typically has white or blue flecks or a blue sheen on the cerata, and rhinophores and oral tentacles that are equal in length.
Size: To 15 mm (0.6 in).
Range: Kayostla Beach, Washington to Los Osos, California.
Habitat: Subtidal.
Remarks: Feeds on the embedded sea fir hydroid, *Thuiaria*. May be difficult to distinguish this species from the sympatric *Cuthonella concinna* without internal examination, but they are genetically quite distinct.

K. Ueda

Cuthonella concinna (Alder & Hancock, 1843) (previously *Cuthona concinna*) — **neat aeolid**

Body is translucent white. White encrustations cover the dorsal surface of the oral tentacles, the distal half of the rhinophores and the tips of the cerata. The smooth rhinophores are generally equal in length to the oral tentacles. The cerata have minute white or blue flecks and often a metallic blue sheen; the cores range from straw-colored to orange, red, purplish-gray, or dark purple.
Similar species: *Cuthonella cocoachroma* has rhinophores that are twice the length of the oral tentacles. *Coryphella verrucosa* has wrinkled rhinophores and the cerata begin far behind the rhinophores. The cerata of *Zelentia nepunicea* each have several large opaque white spots.
Size: To 15 mm (0.6 in).
Range: Lisianski Inlet, Alaska to Coleman Beach, Sonoma County, California; Atlantic.
Habitat: Subtidal.
Remarks: Feeds on the hydroid *Sertularia*.

G. Jensen

Cuthonella punicea (Millen, 1985) (previously *Cuthona punicea*) — **pomegranate aeolid**

Body translucent white to pale peach. Oral tentacles encrusted with opaque white spots dorsally forming a broad line; rhinophores sprinkled with opaque white spots, densest posteriorly and towards the tips and sometimes forming a line. The ceratal cores are dark wine-red to purple and the sheaths may be peach colored. The cerata have a broken line of opaque white pigment, sometimes appearing as a line of spots down their outer sides, and are white tipped due to dense subepidermal glands.
Similar species: *Catriona columbiana* has orange on the rhinophores; *Zelentia nepunicea* has much paler-colored ceratal cores.
Size: To 24 mm (1 in).
Range: Plumper Islands to Discovery Passage, British Columbia.
Habitat: Subtidal in rocky areas, to 33 m (108 ft).
Remarks: Feeds exclusively on the raspberry hydroid, *Zyzzyzus rubusidaeus*.

J. Hildering

Cuthona destinyae Hermosillo & Valdés 2007 (previously *Cuthona* sp. 4) — **Destiny's aeolid**

The body is grayish white with large olive-green to black patches down the midline of the notum, and the body and all appendages liberally sprinkled with white specks. The cerata have a brown core and a clear or white tip. The rhinophores have a dark medial band and a white tip.
Similar species: *Nanuca galaxiana* has dishlike rings on the rhinophores and much longer oral tentacles; *Eubranchus steinbecki* has knobs on the cerata.
Size: To 9 mm (0.3 in).
Range: Ixtapa-Zihuatanejo, Mexico to Costa Rica and the Galapagos Islands.
Habitat: Intertidal and shallow subtidal, specimens were scraped from the bottom of boat hulls.
Remarks: Feeds on encrusting hydroids.

A. Hermosillo

Cuthona divae (Alder & Hancock, 1842) — Rose-pink cuthona

Body is translucent grayish white with a cream to pink cast. Numerous dense rows of long, slender white-tipped cerata begin in front of the rhinophores; cores are red, brown or pink. The rhinophores are nearly twice the length of the oral tentacles and both are smooth without white encrustations.
Similar species: *Cumanotus fernaldi* has rhinophores that are joined at the base, and the ceratal cores have a very knotted and lumpy appearance.
Size: To 37 mm (1.4 in).
Range: Vancouver Island, British Columbia to San Diego, California.
Habitat: Intertidal to 20 m (66 ft).
Remarks: Feeds on the hydroids *Hydractinia* and *Clavactinia milleri*.

K. Lee

Cuthona hamanni Behrens, 1987 — Hamann's aeolid

Body grayish-white with irregular patches of dark-brown pigment and white spots. The top third of the rhinophores and oral tentacles are white followed by a dark-brown band below. Cerata with long, white tips and a granular appearance created by dense white specks overlaying the tan, orange, or salmon-colored ceratal cores; bases of ceratal cores are a dark green.
Similar species: *Trinchesia albocrusta* has much more white and shorter cerata; *Cuthona perca* lacks dark bands on its rhinophores and tentacles.
Size: To 14 mm (0.5 in).
Range: Anacapa Island, California to Bahía de los Ángeles, Mexico.
Habitat: Intertidal.
Remarks: Named in honor of Jeff Hamann.

J. Hamann

Cuthona lizae Angulo-Campillo & Valdés, 2003 — Liza's aeolid

Body bright pink to red, often with a large middorsal white spot following the first group of cerata. The smooth rhinophores and oral tentacles are large, often bright pink, with a thin cream ring followed by a rose band and a cream tip. The cerata are often dusted with yellowish dots with dark-brownish or reddish-brown cores and long, cream-colored tips.
Similar species: None.
Size: To 6 mm (0.2 in).
Range: La Paz, Baja California Sur, to Puerto Vallarta, Mexico.
Habitat: Intertidal.
Remarks: Named to honor Liza Gómez.

A. Hermosillo

Cuthona longi Behrens, 1985 — **Long's aeolid**

Body is pale yellow with irregular lighter patches dorsally on the notum, head, and on the long, smooth rhinophores and short oral tentacles. A pale blue patch occurs near the base of the rhinophores. There are white encrustations on the top third of the rhinophores and forming a line on each oral tentacle. Tips of the cerata are white, followed by a band of red, then opaque yellow-gold, followed by a slightly wider band of pale blue; the cores are granular, fading in color from dark to light green. The entire surface of each is sprinkled with opaque white specks.
Similar species: *Eubranchus* sp. 2 has turquoise tips on its cerata.
Size: To 34 mm (1.3 in).
Range: Isla Raza, Baja California, Mexico to Roca Partida, Islas Revillagigedo, Mexico. One recent record from Anacapa Is., California.
Habitat: Subtidal.
Remarks: Feeds on plumularid hydroids.

J. Hamann

Cuthona millenae Hermosillo & Valdés 2007 (previously *Cuthona* sp. 5) — **Millen's aeolid**

Body and head with broad orange and bluish-white lengthwise stripes. One orange line runs from the oral tentacle to the base of the rhinophore, then to the first ceratal group; another runs laterally from the oral tentacles to the first ceratal group. The cerata are a blotchy green and yellow with an apical pale blue band and an orange tip.
Similar species: None.
Size: To 6 mm (0.2 in).
Range: Islas Revillagigedo and Bahía de Banderas, Mexico, to Costa Rica.
Habitat: Subtidal.
Remarks: Found on hydroids on rock walls.

A. Hermosillo

Cuthona perca Marcus, 1958 — **lost aeolid**

Body translucent grayish-white to cream, occasionally pale orange, often with opaque white spots. The rhinophores are smooth and have numerous small, opaque white spots more concentrated near the tips. Cylindrical, slightly inflated cerata have blunt white tips and few to numerous tiny opaque white spots, and a light band well below the tip; the cores range from light to dark olive-green to brownish.
Similar species: *Cuthona hamanni* has dark bands on its tentacles and rhinophores.
Size: To 15 mm (0.6 in).
Range: On our coast it is only known San Francisco Bay area, California; widespread in various brackish, high salinity areas throughout the Atlantic and Pacific, including the Black Sea.
Habitat: Intertidal.
Remarks: Undoubtedly introduced, but it is unclear where this species originated. Co-occurs with the introduced Asian sea anemone, *Diadumene lineata*.

J. Hamann

Cuthona phoenix Gosliner, 1981 — **phoenix aeolid**

Body is translucent white with varying amounts of suffused pale to dark apricot-orange; head sometimes orange. The long, smooth rhinophores are orange and the shorter oral tentacles may be orange or translucent white. The cerata are orange-brown with randomly scattered small brown spots, brown cores and translucent white tips. There is a large gap between the rhinophores and the first ceratal row that sometimes has opaque white patches; each ceratal row contains a single ceras.
Similar species: None.
Size: To 20 mm (0.7 in).
Range: Santa Cruz, California to Bahía de Banderas, Mexico.
Habitat: Pelagic on floating objects.
Remarks: Feeds on the campanulariid hydroid *Clytia linearis*. It was one of the first organisms to appear after an oil spill, when it was discovered on floating, solidified pieces of asphalt. This resilience was the inspiration for its name, as it rose like the mythical phoenix bird from its own ashes to begin life anew.

R. Agarwal

Cuthona riosi Hermosillo & Valdés 2008
(previously *Cuthona* sp. 2) — **Rios' aeolid**

Body and foot are translucent white, with an opaque white dorsum. The smooth rhinophores, oral tentacles and ceratal cores are salmon pink in color; tips of the cerata slightly lighter in color and there is a black marking at the base of each.
Similar species: None.
Size: To 8 mm (0.3 in).
Range: Known only from Bahía de Banderas, Mexico.
Habitat: Subtidal.
Remarks: Feeds on hydroids such as *Tubularia crocea*.

A. Hermosillo

Cuthona rolleri Behrens & Gosliner, 1988 — **Roller's aeolid**

Body is white; cerata have salmon pink cores, frosted white tips and sprinkles of very fine brown specks. Body is dorsoventrally flattened with a wide foot, round foot corners and a rounded tail. The oral tentacles are joined medially to form a broad frontal veil. Rhinophores are simple, smooth and tapering, and the long, flattened cerata are widely separated dorsally.
Similar species: The oral veil of *Tenellia adspersa* is rounded anteriorly.
Size: To 15 mm (0.6 in).
Range: San Luis Obispo County, California.
Habitat: Intertidal mudflats.
Remarks: Forages by burrowing into the mud for prey.

G. McDonald

Cuthona sp.

This small (to 6 mm/0.2 in) aeolid has a yellow-orange body and a light blue patch edged with darker orange between the yellowish-white-tipped rhinophores. The lower half of each ceras is black followed by an opaque white band, then a blue band and a yellowish-orange tip. It has been found in Bahía Tortugas, Baja California Sur and the Gulf of California, Mexico.

A. Hermosillo

Tenellia adspersa (Nordmann, 1845)
spotted lagoon aeolid

Body color is white, yellowish-white, or pale purple with darker flecks and streaks on the dorsum. There is a circular oral veil without distinct oral tentacles and no foot corners; the rhinophores are simple. Cerata are few and arranged in groups of one or two.
Similar species: The oral veil of *Cuthona rolleri* has a straight anterior margin.
Size: To 7 mm (0.3 in).
Range: Coos Bay, Oregon to Long Beach Harbor, California; native to Europe but widely distributed.
Habitat: Intertidal to 8 m (26 ft).
Remarks: Usually found in bays and estuaries where it feeds on a variety of hydroids. Two genetically distinct groups occur in the Atlantic, but it is not known which of those aligns with the ones occurring on our coast.

R. Agarwal

Tenellia ivetteae Gosliner & Bertsch 2017 (previously *Cuthona* sp. 3) — Ivette's aeolid

The body is translucent white. The cerata are very large and wide compared to the body of the animal and their cores are creamy yellowish-white. The rhinophores and oral tentacles are smooth, small, and their outer two-thirds are encrusted in opaque white.
Similar species: *Eubranchus cucullus* has a brown head.
Size: To 7 mm (0.3 in).
Range: Bahía de los Ángeles, Mexico to Costa Rica.
Habitat: Shallow subtidal.
Remarks: Found under rocks.

A. Hermosillo

Diaphoreolis flavovulta (MacFarland, 1966) (previously *Cuthona flavovulta*) — **yellowhead aeolid**

Body translucent grayish-white to cream; a patch of dark to pale orange coloration covers the base of the rhinophores and may extend onto the head and oral tentacles. The rhinophores and oral tentacles are frosted in opaque white for at least half their length. Ceratal cores vary from pale green to dark green to black, and cerata are randomly encrusted with opaque white spots. An orange line may be present on the lateral edge of each ceras. Cerata tips are white, peach or orange, and there is a white line along the midline of the tail.

M. Passage

K. Fletcher

Similar species: *Diaphoreolis viridis* lacks the orange or yellow coloration on the head; *D. lagunae* has all-orange rhinophores. *Trinchesia virens* (not incl.) lacks the white tail line.
Size: To 10 mm (0.4 in).
Range: San Juan Islands, Washington to La Jolla, California.
Habitat: Intertidal to 18 m (59 ft).
Remarks: Feeds on hydroids.

Diaphoreolis lagunae (O'Donoghue, 1926) (previously *Cuthona lagunae*) — **Laguna aeolid**

Body translucent grayish-white to cream. A patch of orange-red covers the head up to the front of the rhinophores, which are orange-red for their entire length with paler tips. Oral tentacles translucent grayish-white, two-thirds of the length densely covered in encrusting opaque white. Cerata have ochre to nearly black cores and orange-red tips; there may be a few scattered opaque white spots. There is a white line along the midline of the tail.
Similar species: *Diaphoreolis flavovulta* has white on half or more of the rhinophores; *D. viridis* lacks the orange or yellow color on the head. *Trinchesia virens* (not incl.) lacks the white tail line.
Size: To 8 mm (0.3 in).
Range: Coos Bay, Oregon to Ensenada, Baja California, Mexico.
Habitat: Intertidal to 30 m (98 ft).
Remarks: Intertidal specimens found on the hydroid *Symplectoscyphus turgidus*.

K. Lee

Diaphoreolis cf. *viridis* (Forbes, 1840) (previously *Cuthona viridis*)

Body is translucent grayish-white; rhinophores and tentacles are encrusted with opaque white pigment. The ceratal cores are pale or dark olive green interspersed with darker pigment and with large white or yellowish tips; each has a longitudinal broken line of opaque white pigment along each side.
Similar species: *Diaphoreolis flavovulta*, *D. lagunae*, and *Trinchesia virens* (not incl.) have yellow or orange color on the front of the head.
Size: To 11 mm (0.4 in).
Range: Alaska to central Puget Sound, Washington.
Habitat: Subtidal.
Remarks: Found on the hydroid *Sertularella* sp. *Diaphoreolis viridis* was described from Europe and there are internal differences between Atlantic and Pacific specimens.

T. Gosliner

Zelentia fulgens (MacFarland, 1966) (previously *Cuthona fulgens*) — shiny aeolid

Body is translucent gray; rhinophores and oral tentacles with opaque white encrustations. The ceratal cores can vary from yellow-brown to dark brown; there are yellow bands at the bases and near the clear tips and they are liberally sprinkled with opaque white dots. Trailing tail may have a dorso-medial white line.
Similar species: *Diaphoreolis flavovulta*, *D. lagunae*, and *Trinchesia virens* (not incl.) have yellow or orange on the head; *D.* cf. *viridis* has longer cerata bearing fewer white spots.
Size: To 8 mm (0.3 in).
Range: Puget Sound, Washington to San Diego County, California.
Habitat: Intertidal and subtidal.
Remarks: Feeds on hydroids.

R. Agarwal

Zelentia nepunicea Korshunova et al., 2018 (previously *Cuthona pustulata*) — pimpled aeolid

The body is translucent white, often with internal organs and brown jaws visible. Distal half of cerata frosted white and lower half with scattered opaque white spots; cores are granular and vary from dark reddish-brown to pinkish-tan to tannish. The smooth rhinophores and oral tentacles have opaque white encrustations.
Similar species: *Cuthonella punicea* has much darker ceratal cores; *C. concinna* lack the bright white spots on the cerata.
Size: To 20 mm (0.8 in).
Range: Port Hardy, Vancouver Island, British Columbia to Tacoma, Washington.
Habitat: Subtidal to 20 m (66 ft).
Remarks: Feeds on hydrozoans of the genus *Halecium*. Very recently shown to be distinct from the Atlantic species *Zelentia pustulata*.

K. Fletcher

Zelentia willowsi Korshunova et al. 2018 — Willows' aeolid

Body is translucent whitish gray; dark jaws are visible through the body. Ceratal cores are dark olive to dark brown with small, white spots on the tips. Cerata are relatively long and begin anterior to the thick, translucent rhinophores. No white encrustations on rhinophores or oral tentacles.
Similar species: *Cuthona divae* juveniles have thinner, more pointed cerata.
Size: To 9 mm (0.3 in).
Range: Known only from type locality, Port Orchard, Washington.
Habitat: Subtidal to 15 m (49 ft).
Remarks: Feeds on encrusting hydroids.

K. Fletcher

Phestilla lugubris (Bergh, 1870)

coral-eating aeolid

Cryptically colored from pale cream to orange, matching the coral colony upon which it feeds. The knobby cerata have brown, grey, green, or purple cores, with a subterminal clear area and a white or yellow tip.
Similar species: None.
Size: To 30 mm (1.2 in).
Range: Widespread throughout the Indo-Pacific; in the eastern Pacific it ranges from the central Gulf of California and Mexican Pacific to Isla de Malpelo, Columbia.
Habitat: Intertidal to 10 m (33 ft) under coral heads of *Porites* spp.
Remarks: *Phestilla panamica* is likely a synonym.

A. Hermosillo

Fiona pinnata (Eschscholtz, 1831)

feather aeolid

Body is cream to brownish when diet is barnacles; purple if *Velella* is eaten. One variation has an orange patch between the rhinophores followed by an opaque white spot. The rhinophores are simple. The cerata are sail-shaped and positioned laterally, leaving the dorsal surface of the body bare.
Similar species: None.
Size: To 25 mm (1 in)
Range: Alaska to Chile; New Zealand.
Habitat: Pelagic.
Remarks: Found on floating debris with the pelagic barnacle *Lepas*, surface dwelling sea jellies, and the by-the-wind-sailor *Velella*.

M. Chamberlain

aeolid sp.

Photographed at Bird Rock in San Diego, California, this mystery slug cannot be definitively assigned to any particular genus. It has a long, translucent, greenish-yellow body with no markings or spots. The cerata are in groups with granular, tan cores and a dark green band below the bright, white tip. Oral tentacles are the same color as the body and smooth; the rhinophores slightly lighter than body and perfoliate with brown tips.

S. McKim

SELECTED REFERENCES

Behrens, D.W. 2005 Nudibranch Behavior. New World Publication, Jacksonville, FL. 176 pp.

Behrens, D.W., & Hermosillo, A. 2005. Eastern Pacific Nudibranchs – A Guide to the Opisthobranchs from Alaska to Central America. Sea Challengers, Monterey, CA. 137 pp.

Bertsch, H. 2010. Biogeography of northeast Pacific opisthobranchs: comparative faunal province studies between Point Conception, California, USA, and Punta Aguja, Piura, Peru. SMMAC. 221-259.

Bertsch, H. 2019. Biodiversity and natural history of Nudipleura communities (Mollusca, Gastropoda) at Bahía de los Ángeles, Baja California, Mexico. A 30-year study. Geomare Zoológica 1: 89-136.

Bertsch, H. & Hermosillo, A. 2007. Biogeografía alimenticia de los opistobranquios del Pacífico noreste / Feeding biogeography of the northeast Pacific opisthobranchs. Estudios sobra la Malacología y Conquiliología en México. 71-73.

Bertsch, H. & Rosas, L.E.A. 2016. Invertebrados Marinas del Noroeste de México/Marine Invertebrates of Northwest Mexico. Universidad Autónoma de Baja California, Instituto de Investigaciones Oceanológicas, Ensenada, MX. 432 pp.

Camacho-García, Y., Gosliner, T.M. & Valdés, Á. 2005. Guía de Campo de las Babosas Marinas del Pacífico Este Tropical / Field Guide to the Sea Slugs of the Tropical Eastern Pacific.. California Academy of Sciences, San Francisco, CA. 130 pp.

Ferreira, A.J. & Bertsch., H. 1975. Anatomical and distributional observations on some opisthobranchs from the Panamic faunal province. The Veliger 17(4): 323-330.

Goddard, J.H.R. 1984. Presumptive batesian mimicry of an aeolid nudibranch by an amphipod crustacean. Shells and Sea Life 16: 220-222.

Goodheart, J., Camacho-García, Y., Padula, V., Schrödl, M., Cervera, J.L., Gosliner T.M. & Valdés, Á. 2015. Systematics and biogeography of *Pleurobranchus* Cuvier, 1804 sea slugs (Heterobranchia: Nudiplura: Pleurobranchidae). Zoological Journal of the Linnaean Society 174(2): 322-362.

Gosliner, T.M., Valdés, Á. & Behrens, D.W. 2018. Nudibranch & Sea Slug Identification – Indo-Pacific 2nd Edition. New World Publications, Jacksonville, FL. 452 pp.

Hermosillo, A. & Behrens, D.W. 2005. The opisthobranch fauna of Mexican states of Colima, Michoacán and Guerrero- filling in the faunal gap. Vita Malacologia 3: 11-22.

Hermosillo, A., Behrens, D.W. & Ríos-Jara, E. 2006. Opistobranquios de México: Guía de babosas marinas del Pacífico, Golfo de California y las islas oceánicas. CONABIO. 143 pp.

Hoover, C.A., Lindsay, T., Goddard, J.H.R., Valdés, Á. 2015. Seeing double: pseudocryptic diversity in the *Doriopsilla albopunctata-Doriopsilla gemela* species complex of the north-eastern Pacific. Zoologica Scripta 44: 612-631.

Karmeinski, D., Meusemann, K., Goodheart, J.A., Schroedi, M., Martynov, A., Korshunova, T., Wagele, H. & Donath, A. 2021. Transcriptomics provides a robust framework for the relationships of the major clades of cladobranch sea slugs (Mollusca, Gastropoda, Heterobranchia), but fails to resolve the position of the enigmatic genus *Embletonia*. BMC Ecology and Evolution. Retrieved from : https://doi.org/10.1186/s12862-021-01944-0

Lamb, A & Hanby, B. P. 2005. Marine Life of the Pacific Northwest – A Photographic Encyclopedia of Invertebrates, Seaweeds and Selected Fishes. Harbour Publishing, Madeira Park, B.C., Canada. 398 pp.

MacFarland, F. M. 1966. Studies of opisthobranchiate mollusks of the Pacific coast of North America. Memoirs of the California Academy of Sciences 6: 1-546

Marcus, Er. 1961. Opisthobranch mollusks from California. The Veliger Vol 3 (Supplement): 1-85.

Marcus, Er. & Marcus, Ev. 1967. American opisthobranch mollusks. Part I, tropical American opisthobranchs. Studies in Tropical Oceanography, University of Miami, 6(1): 1-137.

Marcus, Er. & Marcus, Ev. 1967. American opisthobranch mollusks. Part II, opisthobranchs from the Gulf of California. Studies in Tropical Oceanography, University of Miami, 6(2): 141-256.

McDonald, G. R. 1983. A review of the nudibranchs of the California Coast. Malacologia 24(1-2): 114-276.

McDonald, G. R. 2021. Nudibranch Systematic Index, Third Online Edition. Institute of Marine Sciences. University of California, Santa Cruz. Retrieved from: https://escholarship.org/uc/item/38n512jw

McDonald, G. R. 2021. Bibliographia Nudibranchia, Third Online Edition. Institute of Marine Sciences. University of California, Santa Cruz. Retrieved from: https://escholarship.org/uc/item/5rx4j4ps

McDonald, G. R. & Nybakken, J. W. 1997. List of the worldwide food habits of nudibranchs. University of California, Santa Cruz. Retrieved from https://escholarship.org/uc/item/0g75h1q3

Thompson, T.E. 1976a. Biology of Opisthobranch Molluscs, Volume I. Ray Society. London. 207 pp.

Valdés, Á. 2019. Northeast Pacific benthic shelled sea slugs. Zoosymposia 13: 242-304.

INDEX

A

Abronica abronia 147
Acanthodoris
  atrogriseata 55
  brunnea 56
  hudsoni 56
  lutea 57
  nanaimoensis 57
  pilosa 55
  pina 58
  rhodoceras 58
Acteocina 12
  cerealis 19
  culcitella 19
  harpa 19
  inculta 20
Acteonoidea 17
Adalaria
  jannae 59
  proxima 59
  sp. 1 61
Adfacelina medinai 141
Aegires
  albopunctatus 61
  cf. *sublaevis* 62
aeolid
  armed 138
  Baba's festive 139
  Bertsch's 126
  Bertsch's rainbow 139
  bonfire 123
  British Columbia 146
  charming 122
  chocolate 147
  colorful 135
  confusing 138
  Cooper's 123
  coral-eating 155
  Destiny's 148
  Doc's 146
  elegant 147
  Elena & Alexia's 141
  feather 155
  Fernald's 129
  galaxy 139
  Goddard's 127
  hakunamatata 144
  Hamann's 149
  Hilton's 144
  homely 131
  hooded 130
  Irene's 135
  Ivette's 152
  Japanese 128
  Laguna 153
  Las Cruces 145
  Liza's 149
  long-mouthed 124
  Long's 150
  lost 150
  Marcus' 125
  Medina's 141
  Millen's 150
  Misaki 129
  Moebius' big 136
  Morro Bay 140
  Moss Landing 137
  neat 148
  Olive's 136
  pelagic 142
  phoenix 151
  pimpled 154
  pomegranate 148
  Price's 122
  red-headed 142
  red sparkly 127
  Rios' 151
  rocky 130
  Roller's 151
  San Juan 131
  shiny 154
  sp. 155
  spotted lagoon 152
  Stearns' 140
  Steinbeck's 132
  sulfur 135
  three-lined 123
  Valdés' 142
  Van Syoc's 126
  warty 125
  white-crusted 147
  Willows' 154
  wine-red 144
  yellowhead 153
  Yolanda's 132
Aeolidia
  loui 134
  papillosa 134
Aeolidida 121
Aeolidiella
  alba 135
  chromosoma 135
  oliviae 136
Aeolidioidea 8
Aeolid sp. 155
aglaja
  Albatross 25
  spotted 24
Aglaja
  diomedea 25
  ocelligera 24
Aglajidae 7
Akiodoris salacia 59
Alderia
  modesta 41
  willowi 42
aldisa
  Cooper's 71
  kings' 72
  red 72
  white-lined 71
Aldisa
  albomarginata 71
  cooperi 71
  sanguinea 3, 72
  tara 72
Anaspidea 5, 8, 9
ancula
  freckled 48
  Pacific 49
Ancula
  gibbosa 49
  lentiginosa 48
  pacifica 49
  spp. 49
Anetarca armata 138
Anteaeolidiella
  chromosoma 135
  ireneae 135
  oliviae 136
Antiopella 118
  barbarensis 119
  fusca 119
  gelida 120
Apata
  cf. *pricei* 122
  pricei 122
Aplysia 3, 8
  californica 3, 28, **29**
  cedrosensis 30
  hooveri 29
  juliana 29
  parvula 29
  vaccaria 28, 30
Aplysiopis enteromorphae 42
Armina
  californica 117
  Armina sp. 117

Arminoidea 9, 117
Atagema
  alba 72
  notacristata 73
  sp. 1 73
Atalodoris jannae 59
Austraeolis stearnsi 140

B

Babakina festiva 139
Baeolidia
  cf. *salaamica* 136
  moebii 136
Bajaeolis bertschi 139
Baptodoris mimetica **73**, 96
Berghia major 136
Berthelinia chloris 38
Berthella
  andromeda 33
  californica 33
  cf. *agassizii* 33
  chacei 34
  grovesi 34
  martensi 34
  stellata 33
  strongi 35
Berthellina
  ilisima 35
  sp. 1 34
biogeography 11
Bornella sarape 107
Brazil spurilla 138
bubble
  cylindrical spindle- 21
  grain barrel 19
  San Diego 21
bubble shell
  glassy 23
  green 23
  bubble snail
  Gould's 22
  Japanese 22
  spotted 22
Bulbaeolidia sulphurea 135
Bulla
  gouldiana 18, **22**
  punctulata 22

C

cadlina
  modest 89
  The Limbaughs' 88
  yellow-spotted 88
Cadlina
  cf. *sparsa* 89
  flavomaculata 88
  jannanicholsae 87
  klasmalmbergi 87
  limbaughorum 88
  luarna 88
  luteomarginata 87
  modesta 89
  sp. 89
  sylviaearleae 87
California
  bonfire 43
  diaphana 21
caruncle 118
Catriona
  columbiana 146
  rickettsi 146
  sp. 1 146
Cephalaspidea 5, 8, 9, 15, 18
Cerberilla
  chavezi 137
  mosslandica 137
  pungoarena 137
  sp. 1 137
Chavez's cerberilla 137
Chlamylla sp. 125
chromodorid
  Agassiz's 93
  Baumann's 90
  California 93
  Cedros 93
  Dall's 92
  Eveline's 95
  Ferreira's 94
  Gale & Alex's 90
  MacFarland's 90
  Marisla's 91
  Norris' 91
  Porter's 94
  Soccoro 91
  Sphon's 92
Chromodoris
  galexorum 90
  macfarlandi 90
  marislae 91
  norrisi 91
  sp. 1 91
  sphoni 92
Chromolaichma
  dalli 92
  sedna 92
Cladobranchia 100
Conualevia
  alba 86
  marcusi 86
convoluted armina 117
corambe
  Pacific 47
  Steinberg's 47
Corambe 3, 46
  pacifica 47
  steinbergae 47
Coryphella
  amabilis 122
  cf. *trilineata* 124
  cooperi 123
  fogata 123
  sp. 124
  trilineata 3, 121, **123**
  trophina 124
  verrucosa 125
Coryphellina marcusorum 125
Crimora coneja 3, **62**
Crosslandia daedali 115
Cumanotus 3
  fernaldi 129
  sp. 129
Cuthona
  abronia 147
  albocrusta 147
  cocoachroma 147
  concinna 148
  destinyae 148
  divae 149
  flavovulta 153
  fulgens 154
  hamanni 149
  lagunae 153
  lizae 149
  longi 150
  millenae 150
  perca 150
  phoenix 151
  punicea 148
  pustulata 154
  riosi 151
  rolleri 151
  sp. 152
  sp. 4 148
  sp. 5 150
  viridis 153
Cuthonella
  cocoachroma 147
  concinna 148
  punicea 148
Cyerce orteai 40
Cylichna
  attonsa 20

cf. *alba* 20
cf. *attonsa* 20
diegensis 21

D

Dendrodoris 7
  behrensi 95
  cf. *fumata* 95
  nigromaculata 95
  stohleri 96
dendronotid
  branched 111
  Dall's 108
  dwarf 109
  Kamchatka 109
  red 110
  Robilliard's 110
  stubby 110
  white 107
  white-spotted 107
Dendronotoidea 8, 106
Dendronotus 3
  albopunctatus 107
  albus 4, 107
  dalli 108
  frondosus 111
  iris 106, **108**
  kamchaticus 109
  nanus 109
  robilliardi 110
  rufus 110
  sp. 111
  subramosus 110
  venustus 111
Diaphana 12
Diaphana californica 21
Diaphoreolis
  cf. *viridis* 153
  flavovulta 153
  lagunae **153**, 163
Diaphorodoris lirulatocauda 60
Diaulula
  aurila 73
  greeleyi 74
  nayarita 74
  nivosa 74
  odonoghuei 74
  sandiegensis 75
dirona
  colorful 119
  golden 118
  white-lined 118
Dirona
  albolineata 7, 12, **118**

  pellucida 118
  picta 119
Discodorididae sp. 80
Discodoris
  aliciae 75
  ketos 75
Dolabella cf. *auricularia* 30
Dolabrifera
  dolabrifera 31
  nicaraguana 31
Dondice sp. 1 139
dorid
  Ali's 75
  Ana's 65
  barnacle-eating 60
  Behrens' 97
  Bertsch's 97
  black and white 58
  black spotted 95
  brown horned 56
  Chan's 71
  clown 69
  Cockerell's 63
  crested 73
  crowned 61
  Ernst's 86
  freckled 82
  Ghiselin's 84
  gland 67
  hairy horned 55
  Heath's 78
  Hedgpeth's 66
  Hudson's horned 56
  hunchback 72
  ink stain 64
  Janna's 59
  Janss' 64
  Kirsty's 66
  Lance's 81
  leopard 79
  look-alike 98
  Lopez's 81
  MacFarland's 84
  McDonald's 63
  mimic 73
  modest clown 69
  Monterey 76
  Mulliner's 82
  Nanaimo 57
  Nayarit 74
  noble 83
  northern leopard 74
  Odhner's 77
  Pickens' 77

  pinecone horned 58
  rabbit 62
  red sponge 84
  ridge-tailed 60
  Rosa's 83
  Salacia's 59
  salt and pepper 73
  sandalwood 57
  San Diego 75
  snowy 74
  sorcerer's 65
  sp. 99
  Spalding's 99
  spotted 70
  spotted foot 75
  Stohler's 96
  Tanya's 77
  three-colored 67
  tiger 7, 67
  truffle 78
  tuberculate 59
  two-spotted 85
  western 70
  white smooth-horn 86
  white-speckled 97
  white-spotted 61
Doriopsilla 7
  albopunctata 96
  bertschi 96, **97**
  davebehrensi 96, **97**
  fulva 96, **97**
  gemela 11, 96, **98**
  janaina 98
  nigromaculata 11, **99**
  rowena 99
  sp. 98
  spaldingi 4, **99**
Doris
  immonda 76
  montereyensis 76
  odhneri 77
  pickensi 77
  tanya 77
doto
  British Columbia 113
  hammerhead 112
  Lance's 113
  seal 113
Doto
  amyra 112
  columbiana 113
  kya 113
  lancei 113
  sp. 1 114

Doto (cont).
   sp. 2 114
   sp. 3 114
   sp. 4 114

E

Edmundsella
   bertschi 126
   vansyoci 126
eelgrass palio 62
Elysia 37
   cf. *cornigera* 39
   cf. *pusilla* 40
   diomedea 39
   hedgpethi 39
   sp. 40
Emarcusia morroensis 140
Embletonia cf. *gracilis* 120
Ercolania cf. *boodleae* 43
Eubranchus
   cf. *mandapamensis* 130
   cf. *rupium* 131
   cf. *sanjuanensis* 132
   cucullus 130
   misakiensis 129
   olivaceus 131
   rupium 130
   rustyus 131
   sanjuanensis 131
   sp. 1 133
   sp. 2 133
   sp. 3 133
   sp. 4 133
   sp. 5 133
   steinbecki 132
   yolandae 132

F

Facelina
   sp. 140
   sp. 1 141
   sp. 2 142
Favorinus
   elenalexiarum 141
   sp. 141
feeding 5
Felimare
   agassizii 93
   amalguae 93
   californiensis 6, 93
   porterae 94

Felimida
   baumanni 90
   galexorum 90
   macfarlandi 90
   marislae 91
   norrisi 91
   socorroensis 91
   sphoni 92
Fiona pinnata 155
Flabellina
   amabilis 122
   bertschi 126
   cooperi 123
   cynara 127
   iodinea 126
   islandica 128
   japonica 128
   marcusorum 125
   pricei 122
   sp. 1 123
   sp. 2 125
   stohleri 128
   telja 128
   trilineata 123
   trophina 124
   vansyoci 126
   verrucosa 125
Flabellinopsis iodinea 3, 6, 12, **126**
fuzzy onchidoris 61

G

Gastropteron 3, 8
Gastropteron pacificum 24
Geitodoris
   heathi 78
   mavis 79
Glaucilla
   marginata 142
   thompsoni 142
Glossodoris
   baumanni 90
   dalli 92
   sedna 92

H

Hallaxa chani 71
Haloa japonica 12, **22**
Haminoea
   cf. *ovalis* 23
   japonica 22
   vesicula 23
   virescens 23
Hancockia 106
Hancockia californica 112
Hansine's egg eater 41
Hermaea
   oliviae 42
   vancouverensis 37, 43
Hermissenda
   crassicornis 3, **143**
   opalescens 3, **143**
Hermosita
   hakunamatata 144
   sangria 144
Histiomena
   convolvula 117
   marginata 117
Hopkins' rose 52
Hoplodoris bramale 78
Hypselodoris
   agassizii 93
   californiensis 93
   ghiselini 93

J

Janolus 118
   anulatus 120
   barbarensis 119
   fuscus 119
   sp. 1 120
   sp. 2 120
jorunna
   Osa 80
   Tempisque 81
Jorunna
   osae 80
   pardus 79
   sp. 1 81
   tempisquensis 81

K

Kynaria cynara 127

L

leather limpet 45
Leostyletus misakiensis 12, **129**
Limacia
   cockerelli 3, **63**
   janssi 64
   mcdonaldi 3, **63**
Limenandra
   confusa 138
   nodosa 138
Lobiger 37
Lobiger cf. *souverbii* 38
Lomanotus
   cf. *vermiformis* 115
   sp. 1 116
   sp. 2 116

Loy 46
Loy thompsoni 48

M

MacFarland's runcina 17
Marionia
  kinoi 102
  sp. 102
  sp. 1 102
Melanochlamys
  diomedea 25
  ezoensis 25
Melibe 3, 106
Melibe leonina 7, **116**
Mexican dancer 39
Mexichromis
  amalguae 93
  antonii 94
  porterae 94
  tura 94

N

Nanuca galaxiana 139
navanax
  California 26
  riddle 25
  white-spotted 26
Navanax 7
  aenigmaticus 25
  inermis 26
  polyalphos 26
nomenclature 4
Notarchus indicus 31
Notobryon 3
  panamicum 115
  wardi 115
Noumeaella rubrofasciata 142
nudibranch
  annulated 120
  cockscomb 119
  Daedalus' 115
  frosty-tipped 120
  giant 108
  Hancock's 112
  hooded 116
  horned 143
  opalescent 143
  orange-peel 102
  sarape 107
  shag-rug 134
  striped 117
  threaded 111
  warty shag-rug 134
  white-and-orange-tipped 119

Nudibranchia 8

O

okenia
  Ali & Orso's 52
  angelic 50
  cat 51
  Cochimi's 51
  flat 51
  Los Angeles 50
  Vancouver 52
Okenia
  angelensis 50
  angelica 50
  cochimi 51
  felis 51
  mexicorum 52
  plana 12, 51
  rosacea 52
  sp. 1 53
  sp. 2 53
  vancouverensis 52
Olea hansineensis 41
Onchidella 37
  binneyi 45
  borealis 45
  carpenteri 45
  hansi 45
  hildae 45
Onchidoris
  bilamellata 60
  evincta 61
  muricata 61
orange blob 35
Oxynoe 37
  aliciae 38
  panamensis 38

P

Pacifia
  amica 127
  goddardi 127
Palio
  dubia 62
  zosterae 62
Panama notobryon 115
Paracoryphella sp. 128
Paradoris lopezi 81
Peltodoris
  lancei 81
  lentiginosa 82
  mullineri 82
  nobilis 46, 83
  rosae 83

Phestilla
  lugubris 155
  panamica 155
Phidiana
  hiltoni 144
  lascrucensis 145
  sp. 145
philine
  ear-shaped 27
  white 27
Philine
  alba 27
  auriformis 12, **27**
Philinopsis
  cf. *speciosa* 27
  cyanea 27
Philinorbis albus 27
Phyllaplysia
  padinae 31
  taylori 32
Phyllidiidae 9
Phyllidiopsis 7, 46
Phyllidiopsis blanca 100
Placida 37
  brookae 43
  cf. *dendritica* 44
  cremoniana 43
Platydoris macfarlandi 84
Pleurobranchaea californica 3, 32, **36**
Pleurobranchida 32
Pleurobranchomorpha 8, 9
pleurobranchus
  California 36
  Diguet's 35
Pleurobranchus
  areolatus 35
  digueti 35
  sp. 35
Polybranchia
  mexicana 41
  viridis 41
Polycera
  alabe 64
  anae 65
  atra 65
  cf. *alabe* 65
  gnupa 66
  hedgpethi 66
  kaiserae 66
  tricolor 10, 67
Polycerella glandulosa 12, **67**
Porostomes 96
Proctonotoidea 8, 118
Pseudobornella orientalis 12, **111**

Pteropods 4

R

radula 5
red thordisa 85
red-tipped sea goddess 92
reproduction 9
respiration 8
Retusa obtusa 20
Rfemsia macfarlandi 17
Rictaxis punctocaelatus 17
Roboastra tigris 67
rose-pink cuthona 149
Rostanga
   ghiselini 84
   pulchra 84
Runcina macfarlandi 17
Runcinida 17

S

Sacoglossa 5, 8
Sakuraeolis cf. *enosimensis* 145
Samla telja 12, 128
sapsucker
   Alicia's 38
   brown-streaked 44
   enteromorpha 42
   green 38
   Hedgpeth's 39
   Olivia's 42
   Vancouver 43
seahare
   black 30
   California 29
   Hoover's 29
   Indian 31
   Juliana's 29
   Nicaragua 31
   padina 31
   Rickett's lined 32
   Taylor's 32
sea slug
   Alder's 41
   willow 42
   winged 24
sensory organs 7
shouldered acteocina 20
sidegill
   California 33
   Chace's 34
   galaxy 33
   Groves' 34
   Martens' 34
   mushroom 36

Strong's 35
umbrella 36
Spanish shawl 126
Spurilla
   braziliana 138
   neapolitana 138
Stiliger 37
   fuscovittatus 44
   sp. 44
striped barrel shell 17
Stylocheilus
   rickettsi 32
   striatus 32
swimming cynara 127
Systellommatophora 45

T

Tambja
   abdere 68
   eliora 68
Taringa aivica 85
Tayuva lilacina 75
telja 128
Tenellia
   adspersa 152
   ivetteae 152
Thompson's corambid 48
Thordisa
   bimaculata 85
   rubescens 85
   sp. 86
Tochuina
   gigantea 102
   tetraquetra 102
trapania
   Goddard's 53
   Gosliner's 54
   swift 54
Trapania
   goddardi 53
   goslineri 54
   sp. 55
   velox 54
Trinchesia
   albocrusta 147
   virens 153
Triopha
   catalinae 3, **69**
   maculata 70
   modesta 3, **69**
   occidentalis 70
Tritonia 3
   diomedea 103
   exsulans 3, 101, **103**

   festiva 103
   sp. 1 103, 105
   sp. 2 104
   tetraquetra 104
Tritonicula
   myrakeenae 104
   pickensi 105
tritonid
   butterfly 105
   festive 103
   Keen's 104
   orange ruffled 104
   Padre Kino's 102
   Pickens' 105
   pink 103
Tritonioidea 101
Trivettea papalotla 105
Tylodina fungina 3, **36**
Tyrannodoris tigris 7, **67**
Tyrinna evelinae 95

U

Umbraculida 8, 9
Umbraculum umbraculum 36
Unidentia angelvaldesi 142

V

Vayssierea sp. 100
Volvulella cylindrica 21

W

white phyllidid 100
white-spotted porostome 96

Y

yellow margin dorids 87

Z

Zelentia
   fulgens 154
   nepunicea 154
   willowsi 154
Ziminella japonica 128

Diaphoreolis lagunae

K. Lee

CPSIA information can be obtained
at www.ICGtesting.com
Printed in the USA
LVHW071152080723
751814LV00002B/14